A PLUME BOOK

THE MAN IN THE ROCKEFELLER SUIT

MARK SEAL is an award-winning veteran journalist, a contributing editor at *Vanity Fair*, and the author of *Wildflower: An Extraordinary Life and Mysterious Death in Africa*, about the murdered wildlife filmmaker and naturalist Joan Root. He lives in Aspen, Colorado.

A *New York Times* Bestseller

Chosen for These Summer Must-Read Lists
O, The Oprah Magazine
ABC's *Good Morning America*
NPR
Newsweek/The Daily Beast
Parade
The Huffington Post

Nominated for an Edgar Award in the Best Fact Crime Category

Awarded *Elle* Magazine's Readers' Prize Grand Prix for Nonfiction Book of the Year

---

Praise for *The Man in the Rockefeller Suit*

"A tailor-made riveting read . . . Forget fiction. Pop this jaw-dropper in your beach bag."
—*USA Today*

"Has all the pace and drive of a suspense novel."
—Michiko Kakutani, *The New York Times*

"Irresistibly lucid and propulsive . . . Impossible to put down—Patricia Highsmith couldn't have written a more compelling thriller."
—*Kirkus* (starred review)

MARK SEAL

The Man in the Rockefeller Suit

The Astonishing Rise and Spectacular Fall of a Serial Impostor

A PLUME BOOK

PLUME
Published by the Penguin Group
Penguin Group (USA) Inc., 375 Hudson Street, New York, New York 10014, U.S.A. · Penguin Group (Canada), 90 Eglinton Avenue East, Suite 700, Toronto, Ontario, Canada M4P 2Y3 (a division of Pearson Penguin Canada Inc.) · Penguin Books Ltd., 80 Strand, London WC2R 0RL, England · Penguin Ireland, 25 St. Stephen's Green, Dublin 2, Ireland (a division of Penguin Books Ltd.) · Penguin Group (Australia), 250 Camberwell Road, Camberwell, Victoria 3124, Australia (a division of Pearson Australia Group Pty. Ltd.) · Penguin Books India Pvt. Ltd., 11 Community Centre, Panchsheel Park, New Delhi – 110 017, India · Penguin Group (NZ), 67 Apollo Drive, Rosedale, Auckland 0632, New Zealand (a division of Pearson New Zealand Ltd.) · Penguin Books (South Africa) (Pty.) Ltd., 24 Sturdee Avenue, Rosebank, Johannesburg 2196, South Africa

Penguin Books Ltd., Registered Offices: 80 Strand, London WC2R 0RL, England

Published by Plume, a member of Penguin Group (USA) Inc. Previously published in a Viking edition.

First Plume Printing, June 2012
10 9 8 7 6 5 4 3 2 1

Portions of this book appeared in "The Man in the Rockefeller Suit," *Vanity Fair*.

Excerpts from transcript of "San Marino Bones" episode of *Unsolved Mysteries*, January 13, 1995. Courtesy of *Unsolved Mysteries* © 1995.

PHOTOGRAPH CREDITS:
Insert page 2 (top): Photograph courtesy of Thomas Shweiger; 2 (middle and bottom), 3 (top): © Argum/Einberger; 4 (middle): Chris Newberg; 4 (bottom): Courtesy Grindhouse Pictures AB and Mats Larson; 5 (top): *San Marino Tribune*, used by permission of The San Marino Tribune Company, Inc.; 6 (bottom): Sue Bermudez Coffman; 7 (top and bottom): Jon Gilbert Fox; 8 (top and bottom), 9 (top and bottom): Laura White; 10 (top): Susan Symonds for Infinity Portrait Design; 10 (bottom): © 2007 Don Harney; 12 (top): Julie Gochar, Obsidian Realty; 12 (bottom): *Boston Globe*/Essdras Suarez/Landov; 13 (top and bottom), 14 (top): *Boston Globe*/John Tlumacki/Landov; 14 (bottom): *Boston Globe*/Essdras Suarez/Landov; 15 (top): Reuters/Brian Snyder/Landov; 15 (bottom): *Boston Globe*/Bill Greene/Landov; 16 (top): Reuters/Lisa Poole/Pool/Landov; 16 (bottom): Reuters/ CJ Gunther/Pool/Landov.

Ⓟ REGISTERED TRADEMARK—MARCA REGISTRADA

The Library of Congress has catalogued the Viking edition as follows:
Seal, Mark, 1953–
The man in the Rockefeller suit : the astonishing rise and spectacular fall of a serial impostor / Mark Seal.
p. cm.
ISBN 978-0-670-02274-8 (hc.)
ISBN 978-0-452-29803-3 (pbk.)
1. Gerhartsreiter, Christian, 1961–   2. Impostors and imposture—United States—Case studies.   I. Title.
HV6760.G47S43 2011
364.16′33—dc22
2010048908

Printed in the United States of America
Original hardcover design by Amy Hill

As always, for Laura with all of my love

Contents

Part Two

Author's Note

This book is the product of almost two hundred interviews with people who crossed paths with the enigmatic man who eventually called himself Clark Rockefeller, both in Germany and in multiple states in America, as he rose through his many guises and identities.

All facts are taken from the author's interviews, police reports, court and grand jury transcripts, and television and other media accounts.

In some instances, names were changed at the request of the sources.

Any re-creations of scenes and characters' opinions were based on information gathered from the aforementioned interviews, police reports, court and grand jury transcripts, and television and other media accounts.

Foreword

The January sun beat down on the superior courthouse in the Los Angeles suburb of Alhambra, where the man calling himself Clark Rockefeller stood in his blue prison uniform. The courtroom was packed with people who had known him during his thirty-year run of adopting different identities. But when the defendant entered, he looked away from the spectators' gallery, not even glancing in the direction of those he had deceived. Now he was locked in a cage, released only briefly to appear in this courthouse and hear evidence of the new charge that had been levied against him.

If this situation perturbed him, which it surely must have, he showed no signs of irritation. Actually, he showed little sign of any emotion. His face was thinner, his complexion more pallid, and the corners of his mouth drawn more deeply into a permanent pout in the two years since his trial for kidnapping his daughter in Boston.

The bon vivant who had traipsed through America's most privileged enclaves for thirty years, using various names and increasingly grandiose personas, eventually crowning himself "Clark Rockefeller," was now facing a murder charge. Twenty-nine witnesses would be called during a five-day preliminary hearing before Judge Jared Moses to determine if there was enough evidence for the impostor to stand trial. For me, it was another astonishing twist in a life rife with surprises. I had spent the previous three years writing about the prisoner. Each time I thought I had the whole story, some event, lead, or newly discovered identity would send me scurrying back to the beat that had become my home away from home.

Now, the shocking murder charge hung over him in the courtroom. Here, the defendant was arraigned under his real name, the name he used when he arrived in Boston from his hometown in Germany in 1978: Christian Karl Gerhartsreiter. His once booming, rich-boy's lockjaw voice had shrunk to a whisper, with which, in court appearances, he could barely cough out the words "Not guilty."

As the legal system prepared to hear another case against Clark Rockefeller, those of us who had become spectators—including people he had duped as well as I and others who had chronicled his incredible story—could only hold our breath and wait to see what the great impostor would do next.

The Man in the Rockefeller Suit

Prologue

The plan was foolproof, the route rehearsed, the cast of characters in place, the itinerary perfectly organized. Outwardly calm but with his heart racing, he was at last ready to accomplish what he had been so meticulously planning for months.

He had come a long way to land in this privileged place, a fifth-floor room in Boston's Algonquin Club, a venerable bastion of the most blue-blooded city in America, a preferred meeting place since 1886 for U.S. presidents, heads of state, and local and national aristocrats. He *belonged* here; he was a member of the board and a familiar presence in the club's impossibly grand rooms, with their tall ceilings, museum-quality paintings, and uniformed staff, all of whom he had come to know and rely upon. His name was James Frederick Mills Clark Rockefeller—Clark to his friends but Mr. Rockefeller to everyone else.

"Good day, Mr. Rockefeller," the waiters would say as he sat for breakfast or lunch in the dining room, with its four fireplaces and a magnificent view of Commonwealth Avenue. Or "Good evening, Mr. Rockefeller," as they fetched him his evening sherry in the book-lined library, surrounded by the portraits of past members, whose ranks included President Calvin Coolidge and a Who's Who of American dignitaries. At forty-seven, he was well entrenched as a link in the country's most fabled family, which traced its lineage back to John D. Rockefeller, who founded Standard Oil and created a dynasty of philanthropists.

Lately, a cloud had darkened Clark Rockefeller's usually sunny façade. This explained why he was living, instead of merely lunching, in the Algonquin, which served its members as a haven not only from the unruliness of the outside world but also from temporarily painful and unfortunate events such as marital separation and, as in Rockefeller's case, divorce. Today, however, he had reason to rejoice. He was going to spend it with his adorable little daughter, Reigh, a precious, precocious seven-year-old he called Snooks.

It was a bright Sunday morning, and he put on his customary uniform: well-worn khakis, a sky blue Lacoste shirt with the crocodile embroidered over the heart, Top-Sider boat shoes (as always, without socks), and a red baseball cap emblazoned with the word YALE. He adjusted his heavy black-framed glasses, which some people thought brought Nelson Rockefeller to mind, and proceeded from his room down the wide wooden stairway. After passing through the club's hallway, redolent of polish and leather, he entered the imposing front lobby, where Snooks was waiting for him, along with the clinical social worker who was to chaperone their eight-hour visit. Even though Rockefeller's ex-wife, Sandra, was just a few blocks away, she had followed a court order to ferry the child through the social worker.

"Hi, Daddy!" Snooks exclaimed, rushing over to hug him. She was small for seven, with a blond pageboy haircut and a crooked smile, wearing a sundress. Around noon, Rockefeller hoisted her on his shoulders and started walking toward Boston Common, where they had talked about riding the swan boats in the Public Garden. "Good morning, Mr. Rockefeller," people said as he passed, for he was well known in this Beacon Hill neighborhood, having lived here for years in a four-story, ivy-covered $2.7 million town house on one of the best streets in the city.

That was before Sandra dragged him through a painful and humiliating divorce, taking not only the Beacon Hill house but also their second home, in New Hampshire. She had also won custody of Snooks and moved her all the way to London, where she now worked, leaving him with only three court-supervised eight-hour visits per year. Today was the first, and his daughter had to be accompanied by Howard Yaffe, the social worker who was tagging behind them like a creaky third wheel.

But Clark Rockefeller still had his name, his intelligence, an extraordinary art collection valued at close to a billion dollars, good friends in high places, and cherished private club memberships along the eastern seaboard, where he could avoid bourgeois hotels and restaurants. Although he'd lost Snooks, he'd gotten $800,000 in the divorce settlement, and today he had his adored daughter back with him.

He turned the corner onto Marlborough Street, the tree-lined avenue where Teddy Kennedy once kept a residence. A black SUV was parked at the curb far down the block. Behind the wheel was Darryl Hopkins, a down-on-his-luck limo driver who had had the good fortune to pick up a Rockefeller in the rain one day. He had been driving through downtown Boston the previous summer when he spotted the dignified gent—soaking wet, dressed as if he had just been sailing—attempting to flag down a cab. Hopkins screeched to a stop and offered him a lift. Since then, Hopkins and his distinguished passenger had become something of a team. Rockefeller didn't have a driver's license but always seemed to have somewhere he needed to go, and Hopkins was more than happy to provide wheels for him.

Mr. Rockefeller had the kind of peculiarities that the driver expected from very rich people. He spoke in a heavy East Coast rich boy's lockjaw and dressed exclusively in the uniform of the Wasp aristocracy: blue blazers and rep ties or ascots, when he wasn't wearing khakis and a polo shirt. Before Rockefeller's wife and little daughter had decamped for London, Hopkins used to drop off Snooks at Southfield, the exclusive private girls' school in Brookline, and pick her up.

Today was a bit unusual. Rockefeller had told Hopkins that he and

Snooks had a sailing date in Newport with the son of Lincoln Chafee, the former Rhode Island senator who was known to be a "Rockefeller Republican." But he said he had a problem—a clingy family friend he would have to ditch before they got in the limousine. He offered $2,500 for Hopkins's help.

Shortly after noon, Hopkins was parked on Marlborough Street when he saw them strolling toward the limo, a short three-person parade—Rockefeller with Snooks on his shoulders, trailed by a compact middle-aged man wearing jeans and a bright yellow polo shirt.

As they approached the vehicle, Rockefeller put Snooks down and stopped to point out one of the street's particularly stunning historic homes. When Yaffe turned to look at the building, the scion of the famous family tackled him with a body block that slammed the social worker to the ground.

Hopkins had already started the engine when Rockefeller snatched open the back door, yelled, "Get in!" to his daughter as he shoved her onto the seat—with such force that the doll she had been carrying flew out of her hands—and leaped in after her.

As Rockefeller yanked the door shut, Yaffe scrambled to his feet, grabbed the handle, and tried to climb inside. "Go, go, *go!*" Rockefeller ordered, and Hopkins stepped on the gas, dragging the social worker several yards before he finally let go, hitting his head on the side of the vehicle before crashing to the pavement.

Inside the limo, Snooks was wailing and holding her head, which had slammed into the doorframe as her father thrust her into the car.

"What happened?" Hopkins asked her, glancing into the rearview mirror as he sped away. "Did you hit your head?"

"I didn't just hit it, I *smashed* it," said the little girl.

"Well, at least we got rid of Harold," said Rockefeller, meaning Howard Yaffe.

"I know, Daddy," said Snooks, her crying subsiding as she began to calm down.

Rockefeller barked orders at Hopkins—*Take a right, then a left, now right, left*—until they were in front of a cab parked outside the White Hen Pantry convenience store on Beacon Hill.

"Stop right here!" cried Rockefeller. The plans for Newport had changed, he announced. He wanted to take his daughter to Massachusetts General Hospital to have her head injury checked, and he would grab this cab. "Wait for me at the Whole Foods parking lot," he said, throwing an envelope containing cash onto the front seat.

Once in the taxi, Rockefeller directed the driver not to Mass General but to the Boston Sailing Center. A few minutes later, he and Snooks were climbing into the back of a white Lexus SUV. In the driver's seat was Aileen Ang, a thirty-year-old Asian American piano and flute teacher and Web designer. She had met Rockefeller one year earlier at a members' night at the sailing center. Ang had found him eccentric but not unexpectedly so, given his pedigree, and as time passed she had gotten to know him fairly well, just as a friend.

Recently, he had told her that he was going to sail around the world with his daughter in his new seventy-two-foot sailboat. He invited Ang to join them, saying she could give Snooks piano lessons. Then, just two days ago, her cell phone had rung when she was in a movie theater. She later found that Clark had left her a voicemail asking, "Are you ready to go cruising?"

She called back to say she couldn't go, and he said fine, but could she drive him to New York City, where his boat was docked? Of course, he said, he would pay for her gas and her time, a sum of $500. Since Aileen knew he couldn't drive, she agreed.

On Sunday, she was waiting in her car outside the Boston Sailing Center when Rockefeller and his daughter rushed over and crawled into the backseat. "If you don't mind, I'm going to sit back here, because Snooks has a headache and I want to take care of her," he said. Ang started the car.

"Where are we going, Daddy?" Snooks asked.

"We're going to our new boat," he told her.

Then the father and daughter both lay down in the backseat. Soon after Ang entered Rhode Island, Rockefeller climbed into the passenger seat and asked to borrow her cell phone. Later she picked it up and saw that he had turned it off.

With pounding rain and terrible traffic, the trip stretched to almost seven hours. At one point Ang turned her phone on and saw that she had four messages.

"Just leave it alone," Rockefeller ordered. Dutifully she switched it off again. As she drove, she could hear Rockefeller and Snooks talking, playing games, and singing songs.

"I love you too much, Daddy," Snooks said at one point.

As they were driving into New York City, Clark told Ang to head toward Forty-second Street and Sixth Avenue, where he and Snooks would catch a cab to Long Island for the boat launch. She got stopped in traffic in front of Grand Central Terminal, and before she could even pull over, he said, "I'm going to get off here and grab a cab." He tossed an envelope filled with cash onto the front seat, grabbed his daughter, and took off without even saying goodbye.

As Ang watched them walk away, she turned her phone back on. It rang almost immediately. "What's your Rockefeller friend's first name?" asked the caller.

Ang was perplexed. "Clark," she said.

"Well, he's just abducted his kid and hit a social worker. They're looking for him all over Massachusetts. There's an Amber Alert."

"They just got out of my car!" said Ang. "What should I do?"

"Call the police!"

Several hours earlier, back in Boston, Howard Yaffe had sat up dazed in the street. His hip, chin, shoulder, and knee were bruised and bleeding, and his head was throbbing. He managed to pull out his cell phone and dial 911. "A dad has just kidnapped his daughter!" he told the dispatcher. Once he'd given the necessary details, he called the Four Seasons Hotel, where Rockefeller's ex-wife was staying.

"Sandy, he's got her," he said. "I don't know what to tell you. He's got her. I'm on Marlborough Street. The police are here."

Sandra Boss, a tall, attractive woman with a usually confident air, rushed to the scene in a cab. Devastated and distraught, she was crying and frantically pacing in the street. Then a thin, grizzled private investigator ran up to her. Boss had hired his company to send someone to watch Rockefeller and Snooks secretly from the park, but the PI had bungled the stakeout. Yaffe and Boss could only stand there, dumbfounded, and wait for the police to arrive. The getaway point was about to become a crime scene.

"I knew this would happen!" Boss told the police when they got there. "You'll *never* find them now!"

"Why?" asked one of the officers.

"Because he's not who he says he is."

After twelve years of marriage, she had only recently come to realize this. During their divorce proceedings, in the summer of 2007, Boss had filed an affidavit calling into question her husband's identity. He shot back with his own legal response, signed, sworn to, and filed in court, under penalty of perjury:

Sandra L. Boss and I met on February 5, 1993, and ever since then she has known me by my one and only name, James Frederick Mills Clark Rockefeller. If I indeed had a different name, one would find it difficult to imagine that in nearly 15 years such a fact would not have come to light, particularly since Sandra throughout our life together met many persons who have known me by the same name for much longer than she has known me.

Now he was sending out another response: Catch me if you can.

An ambulance rushed Yaffe to the hospital with a concussion. Detective Joe Leeman from the Boston Police Department drove the frantic Boss back to her hotel, and she gave him pictures of her daughter and ex-husband, which were quickly distributed far and wide. Meanwhile, at police headquarters, clerks proceeded to enter Rockefeller's name into various databases. They found nothing. One of them called the detectives, who put Boss on the phone. To their amazement, she claimed that Clark did not have a social security number or a driver's license and that she had never seen his tax returns.

What about credit cards and cell phones?

His credit cards had been in her name, she explained. As far as she knew, he didn't have a passport or a checking account. Since their divorce, she had reached him at a cell phone number listed in the name of a friend. She couldn't give them any information that would help trace him.

Twenty-four hours after the kidnapping, the curious case of Clark Rockefeller was being scrutinized by FBI special agent Noreen Gleason. She put in a request for the suspect's records, expecting to receive the usual upper-class profile: Ivy League diplomas, a long string of privileged addresses, tax returns with seven-figure bottom lines.

"There's *nothing*," the investigators told her.

She asked for his social security number.

"Not even that," came the reply.

Gleason was incredulous. She called a Rockefeller family spokesman. Of the 78 direct descendants of John D. Rockefeller Jr. and 140 descendants of John D. Rockefeller, there was not a Clark among them. He might be a distant cousin, the spokesman said, but, given the circumstances of his crime, that seemed highly unlikely. In short, the spokesman declared, "We've never heard of him."

Very soon, however, anyone who watched television or followed the news had heard of him. Gleason and a battalion of FBI agents and police in the United States and abroad would spend the next six days chasing a shadow. Like Darryl Hopkins and Aileen Ang, the authorities quickly realized that they had been duped. Before embarking on the kidnapping, Rockefeller had devised an equally elaborate escape plan. He told his many well-heeled friends that he was taking a trip, in every case to a different destination, in every case a lie. To one, he said he was sailing to Bermuda; to another, flying to Peru; to another, the Turks and

Caicos. From Alaska to Antarctica, the authorities tracked down every lead, and every one turned out to be a dead end.

Because of all the publicity, tips poured in to the FBI and the Boston police from around the globe. But the most valuable one came from a friend of Rockefeller's right there in Boston. Clark had been at his house the night before the kidnapping, the friend told investigators, and had drunk a glass of water. The friend hadn't washed the glass yet, so agents rushed over and got it. Technicians carefully lifted the fingerprints and sent them off to the FBI lab in Quantico, Virginia.

While the prints were being analyzed, Gleason fretted. It wasn't just that they didn't know who in hell the abductor was; more important, they couldn't know what he might do now with his daughter. Gleason was a tough blonde who'd put in seventeen years at the FBI's Boston field office. She knew how badly a parental kidnapping could go. In too many cases the kidnapping spouse, when tracked down, said, "If I can't have her, she's not going to have her either." Such cases often ended with the kidnapper killing the child and then himself. If they let it get to the point where Rockefeller knew he'd been caught and he still had his daughter, Gleason feared the game would be over. All the power would be in his hands.

"We need a ruse," Gleason told her associates. But they had to locate him first.

When the fingerprints came back from the lab, one thing was finally clear: the kidnapper was definitely not a Rockefeller. He was Christian Karl Gerhartsreiter, a forty-seven-year-old German immigrant who had come to America as a student in 1978. Shortly after his arrival, he disappeared into what the Boston district attorney would call "the longest con I've seen in my professional career." The elaborate, labyrinthine nature of Gerhartsreiter's shape-shifting adventures, from the time he set foot in this country as a seventeen-year-old student right up to his disappearance, makes his story more bizarre than any gifted writer of fiction could possibly invent.

It was the summer of 2008, and the economic boom was about to go bust. Housing prices were beginning to sink, investment funds would soon be gutted, and America's New Gilded Age ethos was starting to seem a thing of the past. Within months, of course, the era of excess would be over. The crash would come in a sickening wave, revealing just how much had been built on an illusion. In this, Clark Rockefeller was a man for the times.

It was my longtime friend Roxane West, a woman who divides her time between New York City and Texas, who first told me about Clark, screaming his name to me over the phone the day after the kidnapping. "Clark Rockefeller!" she said breathlessly. "Mark, did you hear about Clark Rockefeller?"

Roxane launched into a wild and improbable story. A vivacious blond Texas oil heiress, she'd recently been living part-time in New York and begun attracting the attention of billionaires, rock stars, UN diplomats, and heads of state. Two months earlier, Roxane and some friends had been touring the art galleries of the Upper East Side, including Steigrad Fine Arts, which was located in an opulent town house on East Sixty-ninth Street and specialized in old masters. There, during the cocktail hour, she met an unusually charming man who said he was an old friend of the gallery's owners.

"Hi, how are you?" he had asked in an upper-crust accent. "My name is Clark"—he paused, then dropped the last name—"Rockefeller."

"Oh, hello," said Roxane.

He certainly looked like a Rockefeller, she thought: the preppy chinos, blue blazer, and red rep tie; the scholarly glasses; the patrician air. Roxane's friend Eric Hunter Slater, a student of bone structure who prided himself on being able to spot a blueblood from across a crowded room, saw the resemblance too. "He's got the Rockefeller chin," Slater whispered to Roxane once the man had turned away. "Notice the jawline: small but strong. It's a dead giveaway."

Almost immediately, Rockefeller began trailing behind Roxane. He invited himself along when she and her friends left the gallery, and when the group wound up at a friend's apartment, he cozied up with her on the couch. At the end of the evening he insisted on dropping her off at her home in a taxi.

She received a text message from him the next day. "Sorry about the impersonal text, but giving a tour of the Met, which frowns on phone usage," he wrote. "Let us meet . . . Please text me . . . I did want to tell you that I find you superbly . . ." Then the text trailed off, leaving it up to Roxane to figure out what he meant.

He called her shortly after that, suggesting they have lunch. They met at a fashionable Upper East Side restaurant, and he told her a little about his life. His parents had been killed in a car crash when he was very young, he said, leaving him with a sizable trust. He was forty, a graduate of Yale, and a single father—his seven-year-old daughter had been produced by a surrogate whose egg had been fertilized by his sperm. He worked as a nuclear physicist and was about to leave for China on a business trip. He'd just come from giving his daughter and her friends a tour of the Metropolitan Museum of Art, whose collection he knew extensively, since his family had donated much of it.

After paying cash for their lunch, Clark said goodbye to Roxane at the curb. Almost as soon as he left, she began receiving e-mails and text messages from him. He called it text flirting. She proceeded to share some examples over the phone:

"Problem: I cannot get you out of my head. What to do? Argh!"

"Just gazed at Saturn for the last ten minutes. Viewing excellent tonight in Brookline. Wish you could see this. Wish I could see you."

"In a submarine. Crowded. Strange. Thought of you a minute ago."

"Sipping strange tropical drink in Nantucket now. Would love to see you. This coming week perhaps go to Central Park and kiss. Sound good?"

But then he complained that he wouldn't be able to make it to Manhattan, because he couldn't find suitable accommodations in any of his private clubs, and he said he would *never* consider a hotel. "Have overnight sitter, but all clubs totally booked for tomorrow . . . annoying."

After reading me a few more messages, Roxane said she never saw the mysterious man after their one lunch together. Then she suddenly shouted, "And now he's kidnapped his daughter!"

That night I turned on the television to discover that almost every channel was talking about Roxane's suitor, but in even more sensational terms.

"International manhunt under way for a Rockefeller!" one news anchor exclaimed.

"Authorities search over land and sea for a man and his seven-year-old daughter," reported another.

Clark Rockefeller was suddenly the most wanted man in America. He'd soon become emblematic of a time when people would believe just about anything if it was wrapped in a famous name. As his story unfolded, it seemed, like its main character, almost too astonishing to believe.

Part One

CHAPTER 1

Christian Karl Gerhartsreiter: Bergen, Germany

T he public's first glimpse of the "real" Clark Rockefeller was on May 28, 2009, at the Suffolk County Superior Court in downtown Boston. Hordes of spectators and press were eager to finally get a good look at the mystery man who had simultaneously fascinated and horrified Bostonians for nearly a year. It was beyond imagination that here, in one of the best-educated cities in America, a smooth-talking German immigrant could successfully pose not merely as a member of the aristocracy but as a *Rockefeller*.

The defendant was hustled in by a group of guards. Seated among his high-priced team of attorneys, he was still completely in character as a Boston Brahmin and gentleman of the world. He entered the courtroom, to paraphrase Carly Simon, as if he were stepping onto a yacht—or into one of the many private clubs to which he had belonged. It was as if his life of wealth and privilege were only being temporarily disturbed by this unfortunate proceeding.

"Hear ye, hear ye!" the bailiff boomed, announcing that court was in session. Then he instructed everyone to rise as the judge, a handsome, no-nonsense Italian American named Frank M. Gaziano, entered the courtroom. From the moment he spoke, in a commanding voice, it was clear that this judge was going to do everything by the book. The defendant stood, buttoning his sports coat. He was wearing perfectly broken-in chinos and Top-Siders with no socks, just as he had been on the day he kidnapped his daughter, but instead of a polo shirt he wore a white button-down, a red-striped rep tie, and a navy blue blazer with brass buttons. He stared straight ahead, sphinxlike, as the prosecutor, David Deakin, began leveling all manner of charges against him.

Clean-cut and straight-talking, Deakin brought to mind Atticus Finch, the saintly country lawyer in *To Kill a Mockingbird*, as portrayed by Gregory Peck in the film version of the classic novel.

"The rules don't apply to Christian Gerhartsreiter," Deakin began.

At this, Rockefeller showed absolutely no emotion.

"That is what the evidence is going to show you he believed."

Deakin addressed the members of the jury, who had been chosen mainly because they had somehow managed to remain unaware of the barrage of media coverage about the incredible case of Clark Rockefeller. For a master con man, duping this group of mostly young, impressionable-looking Bostonians would be the ultimate victory.

However, Rockefeller did not deign to testify; instead, he let his lawyers tell his story *exactly* the way he wanted it told. He sat silently as the prosecution witnesses recounted how he had tricked them, his only shows of emotion an occasional blink or a clench of his jaw.

I had been investigating Clark Rockefeller since the previous summer and was convinced that the trial would answer my lingering questions about his fabricated life. Here, in this courtroom, the people Rockefeller had taken for a ride in his once indecipherable puzzle of a life were set to testify against him—most importantly his ex-wife, the ultra-successful management consultant Sandra Boss. I imagined that it would be like a cafeteria line of information: the witnesses would dish it out and all I'd have to do would be to write it down.

How wrong I would turn out to be.

As the case dragged on for more than two weeks, and as I listened to the parade of people whose trust the defendant had betrayed, I realized that I was as gullible as any of them. I had allowed myself to believe, just as they had, that I actually *knew* the man. In fact I knew only a small piece of the story; despite having spent a year doing research, I had seen only the tail of a whale. The body remained submerged and hidden from view.

"To understand this evidence you are going to have to go back to 1978," David Deakin had told the jury at the outset of the trial, "because it was in that year that seventeen-year-old Christian Karl Gerharts-reiter, born in Siegsdorf, Germany . . . came to the United States on a tourist visa."

He was right. To even come close to drawing a portrait of a phantom, one had to go back to the beginning, to the obscure corner of Germany where the young man supposedly met the first victims of his lifelong con.

One day in the courtroom, as the prosecutor was trying to untangle the jumbled threads of Clark Rockefeller's past, he read a brief letter that the defendant had written to the U.S. Immigration and Naturalization Service in Milwaukee a few years after his arrival in America. It was dated May 26, 1981:

> Dear Sirs: With this letter, I would like to inform you that,
> as of tomorrow, my address is going to be changed. My new
> address is:
>
> > Christian K. Gerhartsreiter
> > c/o Dr. Elmer Kelln
> > [Address withheld]
> > Loma Linda, California 92354

The name was a clue, the first step in what would become a very long and unforgettable journey.

"Hello," a woman answered at the Kellns' Loma Linda, California, home. She stopped me as soon as I said the name Clark Rockefeller.

"Elmer!" she yelled, and her husband came on the line. "It's quite a story," Elmer said, suggesting that I come out to California for a visit.

Elmer and Jean Kelln are still in the same modest home, on a typically pleasant Southern California street, where they lived when they first met the man now known as Clark Rockefeller. Jean, a large, bubbly, hospitable woman, opened the door. "I made a chicken salad," she said, leading me into a sunny living room with an upright piano in the corner. "I hope you'll stay for lunch." Elmer joined us in the kitchen. A short, compactly built man who looked a bit like the actor Mickey Rooney, he had recently retired from his dentistry practice and had become a faculty member at Loma Linda University's dental school.

It soon became clear that although more than thirty years had passed, both of them were still smarting at the way they remembered every detail of their experiences with the future Clark Rockefeller. As Elmer told me their story, his wife got up from the table and returned with a batch of photographs.

"He was *always* posing," she said of the man I had watched sitting mute and stone-faced for weeks on end in the Boston courtroom. She showed me a picture of a teenager with long brown hair, wearing a white schoolboy sweater over a blue shirt and giving the camera a wry smile. Then she flipped through a dozen others. One of the most intriguing photos didn't have anyone in it. It showed a little cluster of buildings with what looked like a totem pole in the middle of them. It was Christian Gerhartsreiter's hometown of Bergen, Germany. After hearing Elmer and Jean Kelln's remarkable tale, I decided it would be the next stop on my journey to find out who Clark Rockefeller really was.

Bergen is a speck of a town—a village, really—home to five thousand people, each of whom seems to know everyone else. I drove from Munich, less than fifty miles away, with a German journalist I had enlisted as my interpreter and guide.

On first impression Bergen looks like something out of a fairy tale, a picturesque hamlet nestled in a verdant valley of the Bavarian Alps.

The focal points of the town center are a church and a beer garden (God and beer being the two pillars of Bavarian life), and towering over both of them is the totem pole from Jean Kelln's photo; it's actually a maypole, I later learned, a common sight in Bavarian villages.

It wasn't difficult to find the house where Christian Karl Gerhartsreiter had grown up, at 19 Bahnhof (Train Station) Street—it was almost the first one off the highway. But as soon as we parked in front of the row of shops across the street from the house, I could literally hear the sound of doors locking and shutters being drawn. In the coffee shop directly across the street from the Gerhartsreiter home, a woman said that Irmengard Gerhartsreiter lived in the house and her son Alexander lived in an apartment in the back. Irmengard's husband, Simon, had died many years ago. The woman knew this, she added, because Irmengard's parents had once run a business where the coffee shop now stands.

The childhood home of Christian Karl Gerhartsreiter is a white two-story house with a starburst over the door and intricate designs around the windows, accentuated by navy blue shutters and a profusion of red geraniums exploding from window boxes. I knocked on the door repeatedly, but there was no answer and no audible movement inside the house. Peering through a window, I could see a tidy kitchen and other obviously inhabited but impeccably neat rooms.

My interpreter and I tried calling Alexander Gerhartsreiter at work. He had been the one to confirm for the American press that the man calling himself Clark Rockefeller was indeed his older brother, after a reporter from the *Boston Herald* knocked on his door and showed him a picture of the accused parental kidnapper. However, he was apparently done talking. "You don't have to go any further—the answer is no," he told us before slamming down the phone.

The Gerhartsreiters' next-door neighbor was more receptive. The door swung open almost immediately, and Helga Hallweger extended her hand in greeting. We explained the purpose of our visit, and she invited us in.

A short, pleasant woman, Hallweger said she knew the Gerharts-reiters well, having lived next door to them for decades. We sat at the kitchen table of her clean, simple house, and she told us about the family. Simon and Irmengard Gerhartsreiter were both natives of Bergen—they had grown up across the street from each other, in fact. While Simon was very outgoing, Irmengard was quiet and kept to herself. They were married in the town church and settled into the modest house that Simon's father, a carpenter, built by hand.

On February 21, 1961, they had their first child, Christian. There isn't a hospital in Bergen, so he was born in the nearby town of Siegsdorf. "Parents: Simon Gerhartsreiter, Catholic, and Irmengard Gerharts-reiter, maiden name Huber, Catholic, both residents of Bergen," read his birth certificate, which I had seen in his police dossier in Boston.

Simon was "a lovely guy," according to Helga Hallweger. He was an artist and housepainter, adept at creating the elaborately filigreed trompe-l'oeil detailing often found around the windows and doors of Bavarian homes, including the Gerhartsreiters'. "He cracked jokes, told stories," Hallweger said. "And he was *so* grateful that we bought one of his paintings." He painted mostly landscapes of Bergen and the surrounding countryside, and Hallweger went to fetch the one that she and her husband had bought. It was a lovely depiction of the Bavarian Alps in winter—Simon clearly had some talent. Not only that, my hostess added, he was admired in Bergen for being a leader, a member of every possible club and cause.

"Irmengard was more reclusive," Hallweger said. The two women would always chat when they were outside tending their gardens, but "she never came into the house." I thought it odd that Hallweger was speaking in the past tense when referring to someone who was still alive and who still lived next door, but I soon realized why. Since October 8, 2008—the day the true identity of Clark Rockefeller was revealed—Irmengard Gerhartsreiter had seemingly turned into a different woman.

"Irmengard went to stay with a friend in the country for a couple of days, hoping the press would go away," Hallweger said. "When she came back, I rang the bell and gave her a flowerpot. She said, 'Thank you for your bravery,' and then she shut the door and she never spoke to me again."

I asked if she had seen her since, and Hallweger told me, "Yes, and I said, 'Good morning, Irmengard.' She didn't say anything, just went straight back into the house." Irmengard Gerhartsreiter had yet to recover, it seemed, from the onslaught of reporters and photographers who had shown up on her doorstep, one of whom had even followed her inside her home. A photo taken by a press photographer at the time of her son's arrest tells the story best. It shows the Gerhartsreiter house with an immaculately kept yard. By the time of my visit, the lawn was overgrown and abandoned-looking. Speaking about Irmengard, Helga couldn't bring herself to say the words that I would later hear from other Bergen residents—disturbed, in need of treatment—but the implication was clear.

An artist father and an introverted mother in a small town where everyone knew about everyone else's affairs—the crucible in which Christian Gerhartsreiter had been formed was coming into sharper focus.

Christian's brother, Alexander, wasn't born until 1973, so for the first twelve years of his life Christian was an only child, the cherished center of attention in a house that included not only his parents but also an aunt and grandmother. They indulged the boy's every whim, including allowing him to watch whatever he wanted on television—even the science-fiction programs that were forbidden by most local parents.

"I thought he had discipline issues," said Hallweger. "My son played with him when he was small, and he would do things with Christian that weren't allowed." For instance, most Bergen parents agreed that the local stream was a dangerous place for young children to play, but it was a favorite spot of Christian's, and he would not hesitate to take other kids there. As he got older, Hallweger continued, he became even more of a hellion. "He would bang his soccer ball against the garage door for hours—for hours! Although they were all at home, there was nobody saying, 'Stop it!' I went over there and complained, but Christian didn't care."

Instead of gratitude for his favored treatment, Christian increasingly expressed contempt. It soon became clear that he wasn't like most of the other residents of this little town, content to live there from humble birth to anonymous death. By the time he reached adolescence, Christian was focused on a single goal: escape.

He separated himself from the rest of Bergen with not only his attitude but also his appearance. "He became addicted to looking *cool*," Hallweger said. "He had to be different. He had a certain hat he wore, and he had sunglasses and long hair. All of this was unusual for Bergen. But Christian always had to be ahead of everyone else in fashion."

She sighed and looked in the direction of the house next door. If I wanted to learn more about Christian, she said, I should walk over to the beer garden and join the *Stammtisch*, the table reserved for local men who come to the tavern daily to drink and trade stories. I looked at my watch: it was only ten in the morning.

"Don't worry about that," Hallweger told me. The *Stammtisch* would already be in session.

She was right. The *Stammtisch* was in full swing when I arrived. There was a group of men sitting at a table beneath the trees in the outdoor section of the beer garden, each with a frosty stein in front of him. My interpreter and I approached the men, who were mostly in their sixties, seventies, and eighties. They eyed us suspiciously. We were two strangers carrying notebooks, and that could mean only one thing: *They've come to talk about Christian.* They had had their fill of nosy reporters. But once my German companion started making small talk and joking with them—and especially once I offered to buy everyone a round of drinks—they loosened up, and the stories began flowing as freely as the beer.

One of the men, Georg Heindlmeir, was eighty-three—he was born the same year as Simon Gerhartsreiter, with whom he grew up.

"If Simon were alive, he would be here now!" Heilmeir said.

"Here?" I asked. "Drinking beer before noon?"

He said yes, and the other men agreed. Simon wasn't merely a member of the *Stammtisch*, they explained, he was the head of it. "Because he was an artist," one of the men explained, "and artists don't have set working hours. He would turn up every day at ten in the morning, on the dot, and he would leave at eleven fifty-five every day to be home for lunch. If Simon Gerhartsreiter opened his mouth, everybody got quiet, because Simon always had something to say." He raised his beer stein and toasted the *Stammtisch*'s late leader, repeating, "He was an *artist*."

As the day progressed, some of the men left and others arrived, and each had a different perspective on the oddball kid who had become, for better or worse, Bergen's most famous citizen. One of them knew Christian from school and recalled, "He always tried to impress the other people in class. He was simply too weird for us."

"He was very clever!" added another.

"Christian read a lot of the classics," the first man said. "When we were eleven or twelve, he would come up with the most incredible quotes. He was a very good speaker. It was easy for him to express himself. But he didn't get good grades in school."

"And he was a mama's boy!" a third man added.

Yes, others agreed, a mama's boy with a locally famous father.

He would try to measure up to Simon. "He came to school in a *suit*," said his classmate. "Not a Bavarian suit, but a proper business suit, the kind you only wore to church on Sundays or to a wedding. But it made his mother proud. Irmengard loved extravagance. She was just a simple tailor, taking in neighbors' clothing to repair, but she tried to behave like a lady."

As lunch hour turned to cocktail hour and cocktail hour to nighttime, the beer drinkers moved from the outdoor table to a bigger one inside the tavern, with a metal sign in the middle of it spelling out the word *Stammtisch*. A friendly waitress kept on bringing beers, the air filled with tobacco smoke, and the stories about Christian got increasingly wild.

Christian inherited his father's creativity, the men said, but instead of painting he went into role-playing, imagining himself far from the small town he seemed destined to live and die in. The family toolshed became his workshop, where he could fiddle with all manner of gadgetry: radios, television sets, film equipment. Among his hobbies were eavesdropping on truck drivers as they chatted on their CB radios and watching old American movies. The more he saw of America on film, the more he felt he needed to escape Bergen.

"His major task became to make fun of our teachers," said Christian's former classmate. "At the start of the day, he would announce to us, 'Watch out!' and you knew something would happen."

"What did he do?" several of the men asked in unison.

"One morning he approached the teacher with his fist closed. 'What is in your hand, Christian?' she asked, and then added, 'Give it to me.' He opened his fist. There was pepper in it, and he blew it in her face."

The men shook their heads. Another beer drinker suddenly remembered another story.

"Simon brought Christian to the *Stammtisch* every Friday night," he said. They would always sit side by side, right where we were sitting now, "and Simon would say of his son, *'Er ist ein verrückter Hund.'*" My companion leaned over to translate: "'He is a mad dog.'"

The man continued, "But he meant it as a compliment. Simon thought Christian was strange, but he was *proud* of his son. He was saying, 'He's mad like me. And in a strange way, he will do well.'" He was proud of his son's nerve and defiance—qualities he knew the boy would need in spades in order to create a life for himself outside of Bergen.

Christian was too big for Bergen, all of the men seemed to be saying, and creating another persona was the only way he would ever leave the little town that nobody ever leaves. To escape the preordained and predictable future that awaited him here, he would have to invent a new self out of whole cloth. After all, his father had also attempted to get away from Bergen, enrolling in art school in Munich, only to be forced to return after the death of his father and his lack of success as an artist. Perhaps that's why Simon was proud of Christian. He was striving to do exactly what Simon himself had failed to accomplish during his short stint in art school: to become a success in a different arena from his forefathers and in a place beyond the boundaries of the little town where he was born and raised.

I mentioned something that one of Christian's childhood friends had told the *New York Times:*

"Christian liked to play games in which he adopted another identity," said Thomas Schweiger, a onetime close friend.

   At thirteen, Mr. Schweiger said, Christian telephoned a government office that registered cars, "and he changed his voice and said
that he was a millionaire from Holland and that he wanted to register his two Rolls-Royces." Although the clerk was skeptical, Christian
persuaded him, his friend said. "He really played this role perfect."

The men laughed. It was yet another illustration of young Christian Gerhartsreiter on his journey to discovering an incredibly gullible
world. Then another man jumped into the conversation with a story
that he seemed certain would trump all the others, but as he started to
tell it, several of the others interrupted, exclaiming, "The hearse!"

One of the beer drinkers took up the thread. "Shortly before Christian left for America, he and his father fell out over something," the man
said. "His father threw him out of the house and told him, 'You don't
sleep here anymore.' Christian bought a hearse and parked it outside
his parents' house. The village was outraged. At first people thought the
grandmother had died. But Christian was sleeping in it! It was the talk
of the village for a long time. He would drive up to the shooting club
in this big black car. He obviously loved to drive it around and bother
people, to scandalize everybody."

Someone else at the table said the man had gotten it wrong: that
there was indeed a hearse parked in front of the Gerhartsreiter house
for some time, but that it was Christian's brother, Alexander, who drove

it. By now it was past midnight, and I didn't care who had the story straight. My belly was full of beer and my mind was reeling with a full day and night's worth of tales of Bergen. I stumbled back to the small inn where I was staying, beneath the colorful maypole painted with idyllic scenes of everyday Bavarian life, and lapsed into a dead sleep in the quiet little town that Christian Karl Gerhartsreiter left behind.

I awoke to another source with further insights into Bergen's way-ward son: Herbert Willinger, the owner of the inn, sitting behind the front desk. He had gone through school with Christian Gerhartsreiter. Like everyone else, Willinger painted a picture of an aloof young man who considered himself destined for greater things.

"Christian would tell us, 'Everything here in Bavaria is shit. If you want a better life, you have to go to America.'" When his classmates would laugh at him, he'd tell them, "You will see." One day, Willinger continued, "Christian announced that he had gotten a job at a radio station in New York," but Willinger was pretty sure that wasn't true. "Pretending to be someone else was totally his character."

However, Christian had apparently been experimenting with the idea of escape for some time. In order to get a taste of the world beyond Bergen, he would simply walk down the street in front of his family home to the nearby autobahn and stick out his thumb. Within minutes, a car, truck, or motorcycle would stop, and just like that, he'd be off to another town, another world, away from little Bergen. At first he would hitch his way to larger neighboring villages such as Traunstein, or to the city of Rosenheim, where he attended classes. His range grew along with his ambitions, and he became a regular presence on the autobahn, looking for anyone or anything that might help him escape. It was there that Elmer and Jean Kelln, the tourists from Loma Linda, California, drove into his orbit.

It was a torrential downpour, so much rain that the windshield wip-ers of the tiny rental car couldn't keep up. Elmer and Jean could barely make out the autobahn through the blinding storm. They were trying to make their way from Munich to Berchtesgaden to visit the Eagle's Nest, Adolf Hitler's majestic country home high in the Bavarian Alps. At around 5 p.m., the Kellns exited the highway near Bergen, looking for shelter.

Elmer was driving, and he spotted a young man on the shoulder with his thumb in the air. He wouldn't normally pick up a hitchhiker, but he had never been stuck in Germany in a blinding thunderstorm before. "Maybe he can tell us where we can spend the night," Elmer said to his wife. Before she could voice an objection, he pulled over and stopped the car. The drenched young man flung open the back door and climbed inside.

He couldn't have been more than seventeen. He was wearing white sunglasses, tight jeans, and a floppy hat, from beneath which spilled a mass of stringy brown hair. His clothing had been plastered to his thin frame by the rain.

"I'm Christian Karl Gerhartsreiter," he said, extending a damp hand from the backseat, and the way he said the name, the couple felt, he was *somebody*. From the moment they met him they were impressed.

Jean was struck by how handsome he was. He had a long aquiline nose and full lips that broke into a wide grin when he began speaking, which he did practically nonstop. He said he worked as a tour guide for English-speaking visitors in Rosenheim and sometimes in Munich, and his flawless English gave the Kellns little reason to doubt him. Now he was heading home to Bergen, just a few miles down the road.

He wasn't just charming, he was alluring. Although he was a foreigner decades younger than they were, Elmer and Jean Kelln somehow felt that they had something in common with him and wanted to get to know the young man better. "Where would you suggest we spend the night?" asked Elmer.

"You will stay at my house," Christian said. The Kellns were hesitant, but he insisted. In any other circumstances they would have demurred, but the rain was unrelenting, darkness was descending, and something about the young man was practically magnetic. So they accepted.

The Kellns were charmed when they pulled up in front of his family home: an adorable, typically Bavarian house with geraniums in flower boxes outside the windows. By then the rain had subsided. The hitchhiker's father was working on the roof and his mother was in the kitchen. Christian said little more than hello to them as he escorted the Americans inside. It was immediately clear that the son was the man of the house.

Jean marveled at how he had taken over the entire living room and turned it into *his* room, apparently with the blessing, or at least the acquiescence, of his parents. He had set up a large desk as his workstation and hooked up all manner of machinery—most important, a film projector and screen. Movies, Christian explained to Elmer and Jean, were his passion. In fact, he was soon heading to America to become a filmmaker. His favorite genre was film noir, in particular the works of Alfred Hitchcock. He said he would show them an example, and he dimmed the lights and flicked on the projector.

Just then Jean's stomach growled. "We skipped lunch, and I guess we're sort of hungry," she interjected before the film began.

The Kellns invited the entire family for dinner in a restaurant. They all declined, except for Christian, who directed Elmer and Jean to a typical Bavarian place, with music playing, where they sat in a wooden booth and, over wurst and beer, talked of America.

"I want to take your picture!" Jean exclaimed once their drinks arrived.

"Wait," Christian said. He turned his head this way and that in an effort to find the perfect pose. "Now," he instructed, his hand pressed insouciantly to his temple. The camera clicked, capturing the young German with his eyes blazing, staring straight into the lens as if he were getting his head shot taken at Twentieth Century Fox.

After dinner they returned to the Gerhartsreiter home, where Christian led the Kellns to a spare bedroom and said good night.

"I feel so uncomfortable!" Jean whispered urgently to her husband. She couldn't put her finger on why. The house was perfectly pleasant, as were Christian's mother, father, and brother. And, of course, Christian couldn't have been nicer or more accommodating to them. But he completely ignored his parents.

"Go to sleep, Jean," Elmer said.

"I don't know if I can." Unable to shake the feeling that something wasn't quite right with this unusual young man and his family, she lay awake all night. "I felt he was living in a fantasy world of which his parents were not a part," she recalled.

Elmer, looking back on the experience, said he was more puzzled than anything else on their one night in Christian Gerhartsreiter's home. "He did mention that he wanted to get to the United States," he recalled. "You can tell when a hillbilly is happy in his log cabin and when he wants to live in New York. In his mind, he had to *be* something someday. You could pick that up in everything he'd say and do. He wanted notoriety, I guess, fame. And there's no question that he felt he had to divorce himself from the German culture 'cause he wasn't going to get anywhere if he remained a German."

The next morning the Kellns were eager to leave, but Christian insisted they stay for coffee and rolls. After exchanging contact information with their young host, the couple said goodbye and drove off, thinking they'd never see him again.

Not long after that, Christian Karl Gerhartsreiter pulled out a piece of paper and placed it on his desk: the application for a tourist visa that would allow him to come to America. On the line asking who would be sponsoring him during his brief visit, he wrote, "Elmer and Jean Kelln."

CHAPTER 2

Strangers on a Train

The court was a circus, a never-ending parade of seemingly good, honest, trusting people who, to varying degrees, had been duped by the defendant. Once so friendly and charming, the man known as Clark Rockefeller respectfully acknowledged the people who would decide his fate, the judge and jury, by standing when they entered and exited. But as for the witnesses—especially those testifying against him—he didn't even look their way.

One afternoon early in the proceedings, as an immigration official gave sketchy accounts of how the defendant had come to America as a young man, I got a tap on the shoulder and a whisper in the ear.

"Are you free for a drink this evening?" asked a man who later requested that I not reveal his identity.

He told me to meet him at a bar near the courthouse after the proceedings ended for the day. I was nursing a drink when he entered carrying a thick brown envelope. He handed it to me and said simply, "Maybe this will help answer your questions." Then he breezed back out the door.

I opened the envelope and gasped. It was filled with more than a hundred documents—immigration papers, court records, police reports—spelling out in intricate detail the life of the silent, stoic defendant, from his birth certificate to the warrant that had been issued for his arrest the previous summer.

I started reading from the beginning: there was a document from his German high school showing that he had graduated; a letter from the company in Bergen where his father, Simon Gerhartsreiter, was employed as a designer, stating that his salary was "1,900 US-Dollar a month"; an Affidavit of Support from Simon, stating that he would support Christian in America with $250 a month "plus health insurance," because, as he wrote, "I wish my son to attend school in the US for one year."

One year, I thought. Then back to Bergen? Back to the little white house and the self-contained little town? It was immediately clear that time limits were not part of the young immigrant's plans. One of the next pages in the sheaf of papers had been written in neat block letters by the defendant himself. It was a request to change his nonimmigrant status. His tourist visa was to expire on April 15, 1979, six months after he had arrived in the United States, and he was applying to extend that stay for another four years. "My educational objective is . . . College degree in Business Administration," he wrote.

Where the applicant was asked how he would support himself during his time in America, he wrote, "I am presently attending highschool as a senior. I am now receiving $250 per month. My father will pay all college costs for the following four years of study." At the bottom of the form was Simon's compliant signature.

I flipped through the papers, trying to figure out where the immigrant had established residence after arriving in the land of opportunity. But there was only a short typed-out time line:

October 16, 1978: Gerhartsreiter arrives Boston via Lufthansa.
October 21, 1978: Enrolled Berlin, CT High School.
December 31, 1979: Granted an extension of stay due to being a student.

Then I came across a police report. "The investigator spoke with Thomas Glavin, principal of Berlin High School," it read, and listed a succession of statements from Glavin: "That Gerhartsreiter arrived at his school in 1978. That Gerhartsreiter's school records from previous school were in German. That Gerhartsreiter's records show no information relative to his parents. That Gerhartsreiter never graduated from the school."

In the same summer of 1978, when Christian Gerhartsreiter met Elmer and Jean Kelln, he also encountered another American, a young man named Peter Roccapriore, who had just graduated from high school in Meriden, Connecticut. Peter was backpacking through Europe for three months, traveling from country to country on a Eurail pass. One day on a train in Germany, he met the friendly, well-dressed, exceedingly polite and erudite Christian Karl Gerhartsreiter.

As a film fanatic whose favorite director was Alfred Hitchcock, Gerhartsreiter must have relished the Hitchcockian undertones of his encounter. It brought to mind the Master of Suspense's 1951 classic *Strangers on a Train*, in which the mysterious Bruno Antony invades the life of a tennis star, cajoling him first into joining him for a drink and eventually into joining him in murder.

Gerhartsreiter was apparently always on the lookout for people who could help smooth his escape from Bergen, and when he found Peter Roccapriore, he introduced himself. As Bruno Antony had done with his target, Gerhartsreiter ingratiated himself immediately, complimenting, entertaining, treating the young American to lunch in a nice restaurant, and then taking him on a sightseeing expedition through the area. He knew everything about Bavaria, and for good reason: he told Peter Roccapriore that he had grown up in the area amid considerable privilege. His father was an "industrialist," holding a position in the highest levels of the Mercedes-Benz auto company. The American was so thoroughly impressed that when it was time to say goodbye, he couldn't possibly refuse his new friend's cordial request to exchange contact information.

"Hey, if you're ever in Meriden, Connecticut, look me up," Peter Roccapriore supposedly said in parting. "You can stay with us."

A scant few weeks later, Christian took Peter up on the offer. According to friends of the Gerhartsreiter family in Bergen, Christian told his parents that he had gotten a job as a disc jockey in New York City, and they agreed to send him $250 per month until he got settled. His elderly aunt, who lived with the family, agreed to send money as well, so he would be receiving even more than $250 on a monthly basis. Once he had obtained a six-month tourist visa (using the names of Jean and Elmer Kelln as his sponsors), he packed up his belongings and flew from Munich to Boston, where he arrived in the fall of 1978. He was seventeen years old.

When he landed in Boston, he called his mother: the airline had lost his luggage, he claimed. Could she please send extra money for clothing and other essentials? Of course, she said. The next day he traveled to Meriden, Connecticut, a city of about fifty-eight thousand people halfway between New Haven and Hartford. It had no particular significance for Gerhartsreiter, except for the fact that one of the three people he knew in America lived there. He called the number of Peter Roccapriore, the student he had met on the train, explaining to his mother the invitation he had so kindly received from her son that summer. "I'm here at the bus station, can you please come and get me?" he asked. Peter was apparently away that day. But his mother rushed right over. If her son had met a nice young man who had shown him some kindness in Germany, how could she not return the favor? She gave him a room in her home and she and her family welcomed the slightly built blond teenager. Peter took him over to Platt High School in Meriden, and helped him get enrolled in the senior class. The outgoing immigrant had already graduated from high school in Germany, but he didn't tell anyone that.

Christian stayed with the Roccapriore family for only a few weeks—according to the documents I read, they were under the impression that he was going to return to Germany immediately thereafter. But a few weeks was enough time for Gerhartsreiter to lay the groundwork for his American odyssey.

"Exchange student seeking room and board," read a tiny classified ad in the local newspaper of Berlin, Connecticut. This was misleading, because the young German was only visiting on a tourist visa. But no matter. The ad caught the eye of Gwen Savio, a librarian at Berlin High School. She and her family had hosted foreign exchange students in the past—most recently a French boy named Dominique—and had enjoyed pleasant and meaningful experiences. She called the number listed in the ad, and soon Christian Gerhartsreiter had his thumb in the air once again, trying to hitch a ride from Meriden to Berlin. No one stopped, however, so he walked the four or five miles to his new home, a town of fifteen thousand with an appropriately Germanic name.

He got there late in the afternoon, lugging his meager possessions and looking like a mess after his trek. Edward Savio, the oldest of the family's four children, who was then fifteen and is now a screenwriter in California, remembered Gerhartsreiter's arrival well. He appeared to be trying very hard to resemble his idea of what an American teenager would look like, Edward said, with white-framed sunglasses, formfitting jeans, and a tight button-down shirt. His long hair was "windblown and spiky." But what struck Edward Savio most was the young man's curiosity. His head moved from side to side, he seemed to want to take everything in. And of course the family was curious about him: who he was, where he had come from, and how he had landed in Berlin, Connecticut, of all places.

"My name's Christian Gerhartsreiter," he said with a light German accent, again the epitome of the friendly, outgoing, accommodating immigrant, eager to please and happy to have a home in the strange new country. The Savios didn't have a spare room, but he said he would be happy to sleep on a couch in the living room.

Gerhartsreiter became the fifth child living in the house. Edward had twin brothers, age ten, and a sister, eight, whom everyone called Snooks. Their father, Jim, was a computer engineer. "On my birth certificate, under my father's occupation, it says 'Computer Operator,' which back then was like saying he worked on the space shuttle," said Savio. The house was full of early computers and video games, which must have delighted Gerhartsreiter, enamored as he was of all things technological.

Upon moving in with the Savio family, Gerhartsreiter transferred his records from Platt High School to Berlin High, one of the best public schools in Connecticut in terms of academics. He said he was a senior, and since his school records were in German, nobody seems to have bothered to verify that claim.

As for his background, according to Edward Savio, "He said his father was an industrialist, and he implied that his father had something to do with Mercedes. He tried to make it sound like he was from a family that had money."

Christian went to school with Edward, a sophomore, but he got his real education in front of the television set in the Savios' living room. His favorite show was *Gilligan's Island*, and he took to mimicking the behavior of Thurston Howell III, the millionaire castaway played by Jim Backus. When speaking, he would stretch out the syllables in each word, attempting to affect an English or Ivy League–type accent. "Ehhhd," he would say to Savio at the dinner table, "paaahhss the breaaahhd, please." Savio recalled, "The accent was like a cross between Thurston Howell III and John Wayne."

Savio tried to help his houseguest adjust to his new school, but he wasn't particularly successful. "The reaction to Chris from most of the guys was, 'What's up with him?' Some of the girls were interested, though. He always gravitated toward the females." One even picked him up in her car to drive him to the senior prom. Gerhartsreiter wore a black suit with brown socks; Savio tried to tell him that brown doesn't go with black, but he refused to change his socks, saying, "It's not a problem."

In those early days, Gerhartsreiter was the caterpillar dreaming of becoming the butterfly, Edward Savio told *Dateline*—he had little of the polish he would later acquire. But despite his awkwardness and his tendency toward faux pas, he was tremendously outgoing, and he tried to get to know as many people as possible in his effort to learn about America.

"I was working at Berlin High School, in the guidance office," said a local woman who came to know him, who is also of German descent. "Mia McMahon, the gal in the library's media center, knew that I was German and that he was German. Mia figured he was lonely and thought maybe he would like to speak German and just be with a German person."

She sighed at the thought of the lonely immigrant boy, adrift in America. "Being a mother, I felt sorry for him!" she continued. "Not that he felt sorry for himself. He was very confident."

"There was a big German community in the nearby town of New Britain, and my mother is very much into her German heritage," the German woman's son told me. "She spoke German to me from the time I was five, and she's a *schuhplattler* folk dancer—the German dance where you slap your shoes. She wanted to keep the German culture alive in our family."

And what better way than to bring a *real* German into their home? "We invited him for a few holidays—Easter, Thanksgiving," said the woman. "He was very sweet, but very lost. He didn't fit in anywhere." In an attempt to ingratiate himself, he embellished his life story. "He kept telling us about his father being a great importer of fine wood from South Africa. And his mother was some kind of professional, I can't remember what."

"He was smart, obviously, but he had this *odd* side to him," the son said. That side of Gerhartsreiter was on display when the family took him to their lake house in New Hampshire.

"None of our children really bonded with him," the mother said. "He had no interest in sports, but he *loved* music, especially classical music. He'd bring a Scottish bagpipe every time we came to the lake, and he loved to play it. And when he would come up for the weekend, he would wear nothing but a bathing suit and cowboy boots, which my boys thought was ridiculous.

"My husband was an attorney, very involved in stocks and bonds," she continued. "He and Christian had lengthy conversations, and Christian was knowledgeable—he knew stocks and bonds and banks." In these areas, Christian knew how to make a connection.

Back in Berlin, Gerhartsreiter parlayed his love of classical music into a part-time job. He had been blowing smoke when he told people back in Bergen that he was going to America to work as a radio disc jockey, but that's exactly what he wound up doing.

"I had just gotten an educational FM station at Berlin High School," said Jeff Wayne, who as the town's media director supervised Berlin's libraries and schools, ensuring that they had top-of-the-line audiovisual equipment. Around the time Christian Gerhartsreiter was at Berlin High, a Hartford radio station donated to the town of Berlin a vast collection of classical music albums, Wayne told me: "The really high-end stuff—Chopin, Mozart. An unbelievable collection of music, cabinets full of it—probably a thousand albums. We couldn't have just anybody spinning these records. They had to know something about classical music. But high school students weren't interested in classical music."

Except for one.

"One day the librarian Mia McMahon showed up with Christian, a long-haired, European-looking lad with a German accent," Jeff Wayne continued. "'He's an expert in classical music,' she said, 'and he's interested in your radio program.'

"I jumped at the opportunity," Wayne told me. Impressed by Gerhartsreiter's knowledge, he put him on the air immediately. "Pretty soon we had a lot of people listening to it, and they couldn't believe that there was a high school student doing it. He'd announce the music, give a little commentary about it, and go right into it—very professional. Not quite NPR, but for somebody his age? If you were an aficionado of classical music, it would knock your socks off."

I tried to imagine Gerhartsreiter at the controls, purring into a microphone in what was left of his German accent: "And now, Charles Gounod's haunting 'Funeral March of a Marionette,' from back in 1872."

Looking back on it, Wayne said, Gerhartsreiter was perhaps too professional, too smart. "I didn't see him blend in or really have friends. He
came across as more mature than the average high school student. I
have doubts that he was really high school age. He seemed older, more
sophisticated."

On some evenings in the Savio house, Gerhartsreiter would join Edward in his bedroom, where there was a writing table, a stereo system, and an upright piano, on which Edward composed songs for high
school musicals. Just as Christian had always been determined to leave
his hometown of Bergen, Germany, Edward was intent on leaving Berlin for new horizons. His dream was to move to Los Angeles and become a screenwriter and director. "I wanted to make movies," Savio
told me. "I knew this when I was in sixth grade. Chris and I would have
conversations about it."

"How could you grow up like this?" Gerhartsreiter would ask Savio.
"I certainly wouldn't want to be here."

"I *love* growing up here," Savio would reply. "I don't want to *live* here,
but this is a great place to be from. My goal is to go to school and get
out to California."

"But New York—that's the city," insisted Gerhartsreiter.

"Yeah, New York is a world-class city," Savio agreed, "but California
is where they make the movies. That's where all the action is." He said
he planned to attend film school at USC or UCLA, then blaze a trail
through Hollywood. As always, Gerhartsreiter paid close attention, absorbing every word.

Even as he tried to befriend Edward, Gerhartsreiter began acting increasingly haughty toward his host family. With his position as a classical music DJ, his weekends in the country with the German family,
and his observations of Thurston Howell on TV, he began thinking of
himself as being more than he actually was, and more important than
those who hosted him in their home. "My *fah*-ther," he would say in a
faux-aristocratic accent, "wouldn't let me speak to peasants."

"We would *never* eat like this," he would complain at the dinner table. "We would have *servants* bring the food." When he grew tired of Gwen Savio's everyday Italian American fare, he would say, "Oh, this is what we're having, *again*?"

"I'd never marry an Italian," he said once. "They're just too emotional."

"Well, thank God for that!" Mrs. Savio shot back. "Lucky for Italian girls."

Time and again, Gerhartsreiter said, "I would *never* live like this," meaning in a modest house in a small town in the middle of nowhere.

"But Chris, you *are*! You *are* living like this," Edward reminded him.

The German teen's transformation extended to his name. "He was Christian Gerhartsreiter when he arrived in our house," explained Savio. "Then it was Chris Gerhart. Then it was Christopher Kenneth Gerhart." He must have liked the sound of that—very American. And how easy it was to take a new name! As with so much in America, all you had to do was *assume* it, grab it, and no questions would be asked.

Still, Chris Gerhart behaved much like Christian Gerhartsreiter, commandeering the Savios' living room, where he watched television day and night from the couch on which he slept.

"Quiet, please!" he would say in the morning as his hosts were preparing for the day and he was still trying to sleep, having been up until all hours watching TV. He needed his rest, and when he awoke he expected his laundry to be done and his meal prepared.

A couple of months into his stay at the Savios', he was reclining on the couch, watching TV, perhaps *Gilligan*—maybe laughing at the way Lovey sucked up to Thurston, or practicing the way Thurston said his lines. He was so engrossed that either he didn't hear a knocking on the door or he heard it and ignored it. Whatever the case, he didn't get off the couch to open the door for Snooks as she stood outside for hours in the cold.

Gwen Savio returned home to find her young daughter shivering on the doorstep. "You're going to have to find somewhere else to live," she told Gerhartsreiter.

"My mom is very polite, even when she is angry, but she was pissed off," Savio recalled. "She told me the story, and I said, 'Yeah, that's unacceptable. But what are you going to do? It's wintertime. Are you going to kick him out on the street?'"

"I need him to leave," she said.

Gwen called around, and Mia McMahon, the school librarian who had made many of Gerhartsreiter's early introductions, offered to let him stay at her house. Christian unceremoniously left the Savio residence.

"I'm ready for something better anyway," he said as he left.

I attempted to reach Mia McMahon, but she declined to speak with me, preferring to keep her memories to herself. However, I found a brief synopsis of an interview she had given to the police years after the young man left her home:

She related: that Chris Gerhartsreiter appeared at her residence back in 78/79, after staying with the Savio family. That Chris indicated to her then that he was from Germany but had left the country to avoid being drafted into the army. That his father was an engineer, with his mother being a South African citizen. That Chris made several lengthy calls to Germany and South Africa during the time he stayed at her residence. That Chris and her departed on bad terms, due to Chris's attitude about paying for overseas telephone calls.

Having left (or been kicked out of) three different homes in less than a year, he was finished with Connecticut altogether. He didn't bother waiting until the school year ended, for he was off to bigger and better things: college. He'd been accepted as a foreign student at the University of Wisconsin at Stevens Point, an extension of the school's main campus in Madison and thus easier to get into.

I studied the application forms that Christian Karl Gerhartsreiter, the name he still went by for official purposes, had filled out. It wasn't clear how he managed to get into the college—he was intelligent and well educated, having spent much of his time reading and studying in the Berlin public library, but he never got a diploma from Berlin High School. Regardless, there was an admission certificate that read, "University of Wisconsin–Stevens Point. The student named herein has been accepted for a full course of study."

Where the F1 immigration form asked the applicant to identify "the person most closely related to me who lives in the United States," Gerhartsreiter gave the name and address of the Berlin woman of German descent with the lake house. "We had one phone call from him," she told me when I asked if she had ever heard from him after he left Connecticut. "He said his mother had just gone through a cancer operation and needed a place to recoup, and could he use the cottage." He was referring to the family's lake house. "He was trying to tell us that he was attending university. He kept talking about stocks and bonds. I just remember it was October and after that he never called again."

Chris Gerhart listed his major field of study as political science and stated that he intended to stay at Stevens Point for the full four years required to obtain his bachelor's degree. By August 1979 he had moved to Wisconsin and was living in a dormitory called Baldwin Hall, which housed many of the university's international students. They were encouraged to participate in social activities aimed at fostering their language and cultural skills—a perfect environment for Gerhartsreiter, who, despite all he had learned, was still working at becoming American.

I contacted the university administrators whose names appeared in the paperwork in my file. No one seemed able to provide any information about the young man. "We wanted to help but have no records in the foreign student office (where I once worked) and have no memory of this guy," Gerhartsreiter's college adviser e-mailed me. Finally, I found his first roommate, Chris Newberg, who had an indelible memory of the freshman, who arrived in the dormitory with new black luggage, a set of golf clubs, and an aristocratic air. "Supposedly his mother or father was an ambassador who had come from back east," said Newberg. "He said he was from Boston, Massachusetts.

"I had a wall where I put my posters and I had a big American flag that was tattered on the end," Newberg continued. "I thought it looked cool, that it represented what our country had been through with battles." But Christopher thought it looked tawdry. "I'm sorry but you're going to have to burn that. It's in disarray," he told his roommate in his formal English accent.

He buttressed his image as the son of a Boston ruling class family by regularly practicing his golf and by what he ate and drank: Irish coffee, exclusively, and Boston cream pie, not on occasion but every single day. "We all thought his dad was in the FBI or the witness protection program because he was so secretive about his family," recalled another fellow student, Richie Riddle. He was *so* secretive that he insisted that his name and biographical details be blacked out from the book that listed Baldwin Dormitory's students—and their emergency contact information—at the dorm's front desk. One night, at a party in the girls' wing of the dormitory, Christopher so adamantly refused to leave when the party ended at midnight that the girls had to call the resident assistant to force him out. "Do you know who I am?" Christopher snarled. "I don't have to take orders from you."

"That was the last time we saw him," said Richie Riddle.

In fact, he spent only one three-month semester at Stevens Point. In January 1980, he transferred to the University of Wisconsin at Milwaukee, where, he wrote in his application papers, his education objective was "a B.A. degree in Communications."

Filed about the same time as his University of Wisconsin transfer application was a flurry of other documents—Application for Change of Nonimmigrant Status, Application by Nonimmigrant Student (F-1) for Extension of Stay. They were all approved with remarkable swiftness, signed by a succession of Johns and Cynthias and Joes, busy bureaucrats who most likely never met the enigmatic young German and accepted what he had written on paper as the truth.

By then Christian Karl Gerhartsreiter—a.k.a. Chris Kenneth Gerhart—was in search of the ultimate document, one that could keep him in America forever: a marriage certificate.

CHAPTER 3

Becoming American

I knew him as Chris Gerhart," said Todd Lassa, who was a student at the University of Wisconsin at Milwaukee when Gerhartsreiter arrived in January 1980. "I was twenty-two and taking film classes. We both were. One of the classes I had with Chris was a class in film noir. He told me he'd spent the previous semester at the University of Wisconsin, Stevens Point. He befriended me."

Lassa, a writer for *Motor Trend* magazine, recalled, "He had a German accent when I met him. It wasn't anything he was trying to hide. He was living in a suburb of Milwaukee, Elm Grove. I went there once. He invited me into the house, an upper-middle-class house, which is the way I saw him. I can't remember if he said it was his parents' house or his aunt's. But there was nobody else there. It would have been a very strange house to rent. It cost quite a lot. Maybe he was house-sitting.

"He and I and another classmate went out for beers a few times, so it was surprising when he asked me to be the best man for his wedding in a civil service in Madison," said Lassa. "This is after I knew him three or four weeks. But I said, 'Sure, I'll do it.'"

The lucky bride's name was Amy Janine Jersild.

Chris Gerhart had met Amy through her younger sister, Elaine, who must have seemed a miraculous gift to him. She was the twenty-two-year-old daughter of a hardworking middle-class couple, Arthur Jersild and Bertha M. Geiger Jersild, of Elkhart, Indiana. He had met Elaine through a church group. She was not a beauty, but she was very spirited and vivacious. More important, she was an American citizen and thus had the power to obtain for Gerhart what he wanted most at this juncture of his life: a green card, which grants permanent resident status to an alien who marries an American.

Chris broached the subject of marriage with her, saying that he wanted to stay in America to avoid begin drafted into the German army, where he would surely be put on the front lines, directly in the line of fire in the cold war against the Russians. Elaine sympathized—the cute, friendly, and diminutive Chris Gerhart would seemingly have no chance on the front lines of any war—but she had no intention of helping him. Though Elaine wasn't game, she said that maybe her older sister, Amy, might be.

I called Elaine Jersild to get an explanation of what happened next. She responded immediately, sunny, cheerful, but as soon as I mentioned Chris Gerhart, her tone turned cold.

"Honestly, hon, I must say *no comment*," she snapped, adding, "I thought this was over, but I guess it's not."

Amy Jersild, however, could not refuse to comment. She was subpoenaed for the trial in Boston, where all the reporters and spectators in the courtroom eagerly anticipated her entrance. Finally, we would hear evidence from someone who had actually known the strange young man in his early, unstoppable years in America.

When Amy Jersild Duhnke walked in, the media pack looked at one another as if to say, *That's her?* She was fifty, weathered and gray, with a long white braid snaking down the back of her drab business suit. The toll of spending several decades in the food service industry—most recently as a cook in a Milwaukee restaurant called the Twisted Fork—

was etched in the deep wrinkles of her face. It was impossible to imagine her as the first wife of the budding bon vivant.

One would expect that the sight of his first wife reemerging in his life after thirty years would elicit some reaction from the defendant. But he stared straight ahead. He registered no emotion whatsoever.

"Describe the first time you met him," asked the prosecutor after Amy was sworn in.

"He came in with my sister to visit me expressly to ask me to marry him," she said in a dry midwestern monotone.

I knew from the documents I'd read that when Amy met Chris, she was earning $5,800 a year as a clerk at a delicatessen called East Side Foods, which meant she had a take-home pay of a little more than $100 a week. I also knew that she was then living in a small apartment near her workplace with her boyfriend. What could have persuaded her to marry a complete stranger? Had he offered her money? In those days, a hungry immigrant would without hesitation have paid for a quickie marriage to a willing young American. Later, the prosecutor would say that Amy didn't recall whether money was ever offered, but she did recall that she never received a dime from the immigrant.

"Who brought up the idea of you marrying him?" Amy was asked next.

"My sister, Elaine," she said.

"And did she tell you *why* she wanted you to marry him?"

"I can't remember verbatim . . . all the information. But because he wanted to stay in this country. He was a foreign exchange student."

Over the course of an hour, she said, she listened to Chris and Elaine explain how Chris could become a resident of the United States if Amy married him. She was not asked in court whether the question of money came up. The prosecutor simply asked her, "Did you come to a decision?"

"Yes," she said, "that I would in fact marry him."

The prosecutor didn't probe any further, and Amy certainly didn't volunteer anything further about her motivation for agreeing. "It was easy," she explained—all she had to do was learn how to pronounce and write her future husband's name. "I just know we made an arrangement for him to pick me up to go to Dane County in Madison, which is in Wisconsin, to get married."

Shortly after Amy said yes, Gerhart asked Todd Lassa to be his best man. The two students had spent a semester studying the great examples of film noir, which usually features conniving people doing dastardly things to one another in a very black-and-white world. Gerhart's request—to have a near stranger as his best man at a wedding that had come out of nowhere—perhaps seemed almost normal compared with what they had been watching in class on film. Lassa readily agreed.

"It was a Saturday afternoon," Lassa told me. "He picked me up, and we drove into an older neighborhood of Milwaukee." They were in Chris's 1980 Plymouth Arrow, and Chris and Todd were both wearing suits. The Jersild sisters were waiting for them at the door. Strangely, though, the sister Todd thought Chris was dating—the younger one—was not the sister he was marrying.

"They seemed in on the joke," said Lassa, "as did Chris. He gave me a crazy explanation that he was marrying his girlfriend's sister for tax purposes, that he had a book he was publishing. And secondly, he didn't want to make a big commitment to his girlfriend. It was obvious that he was bullshitting, that he was out to get a green card."

It was also obvious to Todd back then that Chris was accustomed to getting what he wanted. And why not? He was young, smart, handsome, and on his way. On February 20, 1981, one day before he turned twenty, Chris Gerhart stood solemnly beside Amy Jersild in the Dane County Courthouse as circuit judge Richard W. Bardwell read the simple, straightforward questions and waited for their responses.

"Do you, Christian Karl Gerhartsreiter, take Amy Janine Jersild to be your lawful wedded wife . . ."

Within minutes the modest ceremony was over, and there was no reception. Immediately after saying "I do," the newlyweds went their separate ways. Chris and Todd dropped the Jersild sisters off back home and returned to college. A few weeks later, Chris picked up Amy again and drove her to the federal courthouse in Milwaukee, drilling her on the spelling and pronunciation of his real, full name—Christian Karl Gerhartsreiter.

On April 7, the marriage would be consummated, not in bed but on paper. "He gave me a sheet of paper with his name on it so I could memorize it, because there are quite a few letters in his name," Amy told the prosecutor. "And I had to look at it so I would be able to write it down on the document that I was going to be signing."

"And what would those documents accomplish?" she was asked.

"Getting his legal status to stay in the United States of America."

"Did you have any intention to be together as husband and wife?"

"None whatsoever," she answered defiantly, with the first hint of emotion in her tone.

When the documents were presented for her to sign, she had no trouble and aroused no suspicion that this was anything less than a marriage forged in love. I found the marriage certificate and related papers in my dossier of documents and could see where Amy had flawlessly filled out the affidavit of support, stating that she was "willing and able to receive, maintain, and support" her husband. She filled in her annual salary but left blank the space where the applicant is asked to list savings deposits and personal property. She agreed to the provision that asked if she would be willing to deposit a cash bond, if needed, with the U.S. Immigration and Naturalization Service to ensure that her husband would not become a liability or "public charge" to America.

She wrote as the reason for her filling out the affidavit, "Application for permanent resident status of my husband." Then she signed—under oath—Mrs. Amy Gerhartsreiter, with the same flair and loops her husband used in his signature.

"And after that day in the courthouse, did you ever see him again?" Amy was asked.

"No," she said, adding that twelve years passed before she obtained a divorce so that she could marry a man she actually loved. By then, Chris Gerhart had moved far from Milwaukee, and Amy had no intention of advising him of a divorce that would probably mean nothing to him. All she had to do, she testified, was place a public advertisement in the local newspaper announcing her divorce from Christian Karl Gerhartsreiter and it would be final.

"For the last several weeks of class, he just stopped showing up," said Todd Lassa.

Nobody in Milwaukee ever saw Gerhart again. He had gotten all he needed from Milwaukee, and all he had had to do was say "I do" to Amy Jersild and a circuit judge. With that, the welcoming arms of America opened wide to him.

The documents told the story succinctly:

February 11, 1981: State of Wisconsin . . . Certificate of Marriage, Groom, Christian Karl Gerhartsreiter . . . Bride, Amy Janine Jersild. Marriage ceremony held on February 20, 1981. Duly signed and authorized.

April 7, 1981: United States Department of Justice Immigration and Naturalization Service . . . Application for Status as Permanent Resident. Duly signed and authorized.

Once he had a legal wife, Chris Gerhart climbed into his Plymouth Arrow and hit the road to a better future, barreling toward all he could and would become. There was only one destination for a dreamer of his stature: Los Angeles, where dreams are an industry.

Shortly after he informed the Immigration and Naturalization Service of his new address in California (that of Elmer and Jean Kelln), the most important document of his new life was dutifully signed and filed: "June 16, 1981: Memorandum of Creation of Record of Lawful Permanent Residence, Approved, U.S. Immigration, Chicago, Illinois." The document was signed Christian Karl Gerhartsreiter.

It was the last time he would use that clunky name. Even his new name, Chris Gerhart, was too dull and German for where he was headed. For the new life he was about to launch, he would adopt something regal and wondrous, a name hinting of Old World money, power, and prestige.

He tried on various names for size on his drive west, including Dr. Christopher Rider, which he employed on a brief stopover in Las Vegas. He had the good fortune to meet a cardiologist in that city, which was such a wonderful coincidence, he told the doctor, for he was a cardiologist too. He said he was moving to Las Vegas and was hoping to find an established physician whose practice he might join.

"Do you think we might be a good fit?" the young man asked.

The Las Vegas doctor was charmed by him, so he offered to drive him around the finer residential neighborhoods of the city to help the newcomer find a suitable house. Along the way, Dr. Rider cajoled and persuaded his new cardiologist friend to lend him $1,500. The doctor gladly gave him the money, but before Dr. Rider could repay the loan he left town without a word.

The young man was still searching for the new name when he arrived in Loma Linda, California, at the home of Elmer and Jean Kelln, the couple he had met while hitchhiking in Germany, whose names he had used without their knowledge as his sponsors on his immigration papers. He used them once again, without their knowledge or consent, as his permanent address in California, although he never paid more than brief visits to their home.

They almost didn't recognize him when he showed up. His hair, once long and cut in the popular shag style of the day, was short and businesslike, and his clothing, which had evoked the 1970s American hippie style, was now strictly Ivy League. But there was something still missing in his transformation, his dream of becoming a player in the film industry, he told Elmer and Jean. He needed a better name. Sitting in the Kellns' living room, he began leafing through the San Bernardino telephone book, searching for a new name for himself.

"What's wrong with your own name?" asked Jean, but Elmer understood completely. Chris was going to work in Hollywood, where adopted names are commonplace, where a Bernard Schwartz can become Tony

Curtis, and where the only thing that separates falsehood from fairy tale is the extent of one's success.

"Nobody in the movie business uses their own name!" Elmer admonished his wife. As he later explained, "You have to remember you are in California, where changing your name is not illegal. Many people have aliases. I used to be academic dean at the university and I used to order students' diplomas. If a student came in just before graduation and says, 'This is how I want my diploma to read,' that was how his diploma read for the rest his life when he would be practicing dentistry. Many of them were Asian students. I particularly remember someone's last name was Duc, but they didn't want to be known as Dr. Duc, so they were allowed to change their name. This is legal in California, so I thought nothing of him picking a new name."

"Too German," Chris said dismissively of his real name as he leafed through the phone book, looking for one that would set him apart from the pack.

When he couldn't find a name he liked in the phone book, he began to tick off those of people he knew. Returning in his mind to Berlin, Connecticut, he recalled the teacher of his dreams, Joan Chichester, a class adviser who taught science and biology. She was blond and beautiful, in an almost British sort of way, and the young Gerhartsreiter had had a crush on her. Ed Savio told me so, even though Joan Chichester herself said she had no recollection of the young man. "It's a horrible thing to say," she told me. "I'm older, but I don't think it's senility. I was the class adviser and probably had him in class. He was just not outstanding to me at the time. I really don't have anything to add. *You've* told *me* everything I know about him."

"Oh, she's *so* fantastic!" Chris Gerhart had often told Ed Savio. In addition to her striking looks and intelligence, she had the perfect name: Chichester, which Chris pronounced *Chee*-chester. It was *so* beautifully British, especially when paired with an august first name, like Christopher.

He suddenly had it: Christopher Chichester! And to gild the lily a bit, he threw in a fancy middle name: Mountbatten. Christopher Mountbatten Chichester. Elmer and Jean couldn't help but smile. It was brilliant, and seemingly harmless, and they were happy for him. Their young German friend was ready for Hollywood! He had come so far since that day the couple met him, a soaking wet hitchhiker on the side of the highway in Germany. Since then he had clearly learned how to flatter and acquiesce, when to speak and when to remain silent, and how to work the American system.

In Hollywood, they all knew, reinvention was a way of life. But Christopher Mountbatten Chichester decided not to base his new life in Los Angeles. That would be too "on the nose," to use the screenwriters' term for too obvious, too predictable. Instead, he would launch himself in a bucolic enclave twelve miles to the east of L.A., a tiny, self-contained, all-American town of true-blue believers, all too eager to embrace a stranger, especially one with a stellar name.

CHAPTER 4

Christopher Chichester: San Marino, California

D
eep in the dossier of documents I had been given by my secret source in Boston, an interesting item caught my eye, a report from the Los Angeles County Sheriff's Department, dated July 4, 1994:

> Detectives say that Chichester dresses well, is very clean cut and very articulate. He attends church services and ingratiates himself with older people in wealthy communities. He has passed himself off as a computer expert, film producer and stockbroker. He has told people that his father was a lawyer, an archaeologist or a British aristocrat and his mother an architect, an archaeologist or an actress. He is very knowledgeable on subjects of which he would speak. Although Chichester speaks with what people have described as an English accent, detectives say he is not British. He is believed to be from another Western European nation.

Nearby in the dossier on the young immigrant were the following lines:

May 26, 1981: Moves to California, becomes Christopher Chichester.

February 7, 1983: issued California drivers license No. C309973— sometime between this date and 2-08-85 moves into the rear house at 1920 Lorain Road, San Marino.

I had never been to San Marino, but once I learned more about it, I could see immediately why the German who now called himself Christopher Chichester had chosen to move there. GARDENS OF EARTHLY DELIGHT, read the headline of a *New York Times* article about the place. A 1996 story in the *Los Angeles Times* listed the city's impressive statistics: area in square miles, 3.75; population, 12,959; median age, 41.2; median household income, $100,101.

The story read:

San Marino, known for the size of its estates and incomes, is a city of superlatives.

Consider one of its many distinctions: One of its founders, rail tycoon Henry E. Huntington, ultimately had his name on nearly as much Los Angeles real estate as the county assessor. The city's first mayor was George Patton, father of the famed "Blood and Guts" general of World War II. As a boy the younger George swam in Lake Vineyard, which would become a 35-acre verdant jewel called Lacy Park. . . .

A rigorous set of regulations are enforced to maintain a posh lifestyle: a car can be visible in a driveway for no more than 48 hours continuously, only one family is allowed for each home, trash cans cannot be in view of the street, door-to-door hawkers and chain-link fences are expressly prohibited. The only salvation for some jittery souls is a double espresso, the strongest drink for sale in the city.

One day in the fall of 2008, I took the 110 freeway from downtown Los Angeles until it stopped and suddenly turned into an ordinary road. After I drove through a short and scruffy patch of Pasadena, the sky suddenly opened, the foliage thickened, and the air turned cool and clear. The road widened into a six-lane boulevard. Suddenly I was in a different world, the antithesis of the metropolis twelve miles away. San Marino seemed to be stuck in another era, a flashback to Norman Rockwell's America, a pristine little town framed by the San Gabriel Mountains, dotted with palms and filled with good, honest, churchgoing citizens. The town felt immediately safer than the urban sprawl I had just left behind.

The eyesore double-decker strip malls that had taken over Los Angeles had not encroached here. Instead, the main road, Huntington Boulevard, was lined with tidy and quaint little shops: the Huntington Drive Service Station (with real attendants, not the standard serve-yourself computerized pumps), Diana Dee's Gifts, Carriage Trade Coiffures, the Plantation House, Fashion Cleaners, the Collenette School of Dancing (specializing in ballet), Deluxe Shoe Repair. There were shops offering skin care, ballroom dancing lessons, custom tailoring, arts and crafts, and hobbies. Churches seemed to be on every other corner. I immediately spotted a Christian Science Reading Room alongside the First Church of Christian Science. By noon, the locals had packed the Colonial Kitchen—OPEN DAILY, 7 A.M., SPECIALS! read the sign out front. Through the windows I could see laughing waitresses pouring coffee for proper gentlemen eating bacon and eggs.

Everything about this place instantly put a smile on my face.

This was San Marino, Christian Karl Gerhartsreiter's first real permanent home as an American citizen. Around the time of his arrival, a local wrote a song about the city:

> I've heard of a town
> Where millionaires stay
> That's only 20 minutes outside of L.A.

They've got a Police Force, Fire Department
That they don't need
'Cause there's no crime, no riots, they're
Securitied

There're five limousines
In every carport
The schools are all so rich
They're teaching every sport

The streetlights burn all night
The trees are trimmed just right
What is its name?
San Marino

Christopher Mountbatten Chichester landed here in 1981. Having mastered English, he was ready to launch his most impressive identity to date—not in Los Angeles, where there is a poseur on every corner, but in the gardens of earthly delight.

My first stop was the Jann of Sweden Hair Studio, in one of the charming little collections of shops on the main road. Stepping through the door, I felt I'd stumbled into a saloon instead of a salon. The room was covered floor to ceiling with silver-studded saddles, bronzes of cowboys and horses, mounted deer and steer heads, guitars and mandolins, rodeo ribbons and trophies, and endless framed photographs of a blond, bearded cowboy in decades of Rose Bowl parades.

The proprietor appeared, an enormous man so tall that he practically touched the ceiling, wearing a bright red western shirt, a bandanna around his neck, and snakeskin cowboy boots, into which he had tucked skintight jeans held up by a hand-tooled leather belt with a mammoth silver rodeo buckle. His hair was long and snow white, and I could hardly tell where it stopped and his long beard began. Hanging below the beardline was a swirling walrus mustache. He flashed a big, broad, snaggletoothed smile, and his turquoise blue eyes lit up as he introduced himself.

Jann Eldnor had arrived in the United States in 1971. "I was clean-cut—I looked like Ross Perot," he said, referring to the Texas billionaire and former presidential candidate. Then someone took Jann horseback riding, and he caught the bug that would turn into an obsession. "My hair grew long; my mustache grew out; I started to decorate my shop like the Wild West. I became the Swedish Cowboy!" Ever since then he had been riding on horseback in parades, and once he even rode onto the set of *The Tonight Show with Jay Leno*.

When I asked him about Christopher Chichester, he bellowed, "All right!"—one of his favorite expressions, I soon learned. "He sat right there," he said, pointing to his antique barber chair, which bore a plaque stating that it dated back to 1886.

Having been the town barber since 1972, Jann said he knew almost everyone in San Marino. I laid out for him what little I already knew: that an immigrant calling himself Christopher Chichester had chosen this place because of its reputation as an old-money enclave of wealth and sophistication. I repeated what Elmer Kelln had told me: "He wanted to be where the rich people were." But exactly when he arrived and where he stayed weren't known, it turned out, even by Jann of Sweden.

"I think he was living off a lady down on Bedford Road," Jann said.

"*Off* a lady?" I asked, thinking that the phrasing was due to his broken English, and that he meant "*with* a lady." No, he assured me, he meant *off*. And the ladies of San Marino were happy to have him; they welcomed him almost instantly, because he was a young man of not merely wealth, taste, and sophistication. He was royalty. "He said to people he was from royalty in England and that his name was Christopher Chichester." Jann pronounced the name *Chee*-chester, accent on the *Chee*. "And even though he was only twenty-six, he acted like he was forty. Every time he meets a lady, he takes her hand and kisses it before he presents himself. These ladies were thinking Chichester was sent by God or something," he continued. "Because he acted so well. So *not* like the other guys out in this country. He could talk about the stock market, about politics, about everything. These ladies would invite him to come and stay in their big houses. They always had a guest room or something. And they fed him and bought him clothes."

"How did *you* meet him?" I asked.

He'd heard about him before he met him, he said, and had started seeing his photograph in the local newspaper, always dressed in a suit and a tie. "And I wonder, 'All right, who the hell is this?' This guy Chichester starts showing up at the city council meetings and different things. And then for sure he's all of a sudden at the clubs."

"The clubs?" I asked.

"The City Club and the Rotary and all the others," he said. "I know all the people, and they all told Chichester, 'Since you're British, you should go to Jann for your haircuts, because he's from Europe too!' So suddenly he shows up in his suit and wants a haircut. And then he starts to tell me the stories—that he was a Mountbatten and all that."

Not only was he a Mountbatten, he added, he was the nephew of Lord Mountbatten, which was a *monumental* relative to have, as anyone would have known had they read the biography *Mountbatten*, by Philip Ziegler, whose flap copy reads:

He was born in 1900. His Serene Highness Prince Louis of Battenberg, great-grandson of Queen Victoria, nephew of the Tsar and Tsarina of Russia, cousin of the King of England. He became Lord Louis Mountbatten, the young idol of the British Navy and eventually one of the Three Supreme Allied Commanders of World War II (the others were Eisenhower and MacArthur) with a quarter of a million Americans under his direct command; the last Viceroy of India, who orchestrated, in circumstances of horrifying difficulty, India's independence from Britain. . . .

It is a life that almost defies description. Mountbatten wielded power over millions of people across the globe. Yet this unwavering champion of nationalist freedom and democracy was also extremely royal: best friend of his cousin, the Duke of Windsor; uncle of the Duke of Edinburgh and architect of his marriage to Elizabeth; beloved "Honorary Grandfather" of Prince Charles.

He was glamorous, indecently handsome, married to one of Europe's richest and most beautiful heiresses. . . . Everything about him was on a gigantic scale.

Yet here was a young man claiming to be his nephew . . . in a tiny Southern California town. But no one had any reason to disbelieve him. Everything about him—his clothing, accent, education, and charm—seemed to be real.

Jann pointed to his antique barber chair. "Many assholes have sat in that chair since 1886," he said, which is what he told every new client. Then he made a sweep of his hand, a gesture that I took to mean, "Have a seat and see how it feels." I sat down, and Jann resumed his story: "So Chichester started coming to me for his haircuts, at least twice a month. And like so many other customers, they come to me to tell their stories and talk about their problems. They know that I will listen. They kind of use me like their cheap psychiatrist, like a bartender."

I sank deep into the chair, which was old and creaky but soft and comfortable. Jann, as well as his fellow townspeople, had one hell of a story to tell.

A young man seeking to make his way in the higher echelons of San Marino would do well to start with Kenneth Veronda, a pillar of the local community and headmaster of Southwestern Academy since 1961. Southwestern is an exclusive prep school in San Marino that Veronda's father, Maurice, founded in 1924. As headmaster, the younger Veronda, who earned his master's degree from Stanford University, had guided countless young men and women into adulthood, through both his prep school's rigorous curriculum and his own intelligent and insightful guidance.

One day in the early 1980s a young man named Christopher Chichester walked into Veronda's little office in a quaint cabin on Southwestern Academy's pristine grounds.

"He was new to town, and someone sent him here to ask how he could get a little more involved in the community," recalled Veronda, a heavyset, well-mannered man, sitting behind an enormous cluttered desk. I sat in a chair across from him, in exactly the same spot where Christopher Chichester had sat so many years before, and I could easily imagine the well-dressed new arrival in the business suit in this office, speaking to this friendly, eminently hospitable older man and instantly charming him. "He said that he was a descendant of the Chichester family in England, and that his mother was at the family home in Switzerland. He had come over here to attend USC, to study communications or television. He was relatively modest, saying, 'Oh, yes, we're British nobility, but I am a poor relation.'"

Everyone welcomed him, especially Veronda, who gave the young man his entrée into San Marino society. "I invited him to come to a chamber of commerce mixer, which is simply a meet-and-greet with fifty or so people, which he did," said Veronda. "Then he wanted to join the Rotary, which he did. He came to the weekly Rotary lunches. Of course, he was much younger than most of the guys—most were in their fifties or older. New members have to sit at a back table, where I often sat. He was always well dressed—nicely cut English suits, shirt and tie. And he was polite, pleasant. But at these kinds of meetings, there really isn't much time to talk. Once you get your plate served at the buffet, there's business and announcements, then a program and a speaker."

Soon, Christopher Chichester was a regular at the clubs, the city council meetings, and the parties of the wealthy, well-heeled citizens, who seemed happy to have a royal in their midst.

"This town is divided into three," said Jann Eldnor. "Super Marino, on the hill with houses $5 million and up; San Marino, on the flats, good, big houses for doctors and professionals; and Sub Marino, where the houses are cheaper, for engineers, schoolteachers, and lower income." We were on a driving tour of the three strata of San Marino. I met Jann at his salon and waited out front while he went to pull his car around—a big white GMC pickup truck with a roaring engine, caked with horse manure from his stable. Like everything else about Jann, it seemed out of place in placid San Marino, but the Swedish cowboy had long since become something of a character in the city and people expected him to do the unexpected.

"Before I got this truck, I had a red one, with Texas longhorns on the front," he said. "I kept a double-barreled shotgun on a gun rack in the back and a bale of hay in the bed, just for decoration. The cops were always stopping me to ask, 'Jann, is that gun loaded?' And I'd say, 'It's not a gun if it's not loaded!'" He laughed and told me it was never loaded— he simply liked the look of it.

I climbed in, and Jann, as usual, started talking. We were in the flats of San Marino, with the town's lowest-rung neighborhoods—Sub Marino—behind us. But Jann didn't want to start there. He headed straight to the upper-class areas. As we drove through the town's middle strata, he explained, "The houses are bigger and nicer here—one- or two-million-dollar houses. Doctors and lawyers and everything. But they're not the *big* money, the *old* money. Chichester wrinkled his nose at all of *this*. He wanted to be with the *real* people, the *rich* people."

As the truck climbed into the foothills of the San Gabriel Mountains, the houses grew larger and statelier, and I could make out a grin beneath Jann's Santa Claus beard. This was Super Marino, the rarefied world upon which Christopher Chichester's eyes had been fixed.

The neighborhood begins at the Huntington Library, the 207-acre former home of Henry Huntington, the railroad baron and town patriarch. Today it houses an art gallery, a botanical garden, and a research library containing more than six million rare books and manuscripts, collected by Huntington from all over the world.

It made sense that Chichester had chosen to live in a city with one of the foremost libraries in America, since libraries were a key part of his existence wherever he went. He spent much of his time in them, studying how to become someone else.

The Huntington Library brought to mind San Simeon, the storied castle of newspaper baron William Randolph Hearst, just up the California coast, and I mentioned that to Jann. "Huntington was *bigger* than Hearst, all right," he said with pride. "He owned the Pacific Railroad. He had ranches in Australia, in Washington State—all over the place. He'd go to England and buy up whole libraries for nothing and bring them back to San Marino."

We were heading to the house that Chichester had given as his first address in San Marino: 1405 Circle Drive, which, Jann told me, wasn't merely Super Marino, but *Super* Super Marino, at the apex of the town. "I'm not sure where he lived in the beginning—nobody is," he said. "Before he met people, he was probably living in a motel." Not in San Marino proper, of course, he added—hotels, much less cheap motels, were not allowed there. Most likely, he said, the young immigrant would have had to find a place in the relatively plebeian environs of Pasadena, San Gabriel, or Alhambra—only a few minutes' drive but a world away from lovely, leafy San Marino.

Jann hadn't heard about Chichester's supposed address on Circle Drive, so he was as eager to see it as I was. Circle Drive is a half-moon of a street at the summit of a high hill. Its privileged residents can look out on all of San Marino. I knew that Chichester had claimed to live at 1405 Circle Drive, because he had listed it as his address in one of the documents I had been given. The estate at that address was huge—the biggest estate on a street full of big estates. "Oh, all right!" Jann exclaimed when we got to it. Chichester had presumably lived in the guesthouse out back, near the swimming pool and tennis court—if he had ever really lived there at all.

But if he *hadn't* lived there, where *had* he lived? Jann couldn't answer that question, but the next day I met some people who could.

After my tour with Jann, I dropped by to see one of the many Super Marino matrons who had been charmed by Christopher Chichester. "I met him in church," the woman told me, "the Church of Our Saviour. He was *so* nice. We were on the terrace, having coffee after the Sunday morning service, when he came up and introduced himself."

The Church of Our Saviour lies just across the San Marino line, in the town of San Gabriel, but it was central to the lives of Super Marino's Episcopalians. It had been founded by General George Patton Sr., whose famous son, the World War II hero, is memorialized in the garden, with a statue of him in jodhpurs.

Few people took notice the first time Chichester showed up at the Church of Our Saviour and claimed a seat in a front pew. But when the congregants gathered for coffee and conversation on the patio after the service, he readily shared his story and handed out calling cards.

"Hello, so pleased to meet you," he would chirp, grasping a lady's hand and raising it to his lips. Then he would reach into his suit jacket, pull out a card printed on heavy stock, and present it ceremoniously. It read:

Christopher Chichester XIII, Bt.

SAN MARINO, CALIFORNIA
SAN RAFAEL, CALIFORNIA

The Bt. stood for baronet, he would explain if asked, and the Roman numerals identified him as the thirteenth baronet. (If the citizens of San Marino had been motivated to do some research, they might have discovered then and there that the eleventh baronet, Sir Edward John Chichester, was still alive, which meant that a thirteenth baronet could not yet exist.)

The card featured what appeared to be a family crest—a coat of arms depicting an egret, wings spread, with an eel in its beak—and what was obviously the family motto: *Firm en foi.* "Firm in faith," he would translate for intrigued acquaintances.

Soon the baronet was not only worshipping at the Church of Our Saviour every Sunday but also working on special committees and helping to prepare the sanctuary for services. He was so quiet, so deferential, and so obviously alone that certain of the friendly female parishioners felt compelled to adopt him. Among these was a stay-at-home mom named Betty Woods, who wasn't Super Marino by any measure, but solidly San Marino. She invited Chichester for breakfast, and soon after that, lunch. Eventually she asked him to join her family for dinner on Christmas Eve. "I like to take in the strays for Christmas," she would say.

The literature given to newcomers to the Church of Our Saviour includes the following passage:

> People will welcome you . . . as worship creates an extended family. Last but not least of worship's many gifts to us is community. Sitting around us are imperfect, messy, wonderful people on the same path as we are. They, too, are trying to make sense of life and to be better people. They want to be challenged to grow and to make the world a better place. You will find friends of the heart to travel with over years of dinners and walks and family cookouts.

No one found the residents of San Marino and the congregants of the Church of Our Saviour more welcoming than Christopher Chichester—particularly the town's kindly widows. I spoke to several of these women, who told me that Chichester became a regular at their church, often attending the 7:30 a.m. service, the 11:30 a.m. service, and the 11:45 prayers for healing, which were followed by coffee and desserts.

"I met him at the Church of Our Saviour, and he would be out on the patio after church, talking, looking very dapper, being very friendly," said Meredith Bruckner, a longtime San Marino resident. "He had a very cultured voice and he was very anxious to be friendly and talk to people. He wore a navy blue blazer with a crest on it, not a family crest, just a crest that the manufacturer put on the pocket. He always looked classy. If you're going to get people to accept you in San Marino, you have to look classy. When he was accepted by a few people on the patio, he was accepted by everybody. People were just really nice to him.

"Good old Christopher could talk on any subject," she continued, and his versatility showed most vividly while playing the board game Trivial Pursuit. Meredith Brucker played Trivial Pursuit with him several times, and, she added, Christopher Chichester *always* won.

It was by no means an easy task. Indeed, if someone were seeking a crash course on America by board game, the subjects in Trivial Pursuit would be an excellent choice. I found a few sample questions from the game during the time that Chichester became so proficient at it:

What was Rhoda's maiden name? (Morgenstern)

How many days after John F. Kennedy's assassination was Lee Harvey Oswald shot? (2)

How many original seasons of *Gilligan's Island* were TV viewers subjected to? (3)

What did 100,000 self-conscious American women buy 200,000 of in 1980? (Breast implants)

It wasn't just board games at which the young man was proficient. A letter that Chichester would later write to a friend showed his dexterity with the classics of literature. "So glad to hear that you got into Shakespeare," he wrote. "Probably the best writing ever! Richard II and Richard III count as my favorites. Of course, I can help you. Whenever you need anything, just let me know the play, the act, the scene. Read the line number to me, and I can give you my opinion."

"He knew everything about everything," Bruckner continued of Chichester's prowess. "He knew about sports, theater, movies. . . . He just had a great knowledge about everything. He was fabulous. . . . He was a charmer! A very charming guy!"

Chichester's legend increased when a story appeared one day in 1982 in a local newspaper. It revealed that the young man, who had recently become a resident of San Marino, was a descendant of Sir Francis Chichester, the legendary adventurer who had been knighted by Queen Elizabeth II in 1967 for being the first person to sail alone around the world. One woman recalled Christopher showing her the article proudly. Then he blushed and added that he was also rather embarrassed by the attention the newspaper had brought on him and his famous relative.

"And we all thought, 'Wow! This is exciting! He has credentials!'" said the woman who saw the newspaper. His periodic mentions in the local newspaper made him the talk of the town and a popular dinner guest. He was also a favorite at the San Marino Public Library, where he spent a lot of time. Volunteers there would ask, "Are you really related to Sir Francis Chichester?" The young man would always be eager to fill them in with details.

As luck would have it, there was then a popular song by the rock band Dire Straits called "Single-Handed Sailor," about Sir Francis Chichester and his 226-day journey, which began and ended in Plymouth, England, with only one brief stop, in Sydney, Australia. How could the citizens of San Marino, if they listened to the song, resist the temptation to regard Chichester's grandson as potentially heroic too?

"I was named after the town of Chichester, in England," he told one San Marino woman as she drove him home from a Wednesday night church service.

"Chris, I've been there!" she exclaimed, and they shared memories of the historic town, which is best known for its eleventh-century cathedral.

"I've actually recently inherited the cathedral," Chichester said. "I've been considering bringing it to the United States, but I've found no municipality ready and able to take it on."

The woman apparently didn't consider the incalculable difficulty and expense of dismantling and transporting a medieval cathedral, nor did she stop to consider how preposterous it was to think that such a historic monument could be owned by an individual family.

"Oh, Chris, wouldn't it be wonderful to bring the cathedral to San Marino?" she said, adding that she owned a property that could be an ideal spot for it.

"Well, I would certainly consider a proposal," Chichester said.

The next day the woman lobbied the San Marino city manager, extolling the glories of Chichester Cathedral and explaining that San Marino's illustrious new resident was prepared to bring it to town. It would rival the Huntington Library as a must-see destination in the city! "Is there *any* way we could bring this over?" she asked.

"Not if we have to pay for it," the city manager replied.

"Well, Chris has plenty of money," she said. But when she brought up the matter with him again, he said he didn't think his parents would allow him to take the large sum necessary for such an enterprise out of his trust fund.

No matter what the locals said in hindsight, it was clear that back then much of San Marino was in Christopher Chichester's sway. One afternoon I was invited for tea with a few of the area's prominent matrons. We sat on chintz-covered chairs in the large living room of a grand home in Super Marino. "We've got money on this street," the lady of the house acknowledged. "We've got a billionaire two doors down, a millionaire next door, and a billionaire next to that."

The women were exceedingly friendly and generous. They were determined to remain civil even when we got on the subject of Christopher Chichester. One woman told me that she had driven him to and from church nearly every Wednesday. Because his dilapidated Plymouth Arrow was frequently not running, the ladies of San Marino had taken turns ferrying him around town. Whenever she went to pick him up, she said, he would be waiting for her in front of a lovely Super Marino home, and when she dropped him off, he would say, "Don't turn down the street. Just drop me on the corner." She would roll to a stop as instructed, and the young man would step out of her Cadillac and disappear into the night. After a year of Wednesdays, he still hadn't let the widow know exactly where he lived.

Another woman took up the subject. "We sent out a little bulletin to the local paper, the *San Marino Tribune*, asking anybody who could to help paint the high school," she said. It was a typical San Marino effort, with countless members of the community pitching in. Local mothers delivered home-cooked lunches for the painters, and one resident sent over a jukebox with 1950s music to entertain them. People thought it was absolutely splendid that Chichester, a baronet and scion of the Mountbatten family, would volunteer to perform such manual labor.

"I introduced him around," she continued ruefully. "We were all there, painting, and I would say, 'Do you know Christopher Chichester?' We were all so friendly! He made a *lot* of contacts there at the high school. He was well mannered and dressed so well—there was nothing suspicious about him." She put down her teacup, and I thought for a moment that she was finally going to lose her cool and lay into Chichester. But she retained a firm hold on herself, even as she recalled, "He wasn't a very good painter."

After helping to paint the high school, Chichester inserted himself into the most cherished social event in San Marino: Fathers' Night, in which the town fathers—leading politicians and businessmen, mostly—sang and danced in an original musical show. It had been a tradition since 1932, and the 1982 production featured a hundred of San Marino's most important citizens. They performed numbers from such Broadway classics as *Cabaret*, *Guys and Dolls*, and *The Music Man*, with the lyrics adapted to apply to San Marino. ("You got trouble, my friend. I say trouble. Right here in San Marino!") To add to the fun, many of the town fathers appeared in drag.

In fact, the whole community went a little nutty over Fathers Night. Businesses took out lighthearted ads in the local paper saying "Break a Leg!" and "We Gave at the Office." But the women at tea assured me that the event had a serious purpose; it was a major fund-raiser for San Marino's City Club, which supported local charities and the PTA. Our hostess, in fact, usually organized the event, but in 1982 Chichester had stepped in and insisted that *he* coordinate everything. He was very proficient with computers, he said, and he'd do it all electronically. It would save everyone a huge amount of effort.

But when it came time to actually do the work, Chichester found himself faced with a mountain of paper—production notes, lyrics, cast lists—and he gave up on the project without having contributed anything at all. Then, with no explanation, he showed up at the first week of rehearsals expecting to be in the show. "I said, 'Put him in a dog suit,'" our hostess recalled. So the illustrious baronet came out on the Fathers' Night stage in a dog outfit, and the only thing he had to do was pantomime peeing on a fire hydrant.

"He was a *flake*!" the hostess said, a crack finally beginning to appear in her sunny façade. She pointed to two of her friends, who had introduced her to Chichester, and said, "I *told* them he was a flake. But they said, 'No! He's wonderful!'" She shook her head. "These two Virgos," she continued, "are just so *trusting*! They just love *everybody*! Everyone's perfect, and nothing bad ever happens. The world is just as it should be, in their eyes. We never dropped the atomic bomb and there has never been a war or catastrophe."

I looked over at the two Virgos under attack. They continued smiling as their friend railed away at them. The hostess then pointed to one of the women, who I had been told was among her best friends, and said, "I called *her* one morning and said, 'We had lightning strike last night!' And she said, 'Oh, no, we didn't.' We were the most trusting little town, the most innocent people you'll ever know. We went right along with the gag. That's how he got away with it."

She explained, "I'm from San Francisco, and I turned up my nose at San Marino at first. I thought, 'Who wants to live in this flat, icky place?'" She motioned to her garden outside and the hills beyond. "You see, I settled on the biggest hill I could find. But the people here were so nice. San Marino was charming! That's why he—Christopher Chichester—could get by. I can't say that's true today."

Today San Marino is less homogeneous and likely feels a bit less like a community than it did in the early 1980s. Its population is about half Asian American, mostly affluent Taiwanese, who moved to the city in great numbers in the 1980s and 1990s, attracted by its top-notch public school system—consistently rated among the best in California—and its small-town way of life.

The ladies agreed that a great deal had changed in San Marino in the past twenty-five years. The era of trust, openness, and innocence was over, and it wasn't due solely to demographic changes. In large measure, it ended with the mysterious arrival, and the equally mysterious departure, of the young man who called himself Christopher Chichester.

When the tea was over, I rode home with Peggy Ebright, one of the all-trusting Virgos, a perky blonde. We went to her comfortable house in the flats of San Marino, and she pulled out yellowed newspaper clippings and production schedules.

She showed me an article from the January 15, 1984, edition of the *Pasadena Star-News*. It was a society column about a party given by Joyce and Howard Morrow, the owners of Morrow Nut House, a national chain of roasted-nuts shops. They had donated $40,000 to fly in twenty-two Olympic athletes from San Marino's namesake, the tiny Republic of San Marino, the microstate of thirty thousand people nestled in Italy's Apennine Mountains. While competing in the 1984 Olympic Games in Los Angeles, the athletes were wined and dined by the citizens of San Marino, California.

The party given by the Morrows was attended by 150 people, the paper stated. The fare was "champagne and nuts, nuts and more nuts," the society columnist wrote, but the hosts seemed to take a backseat to the star of the evening:

Another guest with a story was Christopher Chichester, a former member of the British peerage and grandson of the legendary sailor, Sir Francis Chichester, who is now an American citizen and a resident of San Marino.

"I'm the one who put Howard Morrow together with the fundraisers for the Republic's Olympic team," said Chichester, whose mother owns a construction business located in the *other* San Marino.

Peggy Ebright pulled out more clippings, including a newspaper advertisement illustrated with stars and klieg lights shining down on the following copy: "What is everyone talking about? Watch *Inside San Marino* and find out. 7 p.m. on Channel 6—Cable Vision. *Inside San Marino* is a Gipsy Moth Production." Gipsy Moth, the name of the production company, was also the name of the ship Sir Francis Chichester sailed around the world.

It was 1984, and the era of cable television had arrived. The San Marino City Council awarded its first cable TV franchise to a car dealer in Pasadena, mostly as an advertising vehicle for them. The first requirement for a fledgling channel was to produce a local TV show. As he vaulted between church socials, city council meetings, and various clubs, Christopher Chichester heard about the cable TV opportunity—and seized it.

One day, the phone rang in the home of Peggy Ebright.

"Hello, Peggy, Christopher Chichester here."

"Oh, hi, Chris!" she exclaimed. Of course, Peggy knew who he was. By now, everyone in San Marino knew Christopher Chichester; he was ubiquitous. He told her some very exciting news: cable TV was coming to San Marino! And *he* had been given the honor of producing the city's first cable TV show, which he wanted *her* to host.

"Peggy, you're a natural!" he said, and that much was true. Petite and perfectly dressed, Peggy always got the Doris Day roles, people said, because she looked and acted like Doris Day: perpetually cheerful. Peggy would be the perfect face of his show, Chichester said, an interview program he would call *Inside San Marino*. She would be Barbara Walters and he would be the producer pulling the strings behind the scenes.

"Chris, that sounds like fun! I'd love to do it!" said Peggy.

Sitting in her living room on the day of my visit, Peggy Ebright laughed—and kept laughing, her laughter punctuating our conversation, her sunny disposition clouded not one whit by the mysterious stranger. "We just couldn't have believed people would not be telling the truth," she said. "In San Marino? No way."

She joined the show, becoming the face of *Inside San Marino*.

Although it was essentially a three-person shoestring production—Christopher Chichester, Peggy Ebright, and a high school student cameraman—with minuscule viewership, Chichester pursued the program as he did everything: full tilt. "*Inside San Marino*—7 p.m., American Cable Vision Channel 6," read the now-yellowed little ads that Peggy Ebright showed me, which Chichester had placed in the local newspaper. He typed the schedules, which he would give to Peggy, who would pick him up in her car for the day's shooting, and they would meet their cameraman and storm the offices and playgrounds of the Super Marino elite.

Chichester booked all the guests. "Lovely, ten a.m. at your home," one can imagine him telling the mayor's wife, the chief librarian, or the museum curator. "Just dress as you normally do, and don't be nervous, dear. You're a natural."

The guests enjoyed the attention, even though they almost never watched themselves on the show. *Nobody* watched cable TV back then, and *Inside San Marino* wasn't catnip enough to make them subscribe to newfangled channels. But Chris! How could anyone deny sweet, cultured, darling Chris? So many of the good citizens of San Marino wanted to help Christopher Chichester in whatever he wanted to do. And he certainly *looked* like a rising show-business star. On shoot days, he would replace his customary Ivy League jacket and tie with "L.A. casual" attire: white jeans, V-neck sweater over a striped polo shirt, its collar points turned up to frame his neck, and aviator sunglasses.

"Assemblyman Richard Mountjoy will be the featured guest on the May 29 edition of *Inside San Marino*," trumpeted one newspaper article, which included a photograph of Chichester smiling at the camera, alongside Peggy Ebright, with his hands crossed. "Above, Mountjoy discusses the program's format with producer Christopher Chichester."

The local notables Chichester roped into appearing on the show—the mayor, the headmaster, various Super Marino powerhouses—were soon depleted and Chichester began looking beyond San Marino for guests. Within a couple of months his roster expanded to include L.A. luminaries, growing so large in scope that Chichester changed the show's name from *Inside San Marino* to just *Inside*. "Welcome to *Inside*," went one intro. "I'm Peggy Ebright, and today we are in the offices of Mr. Daryl Gates, chief of the Los Angeles Police Department."

Off camera, but always in control, Chichester flashed cue cards and shouted directions. "And, Chief Gates, you are responsible for the safety of how many people?" he instructed Peggy to ask.

After filming *Inside* segments, Peggy would chauffeur her producer home—at least to what she assumed was his home, in lower San Marino. On the day of my visit, Peggy drove me over to the house, which sat on an expansive corner lot. It was "a Monterrey house," she said, referring to its Spanish style: red terra-cotta in color, a haven of arches, lush landscaping, and, most auspiciously for Chichester, she added, stained-glass coats of arms on the windows.

"I would tell him, 'I've always loved that house, I'd love to see the inside,'" Peggy said of the many evenings when she dropped him off at the grand hacienda, which he told her was owned by his parents.

"They let me live in it to keep it properly maintained," Chichester said, before bidding Peggy good night.

"Well, I would love to come in and take a look someday," Peggy said.

"Certainly," he would always reply, "but not tonight. Mother and Father asked me to keep up the house, but I'm not doing a very good job, and I couldn't abide your walking into a messy house. I'll invite you over for tea once I get things in order."

He never did.

"I thought, 'Maybe he's a remittance man!'" she told me, meaning the black sheep of the Chichester family, sent to America to gain education and experience while, best of all, staying out of the way of the working members of his prominent clan. It never occurred to her that he had fabricated the entire Christopher Chichester persona from whole cloth.

In San Marino, where eligible young bachelors were rare, especially one with good manners and a royal pedigree, Chichester found several ladies who accepted his request for a date.

"I produced *The Prisoner*," he told the daughter of one prominent San Marino family. He had met her at a San Marino library event where they were both volunteers, and with her parents' prodding, she accepted his invitation to go out on a date.

"You know, the Patrick McGoohan series," he said. "It was big in Great Britain."

She had never heard of *The Prisoner*, and she never checked to see if Christopher Chichester produced it. If she had, she would have discovered that *The Prisoner*—the classic 1960s British television series about a former secret agent perpetually trying to escape from a congenial community that is actually a prison for people who know too much—was on the air when Christopher was all of seven years old.

"I just love musicals!" another young San Marino woman trilled after her parents introduced her to Chris at the San Marino Public Library Book Fair.

"What a coincidence!" Chichester replied. "So do I."

He was *so* accommodating in that way. Whatever his listener loved, he did too. And he could back up that love with knowledge. In the case of the musicals, he began to rave about the glories of, say, *My Fair Lady* and *West Side Story*, and the subtle differences between them, making his listeners feel that they had something deeply in common with the young British nobleman.

He took the girl he met at the book fair on a date to see the Los Angeles Philharmonic at the Dorothy Chandler Pavilion. He led her higher and higher, until they were in the last row in the highest balcony.

"Darling, you're just going to *love* the *Hebrides* Overture!" he said, once they were seated in the nosebleed section, referring to the Felix Mendelssohn work, composed in 1830. "It will change your world."

It didn't. But he was unrelenting in trying to "educate" her on the finer things in life. A few days later, they were strolling past the shops of Lake Avenue in the nearby community of Pasadena.

"Of course, you've heard of Godiva chocolate?" Chichester asked his young companion.

"Well, no," she replied.

"Come with me," he said, taking her arm and whisking her into the Godiva shop. He led her over to a counter and picked up one of the company's trademark gold boxes of chocolates tied with a big red ribbon.

"They're the best chocolates," he told her. "And gentlemen give them to their ladies, and after they've eaten the chocolates they keep their love letters in the box."

After moving to San Francisco, the young woman opened her door to find a Federal Express delivery from C. Chichester, San Marino, with a gold box of Godiva chocolates inside.

"Enjoy the chocolates and keep the box for your love letters," read the accompanying note.

When Chichester's name hit the headlines twenty-five years after he was last seen in San Marino, none of the young women whom he had squired came forward in the media, save for one: Carol Campbell. A sunny, dark-haired mother of three, she invited me to her solidly San Marino house and gave me a tour of the city.

For Carol, however, her interaction with Christopher Chichester was still a sore wound. It began, she said, when her father met him at one of the local clubs—the Rotary or the City Club—where the men of San Marino had bought the story of the thirteenth baronet. Carol's father, Dick Campbell, decided to play matchmaker. Carol was visiting from Texas, and one day her father asked Chichester, "Hey, Chris, would you like to meet my daughter, Carol?"

"Certainly," Chichester replied.

Introductions were made the following Sunday at the San Marino Community Church.

"And you must be Carol," said Chichester.

"Yes," she said.

"I'd be honored if you would go out with me," he said. "How about eleven-thirty tomorrow?"

Assuming that meant a lunch date, Carol Campbell accepted. But instead of a knight in shining armor on a stallion, Chichester came riding up to her parents' house in his broken-down car. She noticed that his clothes were beginning to show some age. This wasn't a traditional date so much as just going with a guy on a series of errands. They rode around town, getting his mail from the post office, taking his clothing to the cleaners, before he finally dropped Carol back at home—without lunch, without explanation. But what most struck Carol was the interior of his car. Yellow Post-it notes were plastered to every available surface, reminders to himself, she later thought they must have been, about all of the things he had said and done in his sojourn in San Marino.

"Mom, that guy is creepy!" she said when she returned home. That was their one and only encounter. But after she returned to Texas she received a couple of letters from Chichester, expressing his admiration of her in his precise block handwriting. The letters just made her shake her head, she said.

Around the same time, a San Marino friend who worked as a wedding coordinator called Carol in Texas.

"Didn't you go out with Christopher Chichester?"

"Well, I guess."

Her friend told her that Chichester was crashing weddings. She'd been too busy to bust him, she said, and probably wouldn't have anyway, because that wouldn't have been the San Marino way. But the previous weekend, she said, she was coming out of the church to close the doors before the ceremony began, just as he was coming in, dressed immaculately but looking sheepish. When he saw her, he turned around quickly and walked back to his car.

As his star rose even higher in the community, he considered going into local politics, beginning with a seat on the San Marino City Council.

"I'm presently staying with friends and don't feel comfortable asking them if I can use their address," he said, referring to campaign documents he'd need to file for the race. He was in the home of Carol and Joe Iliff. "Would it be too much of a bother if I use your address?"

It wasn't that much of a stretch to use their address, as he was always stopping by their house, inviting Joe to breakfast—and never having cash for the tab, since royalty rarely carries cash. He and Joe Iliff would talk investments; Chichester always had some new and seemingly ingenious idea on how to make money. Like bringing over Chichester Cathedral to San Marino—he wouldn't give up on the notion of that—or all manner of other financial and investment schemes, none of which came to fruition.

He also felt sure he could make a difference in San Marino, either by being elected to the city council himself or by being the puppetmaster of a city council member. "He felt that he had ideas and that if he pushed either me or my husband into running for office that he could sit behind the scenes and tell us what to say," Carol Iliff said, adding that Chichester even suggested moving in with the couple.

"Actually, I'm wearing out my welcome a bit with the friends who have been giving me lodging," he told the Iliffs one day. "Would you mind if I stayed with you for a month or so, until I can get resettled?"

Joe, who was on the road most weeks, didn't think that was a good idea. It was only a two-bedroom house and not nearly large enough for his wife and Christopher Chichester. "My husband traveled every other week and he wasn't going to have some guy living here in the house with me," Carol later recalled.

After his first year in the area, Chichester was growing in confidence and attitude—not just in San Marino, which was becoming too provincial for a man of his name and nobility. With all of his social and television activities, it was a wonder that he had time for anything else. But he was living yet another active life as a student. He loomed extremely large as a big man on campus nine miles down the freeway, at the University of Southern California film school.

"I met Chris through my aunt Victoria," said Dana Farrar, a dark-haired, friendly woman. It was a sunny Southern California afternoon and we were sitting on her back patio staring at a stack of photographs of the young man who called himself Christopher Chichester. She had not seen him for a very long time, but the pictures brought him back in all of his glory.

The first one showed Dana, then a fresh-faced beauty, grinning beside Chichester, an extremely thin young man in tight jeans and a V-neck sweater smirking crazily with three cone-shaped party hats on the top and sides of his head. In a second picture, he was peering contemplatively into a glass of wine, which he held with his pinky extended. In a third picture, he was making a funny face and twisting his fingers menacingly toward the camera—posing, Dana Farrar said, he was always posing.

"Aunt Victoria lives in San Marino," Dana continued. "She's ninety-two years old."

Victoria was a true Super Marino matron. She met Chichester shortly after his arrival, at a Friends of the Library dinner.

"She was sitting with a neighbor, some old man from across the street, and Chris somehow struck up a conversation with her," Dana continued. "At the time he used to give out business cards that said, 'Christopher Chichester, Thirteenth Baronet,' or something."

"The Friends of the Library dinner was some kind of a charity event, where mostly it would be retired people, senior citizens, philanthropists," said Dana. "I don't know how he, Chichester, got there. But that's where she met him."

He had charmed her aunt, convincing her that he was involved in film production or something having to do with the film industry at USC, referring to the celebrated film school. "I was a student at USC at the time in journalism, and my boyfriend wanted to get into the film school very badly. Aunt Victoria thought Chris could help my boyfriend get into film school.

"She took us out to brunch with him," Dana continued. "Oh, he was very charming. He was a lot of fun. He knew a lot about a lot of things." But he was affected. He spoke in a clipped half-British, half-indiscernible accent, she said. "He would draw out the vowels at the end of every word."

"Day-*nahhhhhh*," she said, mimicking the way he said her name. "I think he must have studied American movies or something. It's amazing to me. I speak German. I studied German for six years, and I couldn't pick up a German accent with him at all."

The accent was difficult to pinpoint, as were the details of his studies at USC.

"I can just remember being in the restaurant with Aunt Victoria and Chris and trying to pin him down, saying, '*What are you actually doing? What is your job?*' He kind of just danced around everything."

But he knew enough to keep the interest of his companions. Shortly after that he dropped the name Arthur Knight, the most impressive teacher of that era in the school. Dana and her increasingly starry-eyed boyfriend took him to mean, *I'm a teacher's asssistant in Arthur Knight's class.* Arthur Knight was the famed author, film critic, and teacher who had taught future directors like George Lucas in his fabled Introduction to Film class, and had brought in guest lecturers like Orson Welles, Frank Capra, Clint Eastwood, and Chichester's personal favorite, Alfred Hitchcock.

He gave the impression that he would "have a word with Arthur," meaning he would talk to Arthur Knight about seeing what influence he might be able to bring to help Dana's boyfriend get into film school. After the brunch, which Chichester ate ravenously, the parties said goodbye. Although Chichester never quite got around to introducing Dana's boyfriend to Arthur Knight—or to helping him get into the film school—the brunch was the opening bell on Dana Farrar's increasingly peculiar friendship with the young Englishman.

At USC, Dana began seeing him *everywhere*—in the library, at film screenings, dashing between classes. Always with a film script under his arm, he insisted that he was completing studies for his master of fine arts in film.

Dana and her friends could never bring themselves to ask why he was driving an old Plymouth Arrow if he was so wealthy. Nor did they question why his preppy clothing sometimes smelled from lack of dry cleaning—or was it just the musty scent of old money?—or why he had a habit of showing up unannounced at Dana's apartment at mealtimes. "Oh, that smells so delightful, *Day*-nah!" he would say, until she either showed him the door or, more often, gave him a meal. He would wolf down food as if he hadn't eaten for a week, and Dana thought what everyone else did: it all went with the territory of being rich, royal, and eccentric.

The professors knew him as well, and one of them, his English professor Geoffrey Green, assumed he was enrolled, because he was somehow on his roster of students. "I had a printed list from the registrar, and to get on it he would have had to sweet-talk someone in the registrar's office into letting him into the class," he remembered. "I did not admit him or add him to the class. His name was on the list." However, the USC admissions department had no record of a Christopher Chichester, or a Christian Karl Gerhartsreiter, enrolled in the school or ever paying tuition.

"He came to my attention because he was in my prose fiction class in the English department at USC," Green continued. "He was a very active participant in the class and he came to see me during office hours. He was going by the name Christopher Chichester and he claimed at that time that he was descended from the Earl of Chichester, and he showed me some coat of arms, and he also said he was related to the Chichester who had sailed around the world.

"He told me that he lived in a mansion, that he had an extra room in the gatehouse where someone could stay as a guest, and various other things. He said he wanted to make films. He said he was going to be a significant writer, filmmaker. Like a philosopher of aesthetics. He was very outspoken, and he needed to be right."

Chichester frequently invited Dana Farrar to movie screenings, including repeated showings of his two favorite films—*Double Indemnity* and *All About Eve*—at the art houses he loved, like the New Beverly in Beverly Hills. She went with him often. He also managed to get a friend of hers tickets to a special premiere of Barbra Streisand's new movie *Yentl* at USC, tickets that were very tough to get. But when he asked Dana and her friends to the opening of the Marcia Lucas Post Production Building, a state-of-the-art multimedia facility named for the wife of *Star Wars* director George Lucas, she thought he had to be kidding. Chichester insisted that he wasn't, adding that, of course, George Lucas, Steven Spielberg, director Robert Zemeckis, and other Hollywood stars would also be in attendance.

"I'm getting you in!" he told Dana, and sure enough, somehow he did.

Once inside, Chichester acted the host, as the rail-thin film aficionado in the V-neck sweater went about the fine art of making introductions and excelling at the highest Hollywood art form: the schmooze.

"He loved *dangerous* women," Dana said, recalling the films they saw and discussed when they went for coffee and conversation. His talk usually centered on his obsession with film, especially film noir, and the queens of the genre, like Barbara Stanwyck, whose performances fascinated him.

Someday, very soon, he would direct his own film noir movies on the scale of his heroes; for now, his life was seemingly consumed with watching them and, rather more chillingly, internalizing them.

CHAPTER 5

The Secret Mission

Though everyone in San Marino loved to talk about Christopher Chichester, no one seemed to know where he had actually lived during his sojourn in their community—that is, until the end of his time there. His last known residence in San Marino, 1920 Lorain Road, has since become among the most infamous addresses in the city.

He landed there thanks to the recommendation of two friendly young parishioners at the Church of Our Saviour, the Whitmore sisters, Muffy and Tasha. They met Chichester at a Bible study group and soon felt obliged to adopt the young European, whom they referred to as "cute little Chris." They would invite him over to their house regularly for meals with them and their parents, and he always readily accepted. He would drive over in his clunker of a car, sporting a well-worn tweed jacket and tie—the sisters considered that so typical of the upper classes, where being flashy is looked down upon.

"I'd love to show you my house in Glendale on the Hill," Chichester would tell them, alluding to one of Southern California's most affluent neighborhoods. While they suspected that perhaps he might not really live there, they were too polite to challenge him or invite themselves for a visit.

Once, one of the sisters asked Chichester if he had met their grand-mother. "She moved up from Bermuda to be near us, and she had been living in a lovely guesthouse over on Lorain Road, with slip covers on the sofa and an Oriental carpet on the floor."

"*Had* been living?" Chichester inquired.

"Yes, but not anymore. She moved out, and into the Episcopalian home for the aged."

Not long after that, Chichester knocked on the door of the two-bedroom, Spanish-style house at 1920 Lorain Road, located squarely in Sub Marino, near the border with San Gabriel. It's easy to imagine how the encounter must have gone. He would have flashed his broad smile and perhaps presented his calling card. The woman at the door, whose name was Ruth "Didi" Sohus, would have been dressed, as she almost always was, in a tattered housecoat. She would likely have had a lit cigarette dangling from her lips and, even though it was long before the cocktail hour, a tumbler of her drink of choice—vodka cut with sherry—in her hand.

"Christopher Mountbatten Chichester," the dashing young man would have said, extending his hand. "And you must be Mrs. Sohus." As so many San Marino matrons before her had done, the woman would surely have blushed, smiled, and held out her hand, which Chichester would have grandly kissed. Thus began a most unlikely relationship.

When Christopher Chichester arrived at 1920 Lorain Road, both the house and its owner had seen much better days. Didi Sohus had moved there with her parents when she was two years old, and she'd had a typical San Marino upbringing. A picture of the class of 1935 at a prestigious private girls' school in neighboring San Gabriel shows Didi as a petite brunette in a long white gown, smiling broadly and holding an enormous bouquet of flowers. Her parents gave her a convertible when she was still in her teens, and after being presented to Southern California society as a debutante, she graduated from USC. She went to work for a newspaper and flew her own small airplane—daring activities for a woman of her era.

Men, or her taste in them, would be Didi's downfall. Her first husband was named Barney, but even Didi's oldest friends couldn't recall anything about him, including his last name. Husband number two, Harry Sherwood, was a Marine officer stationed at Camp Pendleton, about seventy miles south of San Marino. Harry had a son, who followed in his father's footsteps and became a Marine, then joined the U.S. Border Patrol and the Customs Service as an investigator. He died young. Didi's third husband, Bob Sohus, was a stockbroker. She was beyond childbearing age when they married, but she desperately wanted a baby, so they adopted a six-month-old boy, John, whose teenage mother had given him up.

They lived in Didi's childhood home on Lorain Road. Didi's mother, Frieda Detrick, whom everyone called Mama D., lived in a guesthouse on the property. It was not at all fancy, just a bedroom and bath, for it would be in violation of San Marino's strict building codes if the Sohuses had rented the "accessory dwelling unit" for money.

One day in 1960, when John was still a toddler, Didi and Bob had a fight during which, according to Bob, Didi slugged him, or as Bob later put it, "She fattened my lip." After that he moved out, leaving her to raise John on her own. Mama D. helped out, but one morning she failed to show up for breakfast with her daughter and grandson. "I'm too frightened to go back there and see if anything's wrong," Didi told a neighbor, who went to the guesthouse and found Mama D. dead. After that, John was all that Didi had left. She took a part-time job in an auto garage in nearby Pasadena to pay the bills, and she spent the rest of her time with her son.

John was something of a mama's boy, smart but shy, a loner who suffered from diabetes and ulcers. His absentee father would remember him as very trusting and easily manipulated. Unlike most boys in San Marino, John wasn't into sports or cars; he didn't even show any interest in getting a driver's license, preferring to ride his bike to school. He didn't find his true passion until he was a teenager, when someone introduced him to computers. He was so fascinated by the machines—primitive though they were at that time—that he stole one from his high school and kept it in his bedroom until school officials realized it was missing and demanded that he return it.

Computers were going to be his life, he decided, and he threw himself into them completely. Rather than going to college, he hung out with fellow techies at the California Institute of Technology in Pasadena. In addition to computers, he discovered with these new friends a second love: the elaborate role-playing game Dungeons and Dragons. Through this game John connected with his future wife.

The redheaded, part–Blackfoot Indian Linda Mayfield, who was more than six feet tall and weighed more than two hundred pounds, dwarfed John Sohus, who stood five feet five. Like him she had been a social misfit, dropping out of school in tenth grade, waitressing and searching for herself, until she got into science fiction. She was a passionate fan of *Star Trek* and Dungeons and Dragons, and she loved to paint and sketch. She drew scores of fanciful ducks and bunnies, but her specialty was horses—usually wildly decorated stallions or unicorns, often depicted flying through the air trailing branches of flowers. Early on, Linda took up horseback riding, and when at age sixteen she moved from her childhood home in Venice Beach to live with her grandmother in the Los Angeles suburbs, her grandmother bought her a horse.

After quitting school, Linda spent a good part of her time at the tabernacle of science fiction, the Los Angeles Science Fantasy Society (LASFS). She became a member in July 1976, when she was twenty. Founded in 1934, LASFS is the world's oldest ongoing science-fiction society. Its members have included author Ray Bradbury and super-fan Forrest J Ackerman, editor of the landmark horror magazine *Famous Monsters of Filmland*. Today the club, housed in a ramshackle building on Burbank Boulevard, is a meeting place for writers and artists, geeks and nerds, Trekkies and conspiracy theorists. Robert Bloch, the author of *Psycho*, was a member, and his book *The Eighth Stage of Fandom*, about the addictive pull of science fiction on its followers, is considered a bible of the society. Bloch described the progression of fandom from the first stage, "Reader interest," to the last, in which the individual is "tottering on the brink of the abyss," trapped in a world of fantasy with "no way to retrace his steps. He can only take the plunge, over the edge of the precipice."

Linda Mayfield may not have been at the edge of the precipice, but she was a serious fan. She took a clerking job in a Los Angeles science-fiction bookstore called Dangerous Visions. There, surrounded by such titles as *The Trouble with Humans* and *Monsters, Mutants and Heavenly Creatures*, Linda found a home.

Whenever she returned to reality, however, she found that she was still unlucky in life, especially when it came to love. She had been engaged at age eighteen, but the groom bailed. Eight years later she was engaged again, to a young man who lived in San Marino. He worked as a night watchman and asked a friend, John Sohus, to stay in the house with Linda while he was away. A friendly little puppy of a man, John Sohus wouldn't be much in the way of a bodyguard. He was short and pudgy, with Coke-bottle glasses, but he absolutely adored Linda from the moment they met. They bonded over games of Dungeons and Dragons and other areas of science-fiction fandom. And when his friend decided against marrying Linda, breaking up with her abruptly just before Christmas in 1982 and leaving her crestfallen and depressed, John was there to offer his support. They made for a somewhat strange, Mutt-and-Jeff pairing, but they soon fell in love and moved into John's mother's house. Christopher Chichester was already ensconced in the guesthouse.

From all indications, Chichester was living there as early as late 1982 and at least by 1983. "I attended a barbecue at the Lorain house on July 4, 1983, and Linda and John were living there by that time," remembered Linda's best friend, Sue Coffman. "That's when Linda mentioned the 'strange boarder' who lived in the back house."

Didi Sohus felt that Linda Mayfield wasn't nearly good enough for her son. As John and Linda spent more and more time together, Didi became more of a recluse—wearing her housecoat morning, noon, and night, letting old newspapers and other clutter pile up to the ceiling. Her life had revolved around John, and now she was losing him. She didn't even attend her son's wedding, which took place in the backyard of Sue Coffman's house at midnight on Halloween in 1983. A few guests showed up as Dungeons and Dragons characters and all manner of monsters. The bride and groom, however, as well as the bride's family, dressed conventionally.

Despite Didi Sohus's disapproval of their union, Linda and John continued to live with her on Lorain Road. As a bookstore clerk and a low-level computer programmer, they earned very little, but they were determined to move into a place of their own—along with Linda's six cats—as soon as possible.

Life with Didi was fairly unpleasant for the young couple. She slept days and drank nights, screaming "Johnny!" at all hours and giving the couple very little, if any, privacy. "God, will she ever stop?" John and Linda would ask each other as her dementia grew. She took to pounding on their bedroom door to get their attention, and they finally resorted to putting a padlock on it. They were desperate to get out of Didi's house—and to get Didi out of their lives—but they had very little money and no stability in their jobs. They were trapped.

Dangerous Visions, the store where Linda worked, was the largest science-fiction bookstore in L.A. It sat on the corner of Ventura Boulevard and Woodman Avenue in the Valley, the flatlands of the Los Angeles basin to the west of the city proper. Named for the landmark 1967 collection of science-fiction stories by Harlan Ellison, the bookstore had been owned and operated since 1981 by a bestselling sci-fi author, Arthur Byron Cover, and his wife, Lydia Marano. On the morning of February 8, 1985, Marano stopped by her store and found it dark and locked. Linda Sohus, the clerk who was supposed to be on duty, apparently hadn't shown up. Annoyed, Marano opened the store herself and dialed Linda's home number.

A seemingly drunken Didi Sohus picked up. "They've gone to Paris," she said.

"Paris, Texas?" asked Marano.

"No, dear, Paris, *France*," Didi said and hung up.

Linda had told her friend Sue Coffman a slightly different but equally improbable story: John had been offered the opportunity of a lifetime, a "top secret" government job in New York. They had to drop everything and fly to the East Coast immediately.

"Apparently it had to do with his abilities as a systems analyst with computers," Coffman would later say. "Linda told me that she had also been hired by the government, but she didn't know what they would want her for. All she could figure was that her artistic abilities might be useful for design or computer graphics purposes. I assumed that since she was married, if the husband was needed, it would just be easier to hire the wife also."

Linda said she couldn't tell Sue anything more about the mysterious job, but she assured her friend that she wouldn't be gone long. She promised to be back in time for the trip to Phoenix the two had been planning. They were going to attend a science-fiction convention, and they would drive there in Linda and John's brand-new pickup truck. Just before leaving San Marino, Linda dropped off her six cats at the local "cat hotel" and paid for two weeks of food and board. She assured the clerk there that she would be back for her precious pets soon.

In fact, John and Linda were back on Lorain Road within days of their supposed trip to New York, but only long enough to pack up a few belongings and excitedly inform Didi that they were off to Paris! Didi was shocked, but she wished them well and they took several of her credit cards to use on the journey.

Over the next two months, the owners of the Dangerous Visions bookstore got two calls about Linda. The first was from someone at Robinsons-May, a Los Angeles–area department store, checking on Linda's qualifications, because, the caller said, she had applied for a job. The second call was from a credit card company; Linda had purportedly applied for a credit card and given her employer as a reference.

There was no word from the missing couple themselves, however.

Linda never returned to pick up her cats from the cat hotel, but just before the proprietors were going to have to have them put down, an anonymous person, claiming to have been sent by Linda, retrieved the animals. Linda's half sister, Kathy, eventually grew concerned and called Didi.

"Is Linda back from her trip yet?" she asked, according to a later report.

"I'm not supposed to tell you anything," Didi said. She paused and added conspiratorially, "They're on a mission!"

"What mission?" Kathy asked. "What are you talking about?"

"Well, that's all I can tell you," said Didi. Kathy's subsequent phone conversations with her were not much more informative; depending on how drunk Didi was, they were sometimes completely incoherent.

Sue Coffman got a similar brush-off when she called Didi. "I wish I could say more, but I'm not allowed to," Didi told her, meaning that any leak of information could "jeopardize" their top-secret mission. "I'm just supposed to say that they're okay and that I don't know when they'll be coming back."

A friend of Linda Sohus's who had met her at Dangerous Visions called Didi after almost a month had passed with no news from Linda. "I looked up the only Sohus in that area, which turned out to be John's mother," the friend, known as "PanLives," wrote on a Web site. "I called, expecting to be embarrassed about being such a worrier. She, Didi, answered. I told her who I was and that I was wondering if everything was okay. She immediately broke down in tears and said that she didn't know where he was or what was going on. It got a little incoherent, and then France came up. I said, 'France? I thought they were working in New York?' She just kept crying."

Finally, more than two months after John and Linda had disappeared, someone called the police. Two officers arrived at Didi's house at 7:30 p.m. on April 8, 1985. They knocked on the door, and Didi opened it a crack. The officers said they'd been told that her son and daughter-in-law were missing. Did she know where they had gone?

"They're *not* missing!" Didi would later be quoted as saying. "Everybody keeps asking me, and I keep telling them they're on a secret mission!"

The cops shot each other a look. "Can you tell us how we can reach them?" one asked.

"I have a source," Didi said, adding that this person could reach John and Linda whenever necessary. Didi said she couldn't reveal who the source was, though, because if anyone else tried to contact the couple, it could jeopardize them and their top-secret government mission.

"Okay?" she said and went back into the house.

Then three postcards arrived, each mailed on the same day and each with a picture of the Eiffel Tower on the front and a Paris postmark. One was sent to the co-owner of Dangerous Visions: "Not quite New York, but not bad. See you later, Linda and John."

Another went to Sue Coffman: "Missed New York—Oops! But this can be lived with. Love, Linda and John."

The third postcard was to Linda's mother, which was odd, since the two had been estranged for some time. "Took a wrong turn in Europe," it read.

Nobody really paid much attention to the missing couple, at least not right away. Almost ten years later, however, when the missing persons case would make headlines, San Marino buzzed with speculation. Why had John left San Marino for New York the day before Linda, as someone familiar with the case insisted? And why had John asked for two weeks' advance pay from his boss at Dual Graphics, the computer programming company where he worked, promising to pay it back, only to abscond with the cash, which wasn't at all like honest Johnny Sohus? Did any of this have to do with their boarder, Christopher Chichester?

For a month after the couple left town, he remained in his guest quarters at 1920 Lorain Road. By this time he seemed to have full run of Didi Sohus's house. He even invited people over to play his favorite board game, Trivial Pursuit.

In John and Linda's absence, Didi let Chichester drive their pickup truck. One day he drove it over to Loma Linda, to the home of Elmer and Jean Kelln, the couple he'd met in Germany seven years earlier. "I've finally arrived!" he told them. "I've finally made it in the movie industry!"

He said he was not merely having success as a film producer but that he had purchased a house in San Marino. He said that the actress Linda Evans, who was then starring in the hit series *Dynasty*, lived right next door, and that the houses were so close he could see over her fence. How could the Kellns know that Linda Evans lived in Los Angeles and had never lived in San Marino? They believed everything Christopher told them, even that he was working in a studio mailroom to make extra cash, and that he clipped unmarked stamps off envelopes and sold them.

Later, he showed up at their house again, this time bragging that he had just made $5,000 by selling film emulsion he had picked up for nothing at USC. Why would a rising producer do something like that? He was on his way to the Cannes Film Festival, he explained with a wink, and needed a little pocket money for champagne and caviar.

The Kellns' son, Wayne, pulled up shortly after Chichester did one day. Seeing the unfamiliar truck parked in front of his parents' house, Wayne got out of his car and looked inside. The driver's seat was empty, but a large woman was sitting in the passenger seat. She was *huge*, he would later recall, a strawberry blonde with a red face, looking as if she had been crying.

Wayne walked up to the front door just as Chichester was coming out, carrying a box of things he'd stashed at Elmer and Jean's for safekeeping.

"Hi, Wayne," he said.

"Hi," said Wayne, sensing that something was strange—not that Chris was at his parents' house, because he visited often, but that he was with a woman. Wayne had never seen Chris with a woman before.

"Unfortunately, this is my last haircut with you," Chichester told Jann of Sweden one day in the spring of 1985.

"Really?" asked the Swedish cowboy.

"Yes, a family member has died in London, and I have to go back immediately and settle the estate," he said. He shook hands with Jann and went downstairs to the street, where he got into John Sohus's pickup truck and drove away. Jann Eldnor, Elmer and Jean Kelln, Didi Sohus, Dana Farrar—none of them ever saw Christopher Chichester again.

Five months after John and Linda left, Didi Sohus broke down and called the San Marino Police Department. Two officers were immediately dispatched to her address. Didi invited them into the house and asked them to sit down. She said she wanted to file a missing persons report.

"I thought I knew what was going on, but now . . ." she began.

"Have you had any contact with John and Linda at all since they left?" they asked.

"Well, I've been sending their mail through my source," she said, "the man who has been in contact with them. He's been the one telling me what's been happening."

He had told her, she said, that John and Linda were working for Dassault Aviation, the French aerospace giant, which his family partially controlled and which had branches around the globe. He had also told her to give him Linda's prized saddle and any mail for the couple, which soon included a flurry of past-due notices from banks, credit card companies, and department stores. And, she added, he was shipping it all to what she presumed was a way station for the couple, in Iredell County, North Carolina. Why there? She didn't know. *He*, of course, was none other than Christopher Mountbatten Chichester.

"We'll need to talk to this individual," one of the officers said.

"You *can't*!" said Didi. "See, that's why I'm worried. He's gone too, just *disappeared*."

After putting the police on the case, Didi Sohus continued her sad descent. Crippled by a stroke and mounting medical bills, she eventually sold her house and moved into a trailer park in La Puente, twenty miles from San Marino. "If Johnny comes looking for me, please tell him where I am, because he'll come to you," she told a neighbor on Lorain Road. "He'll want to know why I'm not there."

She never had any word from her son and daughter-in-law. In the fall of 1988, she had a heart attack and died. Her request to have her body cremated and her ashes scattered at sea was carried out by her designated trustees, Linda and Don Wetherbee, who were complete strangers to Didi before the couple sold her a mobile home near their own.

Though few people had taken much notice of Didi in her decline, her will aroused considerable interest. California reporters Frank Girardot and Nathan Mcintire later reported that she left behind an estate worth approximately $180,000, according to court records. She forgave a $40,000 loan she had made to Linda and Don Wetherbee. She also left them the proceeds from the proposed sale of her mobile home, which would amount to $32,000. As for John Sohus, a year before Didi's death she filed a new last will and testament, disinheriting her only son. Why had Didi Sohus really moved into a trailer home? Why did she disinherit her only son from her will? Why did she leave her entire estate to Linda and Don Wetherbee, whose only apparent connection to the deceased is that they sold Didi her trailer home? These questions were not answered—or even asked—in the mid-1980s.

By then, the man who called himself Christopher Chichester was far from San Marino and no longer needed Didi Sohus or her shelter.

In 1994, six years after Didi's death, the San Gabriel Valley Newspaper Group ran an article with the headline COLORFUL CAST OF CHARACTERS: "Detectives try to unravel mystery of old home on Lorain Road." The story related the unhappy details of Didi Sohus's life and the sorry state of her house. "The cast of characters proved irresistible to the young Melanie Whitehead," wrote reporter Bernice Hirabayashi. "In the 1960s, she stood on tiptoe to catch a glimpse of her neighbors over the backyard fence. 'As a kid, I can remember just peeking over the wall and watching them,' she said. 'Everything was overgrown. I don't think they ever took care of the yard.'"

The article went on to describe the principals in the story: "There was the main character, Ruth 'Didi' Sohus, the USC debutante, who took to drinking and socked her husband, Bob Sohus, in the face during a marital spat. There was the adopted son, John Sohus, and his wife, Linda, who shared an obsession with science fiction and fantasy . . . and then there were Didi's illegal tenants—transients who rented the guest-house in violation of city codes."

It was a perfect situation for a tenant who wished to keep his living arrangements hidden. As one Super Marino widow told me, "You have to give him credit. Was there *anyone* that people in San Marino knew *less* about than Didi Sohus and those two?" By "those two" she was referring dismissively to John and Linda Sohus.

As usual, Jann of Sweden, who had cut John Sohus's hair since he was a child, had a much closer perspective. "Oh, I knew Didi," he told me. "Chichester was living there on Lorain Road with her, and he had plenty of space." He was saying that Chichester was living with Didi first, perhaps as early as late 1982, even before John and Linda moved into the house on Lorain Road.

Jann looked to see if I was getting the gist of what he was trying to say, and when I nodded yes, he said, "All right. So, they move in and they discover the man in the back, Christopher Chichester." He shot me a knowing smile. "The son, John, now starts to put his nose into what Chichester is doing. He sees his mother's condition and starts thinking, 'Maybe this Chichester is taking money from my mother.' And he starts to question Chichester."

Jann seemed sure he was onto the truth as he continued: "Now, for sure, Chichester had his eye on all the ladies, young and old. So right away he maybe kept an eye on John's wife, Linda. And because he treats the ladies really special, it might not take long for Linda to start to have a liking for the guy. Meanwhile, the husband, John, might be more irritated, and Chichester suddenly . . ." Jann pantomimed Chichester picking up a large object and getting set to swing.

I cut him off there, because he couldn't possibly have proof that

Chichester suddenly did anything. However, back in my hotel room that night, I found that Jann wasn't the only one speculating in this direction. A *Pasadena Star-News* account quoted Frank Wills, the former San Marino police chief: "According to Wills, investigators speculated that Chichester and Linda Sohus became romantically involved sometime prior to her and her husband's disappearance. 'There was speculation that [Chichester] was in love with the female,' Wills said. 'He had a very elaborately devised story and convinced her that he was a secret agent.' Wills noted that detectives also believed that Chichester was jealous of John Sohus, and that jealousy may have led to murder."

I pulled out the sheaf of documents I had been given during the trial in Boston and found a neatly typed report from the San Marino Police Department, prepared after officers had interviewed Didi Sohus's next-door neighbor. "Mrs. Sohus seemed to drink a great deal," the woman said. Regarding Chichester, who "taught at the school of filmmaking" at the University of Southern California, she said he was "odd, a real strange guy. . . . He did not discuss his family, except to mention that he was wealthy and well-connected in England. She did not remember seeing any friends visit him. . . . She thought Chichester was having financial problems. She said the mailman would comment on how many bills Chichester received and how creditors frequently asked for him."

There was also a report in which Didi discussed her son and daughter-in-law with the police. "She said that the subjects appear to be in a great deal of debt. She is constantly receiving calls and notices from banks and businesses asking for their whereabouts, e.g., Bank of America, Sears, Broadway, Holiday Hotel for Cats."

I put down the papers and tried to visualize the house at 1920 Lorain Road in 1985: one married couple, six cats, and Christopher Chichester—all strapped for cash—and a lonely, loopy landlady who was pretty wealthy by comparison. This was a setting any true student of film noir couldn't help but relish. And Chichester, who was well versed in the genre, actually found himself living in it.

CHAPTER 6

Christopher Crowe: Greenwich, Connecticut

W hen a crew arrived to clean the dwelling behind the main house at 1920 Lorain Road, where Christopher Chichester had lived, they found it was a single large room with a green concrete floor, a tiny bathroom, and a bed pushed against a wall. The place was a wreck, trashed and disorderly, with litter strewn about on what little furniture there was. It was clear that the last tenant had left in a rush and taken anything that may have been of value with him.

Chichester's disappearance left a void in San Marino. The young man who had been able to talk about *anything*, who knew the answer to every Trivial Pursuit question, had left a couple of bigger questions in his wake: why had he left and where had he gone? No one seemed to have seen him depart. But couldn't he at least have said goodbye to those who had given him their friendship and trust? And couldn't he have at least paid the lunch bills he'd racked up at the Rotary and City clubs?

When he did surface, three months after his disappearance, no one in San Marino would know about it, and wouldn't for years. He drove John and Linda Sohus's 1985 Nissan pickup truck, with a homemade camper on the back, clear across America, toward another coast, where in June 1985 he came to rest in the ultimate bastion of Waspy wealth: Greenwich, Connecticut. There he would once again put to use the knowledge that had served him so well in San Marino: *"The bigger the lie, the more it will be believed,"* as the German propaganda minister Joseph Goebbels is famously quoted as saying. *Gullibility has no limits as to class or pedigree.* This time, he didn't look in the telephone book for a new name. Instead he turned to the movies, particularly those of Alfred Hitchcock, and came up with Christopher Crowe.

It certainly had a nice ring, as it should have. The real Christopher Crowe was an accomplished writer, director, and producer who had just been named executive producer of a new television series titled *Alfred Hitchcock Presents*, based on the original 1955 series, in which Hitchcock had introduced each mystery with his trademark "Good evening," along with the theme music, "Funeral March of a Marionette."

The series premiered in the summer of 1985, just as Christopher Chichester was leaving San Marino. On June 12, when he rented a post office box in Greenwich under the name Christopher C. Crowe, he showed the clerk a document stating that his real name was C. Mountbatten.

Following his successful pattern in San Marino, he promptly made himself known at a local church. In this case, he chose the rich, prominent, very social Episcopal parish of Christ Church. Since its founding in the nineteenth century, Christ Church had included among its members the mother of President George H. W. Bush, several Rockefellers, and many other distinguished figures.

The pastor, the Reverend John Bishop, would later say that Crowe had just appeared at the church one day, saying "he was new to the area and was looking to make friends." The reverend said Crowe "became an active member of the church and held a position of usher." A member of the congregation added, "When Crowe arrived in the area, he was assisted by members of Christ Church. . . . When one of the worshippers posted a note in the church that he had a room for rent . . . Crowe applied for the room, and after checking Crowe's references, he rented the room to Crowe." The room was in a house at 34 Rock Ridge Avenue, and the owner was John Callahan Maddox.

As I drove into Greenwich, I couldn't help but admire the nerve of this cunning chameleon in selecting his next destination. According to a description in a 2008 *Los Angeles Times* story: "The ritzy enclave north of New York City, home to dozens of hedge funds and scores of investment bankers, stands out from other upper-crust communities around the suburbs of New York, even Scarsdale and Chappaqua. Greenwich is the only one, for example, that has white-gloved police officers directing traffic along its lightly traveled main street. . . . The median household income in Greenwich last year was $115,644, compared with $49,314 for the U.S. as a whole." The median price of a house there was just under $1.5 million.

When I pulled up in front of 34 Rock Ridge Road, I was stunned. It was a grand estate on what was surely one of the best streets in Greenwich. The house was a sprawling three-story mansion set on four acres of rolling land. The driveway was filled with luxury automobiles. When Christopher Crowe came to take up residence here, it was the home of an elderly couple, John Maddox and his wife, Gretchen.

I found in the dossier of papers I'd been given the following relevant report: "Mr. John C. Maddox, the owner of #34 Rock Ridge Avenue, was contacted by telephone, at which time he related that the Crowe subject had rented a room from him approximately two and half to three years ago . . . That Crowe was driving a small camper-type vehicle, which looked like Crowe had done some type of work on same to make it a camper."

Perhaps that explained where he had slept during the three or four missing months after he left San Marino, I thought as I read.

"Mr. Maddox further related that . . . he found Crowe to be a compulsive liar, based on past incidents where Crowe lied to several people about his background," the report continued.

These remarks were made by Maddox three years after he had taken Crowe in as a tenant. After checking Crowe's references at the time, however, Maddox had been sufficiently convinced to lease the young man a three-room, one-bath apartment with its own entrance on the third floor of the ten-bedroom house.

Maddox was long deceased by the time I arrived in Greenwich, but his daughter helped me fill in some blanks. Her father was a blue-blooded member of the eastern establishment, she said, a retired advertising executive who belonged to several private clubs, including the esteemed Metropolitan Club, founded by the likes of J. P. Morgan, William K. Vanderbilt, and William C. Whitney in 1891, in an Italianate mansion on East Sixtieth Street in New York City. An inventor, Maddox often spoke about his passion—quantum physics—at Christ Church. He was seventy-four when Crowe arrived in 1985. His children had all left home, so John and Gretchen had the big empty house to themselves. To supplement their income, the couple began "quietly renting rooms for single people," according to Maddox's daughter. When the fraudulent newcomer saw a notice posted on a local bulletin board, he called the number listed and soon after arrived with his few belongings.

"I think my mom mentioned that he didn't have much furniture at all," said the daughter. "But he had lots of electronic equipment. And he seemed to ingratiate himself with the members of the Episcopal church and convince them—now, this is hearsay, through my mom—that he was able to do some computer work for them and maybe get their mailing list computerized."

She took a long breath.

"And, of course, he gets ahold of that mailing list. The names of those people in Greenwich would be a rather refined collection of names, if you know what I mean. This *is* Greenwich, Connecticut! And this *is* the Episcopal church in Greenwich, Connecticut. It's where all the money-bags are! And he seemed to find a way into the local papers whenever there was a picture taken of people who had either connections or political power or something. His picture kept showing up in the paper along with all the well-known people."

Indeed, when I leafed through my dossier of records and found the one pertaining to the young man's time in Greenwich, I discovered this: "During a G.O.P. meeting, Crowe did have his picture taken with members of the G.O.P., including Prescott Bush [brother of President George H. W. Bush]."

I asked Maddox's daughter what her parents thought of Crowe. "They were so *snowed*!" she said. "He was good-looking. He was charming. He was kind of intriguing to them. He had proper manners and he dressed well, and my mom would be impressed with that."

Naturally, Christopher Crowe would have been more than impressed with John Maddox, with his aristocratic connections and his late-life passion for light music boxes. "When he retired, he became this really eccentric inventor," said his daughter. "One of the things he was really excited about was to put music with a visual component. He did the first music boxes or music machines." She described these as a system of lights that would dance along with the music.

"I don't know if Christopher Crowe ever saw my dad's video stuff," she said. "But if my dad had someone who was interested in his conversation about it, well, then that person would be invited immediately to the basement."

I could envision Christian Gerhartsreiter, eyes wide, watching the swirling lights, entranced with the soaring classical music, lucky, as always, to have landed in a privileged place and secured an inside track.

The 34 Rock Ridge address only added to the young man's luster, and the Christ Church parishioners more than likely complimented him on his happy choice of lodgings as he passed out church bulletins and escorted worshippers to their seats.

"He was involved in the Cotton Club, a group for singles," the genteel longtime church secretary told me in the parish office, before directing me to the church's public relations director, who, she assured me, had also known Crowe. I found the PR director in the church's gift shop, with her mother, who runs the store. It was Thanksgiving, and they gave me an ornamental turkey made of Popsicle sticks, in the same spirit of generosity that a young arrival in town who wanted to make friends would have surely encountered.

Christopher Crowe quickly became such an accepted addition to the community that the late Reverend Bishop began to take an interest in him, even introducing him to his son, Chris. "Christopher Crowe was very good friends with the reverend's son, Chris Bishop, who is a priest," one woman said. "You need to speak with him!"

"There is a film producer, a young guy about your age, in our church," Reverend Bishop told his son one evening. "He seems very nice. You should meet him." Chris Bishop was a student at the Columbia University film school in New York City, so he got excited. He told me, "I was like, 'Wow! Sure! Make a connection with a film producer? You bet!' So I met him. He wasn't the sort of person I would normally hang out with—very odd, nerdy in a sense, very preppy in a way. But he knew *a lot* about the film business."

Crowe soon admitted to him that he was the producer of the new series that everyone was talking about, *Alfred Hitchcock Presents*, and then summed up his career. "He had done his homework," Chris Bishop told me. "Christopher Crowe had produced a couple of low-budget TV projects [*Darkroom* and *The Hardy Boys/Nancy Drew Mysteries*]. Then he was hired as the director of the new *Alfred Hitchcock Presents* series." There was nothing, it seemed, that the Christopher Crowe of Greenwich didn't know about Alfred Hitchcock, the reverend's son added. "He would talk to me about it like he was doing it. He knew endings, he knew people, and he showed up with a bootleg copy of the pilot episode before it was even on TV—and he showed it to me."

What's more, Crowe seemed eager to help Bishop find *his* way in film. "I gave him a couple of the early screenplays I'd written," said Bishop. "His critiques were very intelligent and useful. He'd certainly studied in film school. He had a 16-millimeter film—no sound, very well shot. He brought it up to my house when I was editing my student film. I had a 16-millimeter projector, and he showed his film to me."

He paused, thinking back before continuing. Then he said, "He's very good at what he does. He's a very competent bullshitter. Every utterance out of his mouth is a lie. But he's good at it."

One day Crowe asked his new friend to drive him to Lincoln Center in New York City, where he was directing an episode of the new series. Bishop eagerly consented. "He was walking around in expensive suits—he went to the umpteenth degree with this," said Bishop. Sure enough, when Bishop dropped him off, there were crew members all around with the Hitchcock logo on their jackets. Crowe grabbed his briefcase, thanked Bishop, and ran off, presumably to lead the extensive crew in turning out another episode. In fact, he wasn't producing anything but an elaborate series of lies.

"He was really good, an absolute psychopath, sociopathic liar," said Bishop. "He gave out to me that he was from a wealthy family in L.A., and he did say he had relatives in Bavaria, but he was from the U.S. One of the weirdest incidents that ever happened: we were in Greenwich, and he said, 'Can you give me a lift somewhere?' and I said, 'Sure.' Then he said, 'I need you to drop me off at my mom's house. She married this really rich guy.'"

Bishop continued, "I'm a pretty good judge of character. I have a pretty good ear for bullshit. But this guy had me completely snowed, just like everybody else. So I drove him and dropped him off at a house in the backcountry of Greenwich."

It was dark. Nobody seemed to be at home. It was in the middle of nowhere.

"I'd love to meet your mom," said Bishop.

"Another time," said Crowe before he bounded off into the night.

I asked Bishop to go on.

"Later on, my relationship with him was fairly sporadic," he said. "I mean, I enjoyed the guy. He was very bright. He knew the jargon. He knew how screenplays work."

Then I asked him how he thought Crowe supported himself. "He said he was working," he replied, "but what he was working at, I never really knew. He did tell me that he had decided to get out of the film business and trade bonds, and I was like, 'Oh, I'm sure you can do it!' Because he was a computer whiz."

Bishop said that whenever he had problems with his computer, on which he wrote his screenplays, he would turn to Crowe. "And zip, zip, zip, he had it fixed," he said. "He was very fast and ahead of his time. He had a Compaq computer and he just knew it all. That's the number one thing about Christopher Crowe: he is smarter than hell."

The mysterious young man was about to use that intellect, coupled with the computer, in his most audacious mission to date. "A bond trader" is what he told Bishop he was about to become. How hard could it be? Of course, he would need the proper connections, but connections came easily to the bright chap with his hands full of prayer books at the back of Christ Church.

Still, his becoming a bond trader seemed like an oceanic leap, especially considering the information in a statement from Lewis Krog, a Greenwich man who later rented a room in *his* large home to the increasingly baffling Christopher Crowe:

"Mr. Krog continued to relate that Mr. Crowe had indicated to him that he was involved in the production of movies, having some association with the late director Alfred Hitchcock," read a police report in my dossier of papers. "Mr. Krog further related that Crowe worked for a place called The Junk Barn on Milbank Avenue, but left to work for a Japanese firm at the World Trade Center in New York City."

I had to read the sentence twice: how did Christopher Crowe rise from working at The Junk Barn—which sounded like a secondhand store—to becoming employed in the upper echelons of the financial community of New York City?

For Crowe, the doors to Wall Street began opening at the Indian Harbor Yacht Club in Greenwich. One warm summer night, I visited the club, a white stucco building festooned with yachting flags. The club was throwing its biggest party of the year, but there was no security at the front door, just two valet parkers in Ralph Lauren attire booming "Good evening!" and smiling.

"Imagine hundreds of people here for a regatta," said my local guide, whom I'll call Samantha, as we walked in. "You know, nobody would know anything. The guy could sneak in, coming up from the shore." Crowe could materialize from out of nowhere and start spouting platitudes and pedigrees, and no one would say anything except "Welcome!"

A dance was in progress, with men in white pants and blue blazers and women in chiffon, twirling to classics such as "It Had to Be You," surrounded by models of ships and portraits of past and present members dating back to the club's founding in 1889.

Outside was Indian Harbor, which is fed by Long Island Sound, studded with sailboats belonging to the members. It was a picture-perfect setting, home to a small segment of privileged America. How did Crowe have the guts to pick this posh community?

Samantha had a partial answer to my question. She was a member of Indian Harbor, a longtime resident of Greenwich, and a veteran banker and Wall Street player—all of which made her inclusion in the immigrant's growing list of dupes seem pretty intriguing.

"Press reports explained that Christopher had walked into the Indian Harbor Yacht Club 'like he owned the place,'" I said. Yes, she responded, that was most likely true. "I'm not exactly sure how he found Greenwich," she continued as we walked through the well-appointed club, "but his story was that he lived in L.A. with his dad. Both his mother and his sister lived in Paris. His parents were divorced. For whatever reason, he headed east. There was a bit of arrogance and attitude. I mean, he gave everyone the opinion that he came from incredible wealth."

He had pictures, she added, of what he said was his home in Los Angeles, but the photos seemed devoid of personal touches. "It was almost as if he had gone to the Vanderbilt estate in Hyde Park," she said, suggesting that he had purchased pictures from a gift shop and claimed that they were photographs of his own home. "He seemed very impressed with himself. Besides, he looked like he walked out of a magazine. He always had his Burberry winter coat, the Burberry umbrella, the very fine cotton button-down white shirts, with CCC monogrammed on his pockets. Always pristine, always perfect."

"CCC?" I asked, interrupting her.

"Yes, for Christopher Chichester Crowe," she said. "Always the part."

I looked around the yacht club. Many of the men were dressed exactly in the style she was describing. But the newcomer had sucked them in by acting as if he were even *better* than they were. "He's talking to you as if he's smarter than you, more wealthy than you, more connected, more *everything* than you—no matter *who* you are!" said Samantha. "So he comes into S. N. Phelps and Company, and he's going to be our technology guy. He's this whiz with technology."

I recognized the company name, as most people familiar with the world of finance would. Samantha, a graduate of the Wharton School at the University of Pennsylvania, was a vice president at S. N. Phelps at the time Crowe finagled his way into the respected firm. She directed me to a 1990 *Forbes* magazine story about its founder, Stan Phelps, entitled "Pay Up . . . Or Else":

Meet Stanford N. Phelps, 56, owner of a thriving investment business headquartered modestly in Greenwich, Conn. Phelps is reveling in the junk bond mess like a pig in a mudhole. He has brought bondmail to a fine art. He will go into the market, buy a bunch of the distressed bonds and then tell the issuer: Pay up or I'll throw you into bankruptcy, and you'll lose the company. It often works. The folks who control the company give Phelps—and sometimes all the bondholders—a better break. If not, Phelps drags the company into a long and painful bankruptcy. Among the companies that have felt his wrath: MGF Oil Corp., MCorp., SCI Television Inc. and AP Industries Inc. . . .

One of the more colorful characters in the bondmail business, Stan Phelps is also one of the toughest and meanest. His usual tactic is to seek to control strategic blocks of bonds . . . Phelps then says: Change the terms to give my bonds a better deal or I'll tie you up in the courts. Indefinitely . . .

Phelps is a member of the old Eastern Establishment. Born to a father who was a prominent accountant and a mother whose family owned a shoe manufacturing company in Rochester, N.Y., Phelps was educated at Exeter, Yale and Harvard Business School. After getting his M.B.A. in 1960, Phelps headed for Wall Street, which at the time was dominated by men of his background and breeding.

The story went on to detail how Phelps had established the bond department of the firm that would soon be called Drexel Burnham Lambert, which virtually created the roaring junk bond business of the 1980s:

Phelps was fired in mid-1972 . . . Stan Phelps is a man obsessed, not only with making money, but also with getting back at his former Drexel associates. He often speaks of the latter in terms that are offensive to decent people. His personal vendettas are of little interest to the world, but in helping redress the balance in favor of the world's much abused junk bond holders and against the powerful dealmakers, he is rendering a public service.

The story noted that Phelps had hired a brilliant young man named Michael Milken straight out of Wharton, only to have his young protégé take over.

"So how did the great, brilliant, and powerful Stan Phelps come to hire the absolutely inexperienced Christopher Crowe?" I asked Samantha.

She said she wasn't sure exactly, but she was certain of how Crowe had found his way to Phelps. It wasn't through past jobs or Ivy League connections. It was through a woman who worked at S. N. Phelps, a woman named Catherine.

"Catherine met Chris at Indian Harbor," Samantha continued. "I heard that she introduced him to Phelps and Company with the idea that he was going to be a computer jock."

"Just like that?" I asked. Someone with no background in finance whatsoever was hired by a major East Coast brokerage firm and allowed entrée into its computer system, where reams of confidential information were stored?

She seemed at a loss for words.

"Yeah . . . but . . . um . . . Stan had flavors of the week. Stan was like Baskin-Robbins. And to tell you the truth, Catherine convinced Stan to hire Christopher. Somebody that's going to be a techie is maybe one step above an amoeba. Somebody who's going to be doing technology—who cares?"

But Christopher Crowe was no amoeba. The brilliant swindler could morph into whatever he wanted to be. Having worked his wiles on Catherine, he would speedily go to work on the other affluent young men and women at S. N. Phelps. Catherine just happened to come first.

"He was going to marry some girl in Greenwich," Chris Bishop told me, "some Wall Street woman. I had met her a bunch of times. Yeah, that was Catherine. I remember at one point he showed up with this diamond—not a ring, just a big diamond."

That night at the Indian Harbor Yacht Club, I asked Samantha where the S. N. Phelps and Company offices were.

"I can show you," she said. "It's right up the street."

We retrieved her car from valet parking and drove a mile away to a modest little building painted green. Not only was the outside of the building green, Samantha said, the inside was green too—walls, ceiling, even the desks. Everything was the color of money.

Crowe not only had to get through his personal interview with the shrewd Stan Phelps but also had to pass difficult tests. Everyone who works at a broker-dealer company must get certain accreditations. "We were regulated by the SEC and the North American Securities Administrators Association, so of course I had a file on him," said Samantha. "You have to fill out what's called a U4. The U4 form has your name, address, social security number. Then you have to give your history: Where did you work over the last ten years? What are the dates and what was your job there?"

Samantha added, "Often, Stan would have you take a personality test too."

"Did Crowe take one?" I asked.

"I think he did."

Samantha continued, "Your job history is on the first page. On the next page you have all the other questions: *Have you been arrested? Have you ever been convicted?* A whole page of questions, and hopefully you are able to answer no to all of them. That's just for you to be associated with a broker-dealer; that has to go through the SEC."

She assured me that he had dutifully filled out all of his forms and that his personnel file was in order—although since she had left the firm it was no longer obtainable. But the forms were just a preamble to the tests, she said, the Series 7 and Series 63 tests, which consist of more than seven hours of questions, and which an applicant must pass before being allowed inside a firm that deals with securities.

The Series 7 test, which has 250 multiple-choice questions, alone takes about six hours to complete; Crowe most likely took his test at One Police Plaza in New York City. "In those days, you took it by hand. Two three-hour parts, with a one-hour break. That's for your Series 7. Some people take it two or three times, because they don't pass it the first time. I've taken this test. It's not easy."

Did she remember how Crowe had done on his Series 7?

"He passed," she said. "He might have been odd. He might have been arrogant. But he wasn't stupid. He's *smart*."

After passing the stringent tests, facing his colleagues at S. N. Phelps must have seemed easy. "It was very close quarters," said Samantha. "Everybody's friends with everybody else. Some were childhood friends. They went to Brunswick [the exclusive Greenwich Prep School for boys, dating back to 1902] or Country Day [an equally exclusive Greenwich prep school that opened in 1926, in a barn on the property of William A. Rockefeller]. They would go skiing together. It was a club."

"And Christopher Crowe?" I asked.

"Christopher was odd. It was like the ugly duckling waiting to become the swan, but in his mind he thought he already *was* the swan."

He let Samantha and everyone else at S. N. Phelps know that in addition to being a techie he was also the producer of the new *Alfred Hitchcock Presents* series. "And if you looked at the credits, you would see Christopher Crowe," said Samantha. "I asked him one time, 'Christopher, it's illogical to me. You're a *producer*. And you become a techie at a junk bond shop making $24,000 a year?' He said, 'I wanted to try something different.'"

He would regale her with stories of his glory years as a Hollywood producer, giving her the inside dirt on his favorite *Hitchcock* episodes. What Samantha found strange, however, was his behavior in the tech department. "When I walked into his room, he would always hide his screens. Every time I walked in there, he did this. And I thought, 'He's doing something that has nothing to do with what he is supposed to be doing.' Later, when the detectives came and started asking all their questions, the first thought that came into my mind was, he was going into people's accounts and skimming off a half cent in volume, and that's how he was supplementing his income. Because he always had this stuff. Stuff that costs money! It was Burberry this and Brooks Brothers that, and all these tall tales. He told me he lived in rooms above a garage on North Street. So I'm thinking, 'How?'"

Having seen Crowe's first palatial abode, on Rock Ridge Avenue, I asked Samantha to describe his subsequent residence on North Street.

Her eyes brightened, and she said, "Oh, it's *beautiful*! North Street has all these mansions. North Street parallels Round Hill Road." Round Hill is the most distinguished district of Greenwich, home to film stars and billionaires, listed on the National Register of Historic Places.

During Crowe's tenure at S. N. Phelps, which lasted less than a year and ended in the middle of 1987, Samantha recalled, he didn't have any plans for Christmas 1986.

"Are you going back to Paris to see your mother and sister?" she asked him.

"No."

"Well, would you like to come to my house for Christmas Eve?"

"Okay."

"He walks in and says, 'You know, Samantha, my mother and sister and I looked at the house right next to yours when it was on the market. We could have been neighbors.'"

"The house next door to ours had been on the market for six to eight million," Samantha told me as we sat outside the green office building. "But Christopher always had a story, and it always concerned wealth. He was better than everybody, more affluent than everybody. It was just arrogance. Although he was shorter than me, he always had the attitude that he was looking down at you. I started thinking to myself I'm really sorry I asked him here to my house."

Soon this arrogance wore thin with his colleagues, starting with Samantha, who grew tired of his haughty attitude, of his saying to her dismissively, "Well, Samantha," and then attempting to say something glib or funny. The traders his age in the company were all close friends, and Crowe was never part of their clique. "It's not that they excluded him, but I don't think he ever felt included," said Samantha, adding that finally he began to grate on the man you didn't dare offend: "Stan didn't like him anymore. He was annoying, and he got on Stan's nerves until Stan just didn't want him around."

The final straw for Stan Phelps was when Crowe wouldn't tell him how to access his computer, someone else insisted. For a hands-on business titan who ran a very tight ship, this was blasphemy. Was Crowe trying to make himself invaluable and irreplaceable? Some would later say that was the plan. But Stan Phelps didn't give him the chance.

Samantha couldn't remember if she had personally fired Crowe, but she thought she had. She did remember that the aftermath of Christopher Crowe at S. N. Phelps was even stranger than his presence there. That, however, was still several years away. At the time, he merely picked up his personal things, draped his Burberry trench coat over his shoulders, and walked out.

Two years after he left, an interesting item on his job application came to light. In the space provided for his social security number, Crowe had written what would turn out to be a curious number. When it was finally run through the system, it came back as the social security number not of Christopher Chichester Crowe but of a David Berkowitz, the name of the serial killer known as Son of Sam, who had terrorized New York City and murdered at least six people in 1976 and 1977.

CHAPTER 7

Wall Street

I n the summer of 1987, Nikko Securities was on the move. One of Japan's "Big Four" brokerage firms, the company was intent on getting into the booming American securities market and planned to increase its U.S. workforce from 250 people to 500. As part of that expansion, Nikko created a corporate bond department, which was announced in a press release on July 13, 1987. After describing the particulars of the new department, the release stated, "Christopher Crowe, who formerly ran the Battenberg–Crowe–von Wettin Family Foundation, will lead the endeavor as vice president."

The Christopher Crowe who presented himself to the brass at Nikko Securities was, on the surface, a perfect candidate for the roaring 1980s Wall Street. He seemed smart, educated, connected. He knew the lingo of the long bond and the short sell. He had a résumé with experience at one of the East Coast's most esteemed securities firms, S. N. Phelps and Company, and boasted of running a family foundation with royal names and seemingly deep pockets. Most important, he dressed the part perfectly, impeccably attired in suits from J. Press and Brooks Brothers. In the blizzard of money that typified the time, Christopher Crowe was like so many others dressed for success and ready to make some serious cash.

He left his failures at S. N. Phelps behind in Connecticut. Not only did he survive, he landed at a bigger, more prestigious firm, in a much more senior position. He would be running an entire department, responsible for trading extremely high-value financial instruments. As one corporate bond trader told me, "The minimum sale you're dealing with is a million dollars." According to his former coworkers, Crowe's annual salary was probably about $125,000, not including perks and bonuses.

How did he wind up in such a position? As usual, his entrée came through a single impressionable individual, in this case a man named Don Sheahan. Now deceased, Sheahan had worked in the securities business for years, and Nikko's Japanese executives entrusted him with assembling much of their New York team. "Apparently Crowe met Sheahan at a cocktail party and sold him a bill of goods," said Richard Barnett, who worked under Crowe at Nikko.

Another Wall Street veteran who worked with Sheahan and Crowe at Nikko told me of Sheahan, "He wasn't some kid, wet behind the ears. Don was a former Air Force pilot, he'd been with Goldman Sachs—he was not a dope." So how did he get taken in by a charlatan? "This guy, Crowe, had a fantastic gift about him," said the Wall Street veteran. "He was like that character Tony Curtis played in *The Great Impostor*, passing himself off as an airplane pilot, a doctor, and everything else. I think the reason Don fell for it was because Don seemed to be impressed by anybody that was either extremely wealthy or had some type of family background. A name like Mountbatten would have caught his attention immediately." (Although Gerhartsreiter had left his San Marino identity behind, he hadn't abandoned the names he had invented for himself; according to my sheaf of documents, the birth certificate he presented to Nikko identified him as Christopher Chichester Crowe Mountbatten, born in Los Angeles.)

"Don Sheahan was taken by people who seemed to be blue-blooded," said Bob Brusca, who worked for the New York Federal Reserve before becoming chief economist at Nikko during Sheahan's tenure. "He wasn't the type of guy who would necessarily check references. Someone may have told him that Christopher was a good person, and that would have been enough for him."

But, I asked, would Sheahan's hunch have been enough for Nikko? Didn't his Japanese bosses have any say in the hiring of this rank amateur? "The Japanese have this thing called shadow management, where for just about every position in the firm where there was an American, there was a Japanese who looked over his shoulder," said Brusca. "Don Sheahan was allowed to run the operation subject to the oversight of the Japanese. That meant Akira Tokutomi [an executive vice president at Nikko] shadowed Sheahan, and he would have had to have said yes to the hire of Christopher Crowe."

His appointment was the subject of an article in the *Bond Buyer*, a trade periodical, under the headline NIKKO SECURITIES INTERNATIONAL ENTERS CORPORATE ARENA WITH INDUSTRIAL FOCUS:

Christopher Crowe, who will head the new corporate bond department as vice president, said the department is currently testing the syndicate waters, participating in a $250 million Chevron Capital USA deal that came to market yesterday, as well as a $150 million Colgate-Palmolive Co. offering that was scheduled for pricing last evening. Further down the road, he said, he hopes to lead the department into corporate underwriting.

He said the department will work most heavily in the long-term industrial sector and will structure its portfolio more or less according to the following mix: 65% industrials, 25% utilities, and the rest a mixture of banks and finance and transportation. "Customers like industrials," he said, adding that "they've been oversaturated with banks and finance."

To date, the department's staff numbers just five, including Mr. Crowe, who formerly ran the Battenberg–Crowe–von Wettin Family Foundation. . . . By the end of the year, Mr. Crowe said, the department should total 15 staff members.

Not yet out of his twenties and with little experience or knowledge, Crowe was in charge of staffing Nikko's new department, and he sought out seasoned finance professionals. Richard Barnett, who had just left a research analyst job at the respected brokerage firm E. F. Hutton, was one of Crowe's first hires. "The head of research at Merrill Lynch gave my name to Christopher Crowe," Barnett told me, and soon he met the well-dressed young supervisor, whom he described as "erudite" with "an aristocratic air." "We met in the lobby of the Grand Hyatt on Forty-second Street. He told me, 'The Japanese are assembling a corporate bond operation. They've asked me to put together an operation rather quickly.' The interview lasted twenty minutes, and I was hired on the spot. He said there was the potential for a lot of money, and he told me what the plans were: to create a full trading operation in corporate bonds and also research. He told me I'd be hiring a number of analysts."

They worked in a trading room in Nikko's offices in the World Financial Center, adjacent to the World Trade Center in downtown Manhattan. As at S. N. Phelps, the quarters were tight, and everyone knew nearly everything about everyone else—except their boss, who usually sat alone, often staring into space, in his sizable office.

"I remember he came up to me one time and asked, 'Do you know anybody who buys this type of Eurobond?'" said Bob Brusca. "I just looked at him and said no. I thought it was so odd. That was supposed to be his job! It would be like somebody who is supposed to be a dentist coming up to you and asking, 'Do you know what a bicuspid is?'"

Yet Crowe led the department, at least for a while. Things soon began to stall, however. "Nothing was being done—there was no trading going on whatsoever," Barnett told me. "We were just sitting and twiddling our thumbs. He went out with me on one account. He tried to bullshit, and you can't do that when you're dealing with people who have been in the industry for ten or fifteen years."

Yet the men who worked with him at Nikko agreed that a certain amount of swagger was an important asset for bond salesmen in those days, and Christopher Crowe had swagger in spades. The ability to tell high-flying, almost inconceivable stories about one's business experience and personal life "frankly can be a great quality for a salesman," said Brusca. "They'll say things that are just utterly fantastic and ridiculous, but they're able to be successful as salesmen."

No one called Crowe out, however, at least not at the beginning, because either they believed him and his story to be real, or they were all busy worrying about their own careers, according to another of Crowe's Nikko colleagues, Stan Forkner. "I was concerned with my own stuff, not really paying him much attention," he said. "I suppose he did what he could to get up to speed and sort of play the role."

Central to the role was making money, and Crowe must have realized that in order to do that he would need help. He got it in the person of a finance pro I'll call Jim Rivers.

"Jim's a character," said Richard Barnett. "One of the trade magazines did a piece on him. They called him the Mayor of Wall Street. We'd go out and a homeless guy would ask him for money, and Jim would put him up in a hotel for the night. Jim knew every bartender in Manhattan—not only knew them, he knew their kids. He was an ex-Marine, and as soon as he would walk into a bar they would start playing the Marine Corps Hymn."

I called Jim Rivers, and, sure enough, he asked me to meet him in a bar. There was no Marine Corps Hymn playing, just a big, affable fellow nursing a drink and dolefully recalling the man nobody really knew.

"I was hired to run the corporate trading desk in August 1987, and he was there," Rivers said of Crowe. "He was supposedly in charge of the three salespeople. They were all pretty inexperienced, but he was the most inexperienced of all." By then Nikko had brought in Mary Clarkin, who had spent twenty-seven years at the Federal Reserve Bank of New York, to help oversee the operation, and her job eventually included overseeing the sales manager, Christopher Crowe.

"He reported to Mary, but he sat directly across from me," Rivers said. "I used to joke with him. He never took his jacket off, and he'd make announcements about his clothes: 'Look at my new suit from J. Press,' or wherever—always a top-quality company."

Two months after Rivers went to work at Nikko, the world's stock markets crashed on the day known as Black Monday, October 19, 1987. It was the largest percentage drop in a single day in stock market history, and by the end of the month the markets had fallen by 45.5 percent in Hong Kong and 22.68 percent in the United States.

The crisis made the executives in Nikko's Tokyo headquarters "petrified of any kind of risk after that," said Rivers. But Black Monday was just another day for Crowe. "He just sat there in his office calling people up," Rivers remembered. "That's all he used to do. He'd sit there all day long. Who he was calling, I don't know. Half the time he'd be speaking German to people."

While playing the part of a high-flying Wall Street executive, Crowe also continued to impersonate a fabulously wealthy aristocrat, making liberal mention of his relatives Lord Mountbatten and the Battenberg family, and of the Battenberg–Crowe–von Wettin Family Foundation, which he had formerly run, supposedly. He said the foundation owned a huge collection of luxury cars and European castles. (In truth, the foundation did not exist.)

One evening, Rivers told me, he and the boss, Don Sheahan, were heading to Sparks Steakhouse on East Forty-sixth Street to interview prospective salesmen. "We had a limousine waiting for us, and Crowe asked if he could hitch a ride. I said, 'Fine.' It was right before Thanksgiving, and Don and I were talking about our plans. I said to Crowe, 'What are you planning on doing?' And he said, 'I'm going to stay at home and read prospectuses'"—detailed business reports and analyses of securities. "I said, 'That sounds like a *great* Thanksgiving. You don't have anywhere to go?' He said no, so I invited him to my house. He took up the invitation as fast as a greyhound, and he said, 'I'm going to come down in one of my cars.' I asked, 'How many cars have you got?' He said, 'I've got a whole car collection—Ferraris, Alfa Romeos, Lamborghinis.' I said, 'All right, pick one out and come down. I'd like to see it.'"

Rivers drained his drink and laughed. "He showed up in a '65 Chevrolet that was belching more smoke than Mount Saint Helens. I'm not joking. The paint was so faded that you could see the body right through it. I said, 'Where's your Lamborghini or your Ferrari?' He claimed there was a power failure and he couldn't get the garage door open, so he had to borrow the car from his maid."

Crowe wore an ascot to the Riverses' Thanksgiving dinner—"You would have thought he was at the Kentucky Derby"—and regaled the family with tales of his relatives. "He went on and on with this whole shtick: 'Lord Mountbatten is my [uncle], and I come from a long line of royalty.' He had a stack of pictures with him, which he said were pictures of his houses. Some of them were of a mansion in Greenwich, Connecticut. He said he was having it refurbished and a new pool put in." Of course, Crowe told the Rivers family about how he had been a movie producer and was responsible for the new version of *Alfred Hitchcock Presents.*

Rivers shook his head. "He ended up staying not just for Thanksgiving but for a few days. He had CCC monogrammed on everything, even on his slippers, bathrobe, pajamas. My son was about sixteen at the time, and he asked him, 'Do you have your underwear monogrammed too?' Crowe said, 'Absolutely.'"

A different side of Crowe emerged when a securities salesman whom Rivers was friendly with visited the Nikko offices. "My friend's about six foot six, and Crowe is five-seven, give or take an inch. There was something on the desk that belonged to Crowe—a souvenir or something. My friend picked it up, and Crowe went nuts and started hollering at him. My friend said, 'I'm sorry, I didn't know it was yours.' When I walked him to the elevator, my friend said, 'That guy's got a screw loose. You better watch your back.' I went back and said, 'Christopher, we don't talk to anybody like that!'"

Crowe snapped back, "If you ever touch anything on my desk again, I'll bring in my Luger!" Rivers found the threat strange, because a couple of weeks earlier the guys in the office had been discussing guns and Crowe had insisted that he knew nothing about weapons of any kind.

"I said to him, 'What caliber is your Luger?' He said, 'Nine millimeter.'"

"You know a lot more about guns than you admitted," Rivers told him. He shot me an uneasy smile. "That's when I started worrying a little more about this character," he said.

He was living the life of a Wall Street player: a six-figure salary, an office in the World Financial Center, and an estate in Greenwich—or at least a few rooms behind an estate in Greenwich. A list of some of the charges on his American Express card (issued in the name of CCC Mountbatten) from 1987 to 1988 shows his increasingly lavish lifestyle. He dined in Manhattan's finest restaurants: the "21" Club, Le Bernardin, the Quilted Giraffe, and Bellini by Cipriani, among others. He was a regular on Broadway and at the opera, charging tickets to shows including *Phantom of the Opera* and *Madame Butterfly*. There were numerous charges for clothing, from such stores as Burberry, Church's English Shoes, and J. Press, the Ivy League–style clothier that seemed to be his favorite—his Nikko colleagues told me he would frequently get packages from there delivered to him at the office. He bought chocolates or flowers on almost a weekly basis—gifts, presumably, for people with whom he wanted to ingratiate himself.

Crowe invited several of his coworkers to visit him at home, telling them that he was living temporarily in his pool house while the main house was being renovated.

"That house in Greenwich had all the trappings," said Stanley Forkner, who, like Crowe, was a vice president in Nikko's corporate bond operation. Forkner said he hadn't actually been to Crowe's home, but I soon had the names of others who had, people who would sit in the pool house with Crowe and watch movies that he claimed to have written and directed. My requests to speak to these people went unanswered. One obvious reason could have been their embarrassment at having been duped into believing the charade. After all, they worked for him and some were even hired by him. Despite Crowe's speaking German on the phone and mentioning his

Luger (the German military's pistol of choice in the world wars), no one could have guessed that he was actually a no-name immigrant.

"He spoke the most perfect English I can imagine. Any traces of an accent were gone," said Wayne Campbell, a longtime librarian at the Greenwich Public Library. He got to know Crowe fairly well, because Crowe made frequent visits to the library to check out old movies—film noir, mostly. He would usually show up on Saturdays, taking a break from the pressures of Wall Street, and was a regular presence at the Friday night movie screenings that Campbell organized in the library's theater.

I visited Campbell, a veteran librarian with white hair but a youthful air, in the Greenwich library, which today, thanks to a $25 million donation from a longtime Greenwich resident, is a sprawling white modern edifice. Although now the library's film collection consists mostly of DVD discs, two racks of the boxy VHS tapes that Christopher Crowe checked out remain. Campbell took me over to the two large shelves where the tapes are stored, and where Crowe, who said he was a Hollywood director in addition to being a Wall Street powerhouse, spoke often to Campbell about his love of film.

"I knew the film business was in Hollywood, so what was he doing in Greenwich?" Campbell asked. "But he seemed to know so much about film! The directors. Filmmaking technique. Which I don't know where he got—unless he was a voracious reader."

He began rifling through the old tapes, picking out what he remembered as Crowe's favorites. "The classics," he said. "Alfred Hitchcock and Orson Welles. Critically acclaimed films. We had a three-day turnaround. He would check out one and then check out another when he turned the first one back in. Until he went through a lot of our collection of fifteen thousand titles."

He knew as much about high finance as he did about film, Campbell continued. "I'd say, 'Hi, Chris, what's up?' He'd say, 'Well, the long bond has gone up to four or five percent and the yield is this or that.' I would just sort of nod, waiting for him to finish so that we could go on to a film subject. But he would reel off some spiel about bonds that was very convincing." However, Campbell said, some things about Crowe didn't make sense. For instance, he said he lived with his mother in Greenwich. But why would a successful executive in his late twenties be living with his mother? And why did he never say what her name was?

Then there was his taste in women. "He was very interested, hormonally, in a girl who worked in the film department," Campbell remembered. "She was very pert, vivacious, cute, intelligent."

I found some information about her in my dossier of papers:

She met Christopher Crowe while she worked as a projectionist at the Greenwich Library. Crowe would attend screenings of old black and white movies approximately once a month.

Crowe told her that he was the director of the new *Alfred Hitchcock Presents*. He told her his mother had been a silent screen actress. If this is true, she would have been in her early 50's when Christopher was born. He said his mother lived in an area of Greenwich that was only accessible by a private road.

She went out for coffee with Crowe on a couple of occasions. She felt comfortable doing this because Crowe knew she was engaged to be married and never made a play for her.

Crowe once offered her a job with a Japanese financial firm he was supposedly working for. He told her the company needed new people. Although the salary would be $40,000 per year, she knew how expensive it would be to live in Manhattan and turned down the job.

It wasn't difficult to imagine Christopher Crowe standing in the middle of the old film tapes, pursuing the greats of film noir, sucking up the plots and characters like a sponge, more clay to build the character he was playing then and would play in the future. There was *Psycho*, *Chinatown*, and *Cape Fear*. "That would have been right up his alley," Campbell said. "An edginess, good technique, and riveting suspense."

Even murder?

"I'm not going to say that," Wayne Campbell replied.

The securities business being a small community, someone eventually remembered Crowe's torturous tenure at S. N. Phelps and Company—and not just anyone, but the big man himself. "Stan Phelps called me up," Jim Rivers told me over drinks. "He said, 'How the hell did you hire this guy Crowe?' I said, 'Wait a minute, Stan. I didn't hire him, and also I heard you hired him and you fired him.' And he said, 'Yeah, I fired him because when we got his social security number back, it was Son of Sam's.' I said, 'David Berkowitz?' He goes, 'Yeah.' I said, 'Does Sheahan know this? I don't think he does.'"

Rivers reported to Don Sheahan that Crowe had used the social security number of the deranged serial killer who claimed to have been taking orders from his dog. "Don said, 'We'll check into it.' It took him a long time, because Crowe was there for at least another six months before he got blown out."

In fact, according to Bob Brusca, Phelps's warning and the bogus social security number weren't the real reasons for Crowe's demise at Nikko. "Basically, Crowe wasn't successful because he didn't have customers," Brusca said. "He was just this lone guy. No matter what your background is, no matter what your pedigree, at some point you've got to contribute something—you've got to do some business. You've got to do *something*."

Everyone's patience with him wore thin, I was told. "I recall him getting chewed out a couple of times," said Stan Forkner. "You know, by the senior guys, or by the traders, who by nature are kind of belligerent." Still, the Nikko staff was surprised when the axe fell, because the Japanese *never* fired anyone. They believed in a job for life, at least back then, before the country was laid low by an economic tidal wave that washed away ancient traditions.

"Right after he left, I was at the Museum of Modern Art, and I was very sure that I ran into him," said Bob Brusca. "I was, like, five feet away from him, and he just walked on like he had never seen me before."

By then Christopher Crowe was already in the process of becoming somebody else.

CHAPTER 8

Missing Persons

As he had done since entering the finance industry, Christopher Crowe continued failing upward. His tenure at Nikko, disastrous as it might have been, was merely a prelude to even bigger things.

Kidder, Peabody & Co. was a venerable, all-service American securities firm, established in 1865 and known for its stellar investment banking division. (It no longer exists as an independent entity, having been acquired in 1994 by PaineWebber, which itself has since been folded into UBS.) One day in the summer of 1988, Crowe showed up at the headquarters of Kidder Peabody, located in the heart of the financial district in lower Manhattan, and walked unannounced into the office of Ralph Boynton, who had recently left Goldman Sachs to run Kidder Peabody's international bond operation.

"In those days there was no security in the building," Boynton remembered of the years before September 11, 2001 (and before the 1993 World Trade Center bombing), when office buildings were not considered potential terrorist targets. "He knocked on my door and said he was looking for a job. I was new to Kidder, and I was looking to build a small team in New York to distribute or sell Eurobonds [a type of bond issued by multinational corporations and subject to little regulation]. I didn't have a budget to do this. Kidder, unlike Goldman, was a strict commission house."

Crowe came off as smart, humble, well mannered—even a bit *too* formal, Boynton thought—and keen on coming to work for Kidder. Despite the fact that he seemed to have wandered in off the street, he made a very favorable impression on Boynton, at least in the beginning. "I thought he was good—bright, polite, presentable. Selling Eurobonds doesn't take a rocket scientist. He didn't look too bad compared to some of the salespeople."

So Boynton, like so many others before him, decided to give this guy a chance: a two-week tryout. "We didn't do a background check, because we never got that far," he said. "I took him to Los Angeles for a meeting with several clients who bought Eurobonds. I was trying to determine his skills as a salesman, to judge whether he was the right guy to deal with these people."

They flew to L.A. on the same plane, Crowe in his typically preppy coat and tie.

"How did he act?" I asked Boynton.

"He was intelligent, articulate; very pleasant, not gregarious or presumptuous. He was a pretty nice guy from a personality point of view."

Having apparently won over yet another potential employer, he seemed on his way to landing his third prestigious job in the financial sector. Then his past came back to haunt him.

The police reports tell the story, starting with his credit card activity between the time of his firing from Nikko, in July 1988, and his arrival at Kidder Peabody. The charges are mostly plebeian: gas stations, delicatessens (the famous Zabar's in New York City being a favorite), and downscale restaurants such as Ham Heaven and Curry & Tandoor. On September 12, the day he began his job at Kidder Peabody, he ate at Popover Café, a popular brunch spot on Manhattan's Upper West Side known for the airy, bulbous pastries it is named after.

Two months later, on November 3, 1988, the Greenwich Police Department received a message via Teletype from the San Marino Police Department, requesting assistance in an old missing persons case. The officers from San Marino were seeking "individuals who might have information relative to the whereabouts of John Robert Sohus, w/m— DOB 12/20/57, and his wife Linda Christine, w/f—DOB 9/17/56." One such individual was "Chris Gerhartsreiter / AKA Chichester—w/m, DOB 02/21/61, Connecticut OP # 024192788, [who] lived with the Sohus family, but also disappeared a month later." The message mentioned the Sohuses' 1985 Nissan pickup truck and provided its vehicle identification number.

The detective who received the Teletype was Daniel Allen. A lieutenant by the time I saw him in Greenwich, Allen met me at the police station and took me to breakfast at a little café on Greenwich Avenue, the rich town's main drag. I felt like I was back in San Marino, for Greenwich is also a tidy, affluent place with clean, crisp air and Norman Rockwell values. As we sat eating bacon and eggs, Allen, a lifelong resident of Greenwich, told me about the day he first heard the name Chris Gerhartsreiter.

"It was a routine job, another department seeking information—a typical missing persons request," Allen said, adding that it was just one of dozens of messages that came across the Teletype during his 4 p.m. to midnight shift that day. "A missing persons case is a noncriminal matter. Once you become an adult, if you decide to pick up and move and not tell anybody—well, that's not a criminal matter."

Of course, the story of Linda and John Sohus was much more complex than that, but Allen could not have guessed that at the time. "People disappear for many reasons," he said, trying to impress upon me how what I was seeing as an extraordinary case had a very ordinary beginning. "This was a three-year-old California missing persons case. San Marino was looking for information to make sure the missing couple was okay. Since the couple's truck showed up here in Greenwich, they thought someone might know their whereabouts."

Allen thought it would be a quick, simple job: interview this individual—"Chris Gerhartsreiter / AKA Chichester," as the Teletype had identified him—and report his findings to California. Allen soon discovered that the man was by that time going by the name Christopher Crowe, but the more information he compiled, the more he got the same feeling I'd been having. As he put it, "I just didn't know who this guy really was."

After breakfast, Allen drove me to the place where his investigation into the missing couple began: Christ Church, the imposing stone edifice where Christopher Crowe had found a spiritual home and where, on the day before our visit, President George H. W. Bush's brother Prescott had been memorialized after his death at eighty-seven.

Allen had gone to the church in 1988 to interview the Reverend John Bishop and his son, Chris, the film student, who had befriended Crowe. The reverend was on vacation, but Chris told the detective all about the truck with the missing title. I had read Allen's report detailing his interview with Chris Bishop: "Some time in July of this year, he approached the Crowe subject about needing a truck for an upcoming film that he was in process of making. Crowe indicated that he did have a truck for sale but had no title."

The title was "out of California," Crowe had told his friend, so if Chris Bishop wanted the truck, he would "have to make an effort" on his own to get the title from the California Department of Motor Vehicles—Crowe didn't have the time or inclination to do it himself.

Chris contacted the California DMV and was told that he would have to send a check for $10 to cover the processing fee for a title search. Chris, at age seventeen, didn't have his own checking account, so he asked his parents to send a check from their account, which the reverend and his wife did. Shortly thereafter, Chris received a call from a bank. He was told that, contrary to Crowe's assurance that he owned the truck free and clear, payments on it had stopped, so there was a large outstanding loan on the vehicle. The entire balance of the loan would have to be paid before the title could be released.

Chris confronted Crowe. "You're trying to rip me off!" he said, but Crowe professed to know nothing about the title mess.

From there, things got even stranger. Allen interviewed Crowe's various landlords in Greenwich, one of whom "related that during a conversation with Crowe one day, he learned that Crowe had a pickup truck. He never saw the truck, as Crowe had it garaged at an unknown location." A check of the records of the Connecticut Department of Motor Vehicles showed that, indeed, a Christopher K. Gerhartsreiter was residing or had at some point resided in the state, but his driver's license had expired and he had provided no forwarding address. According to a police report, "The investigators called the telephone number for Crowe . . . but the New York telephone company indicated that the number . . . had been disconnected."

Detective Allen spoke to people who had known and housed Crowe. Over and over Allen heard the bizarre assertion that Crowe was the director of *Alfred Hitchcock Presents*, which he quickly realized did not add up. He discovered that the man he and his colleagues were seeking—with his multiple names, dubious occupations, and ever-changing addresses—had not left any sort of trail that police could use to track him down.

Allen and other investigators must have turned to one of the few sources of clues they had: a list of American Express charges made by Christopher C. Crowe Mountbatten, compiled by the Los Angeles County Sheriff's Department. From the list of charges:

On Sept. 28, 1988, Crowe shopped at Bloomingdale's in New York City.

On Oct. 3, 1988, Crowe took in a play at the Eugene O'Neill Theater on Broadway.

On Oct. 4, he moved from his last known address in Greenwich—#7 Loch Lane—forwarding address unknown.

On Oct. 14, he reported his vehicle, a Chrysler station wagon, stolen in Stamford, Ct., where, he told police, he had parked the car to take a train to Boston. Six days later, the station wagon was recovered in New York City. But Crowe would wait almost a month before showing up where his car was towed, paying the towing charges but refusing to retrieve the car. (On the advice of his attorney, Crowe said, adding that his attorney was named Solomon Rosenbaum, but giving no contact information for the individual.)

On Oct. 22, 1988, he picked up his mail for the last time from the post office box he had rented in Greenwich.

It quickly became clear that this Christopher Crowe didn't want to speak with Daniel Allen. The detective tried to reach Crowe by phone, but his calls went unanswered. Every time he got close, the trail would turn cold. The information Crowe had provided on various official documents turned out to be largely fictitious. The last Greenwich address he had given, on Loch Lane, did not exist. "Crowe had made up the street number 8 when he had the phone service put in at 7 Loch Lane," Allen wrote in one report. When they ran the social security number Crowe had written on various forms, they discovered that it wasn't assigned to Christopher Crowe, but to a Steven J. Biodrowski, a USC film student who had met Chichester when he was a regular presence at the school. Biodrowski had no inkling that Crowe/Chichester was using his social security number.

When the police contacted Chrysler Financial, from which Crowe had leased the vehicle he later reported stolen, they learned that "Crowe indicated on his credit sheet that his father's name was H. Crowe, of #34 Rock Ridge Ave., Greenwich, Ct. It should be noted that #34 Rock Ridge Avenue is the residence of Mr. [John] Maddox, previously identified in this report."

The identity of Crowe's purported mother was equally nebulous, Detective Allen learned after contacting the woman who knew him at the Greenwich Public Library. Crowe had told her that his mother was an actress whose stage name was Gloria Jean. There was indeed a Hollywood actress and singer named Gloria Jean, who appeared in twenty-six films between 1939 and 1959, including *Never Give a Sucker an Even Break*. But when Allen contacted Actors' Equity looking for information about her, he "was informed that Gloria Jean was a member but had discontinued her membership in 1956." Another dead end.

The good people at Christ Church had a work address for Crowe, but it was presumably S. N. Phelps and Company, which he had long since left. Investigators in San Marino checked an early address he had once given in *that* city—for the beautiful estate on Circle Drive—but discovered that the house at that address hadn't been occupied since 1977, a year before the immigrant's arrival in America. Investigators contacted a woman I'll call Rose Mina, with whom Crowe had reputedly been staying in New York—she worked at Moody's Investment Services—but she "related that she had not seen him since giving him the message to contact the investigator." A call to the Immigration and Naturalization Service in Hartford was similarly unhelpful. "The department had no record of the individual Gerhartsreiter, Chichester or Crowe with the DOB 2/21/61," wrote Detective Allen.

"When I reached out to Crowe and he wasn't forthcoming, I let the authorities in California know that it seemed that he wasn't going to voluntarily come and see me," Allen told me. "They asked me to make personal contact with him, and that's when I went to Kidder Peabody, his place of employment."

I said my understanding was that Crowe had been at Kidder strictly on a trial basis. Allen shook his head. "My impression was he was working for the company," he said. "His actual place of employment was Kidder Peabody. I went down to New York. It was a big investment company. I waited for him to come to work, but he ended up calling in sick that day."

At this juncture in our morning together, I began to press Lieutenant Allen a bit. I didn't understand how he could be so calm and matter-of-fact about a case that had been driving me crazy. "Weren't you obsessed with the case?" I asked.

"No," he said.

"Did you feel you were chasing a ghost?" I asked, telling him that that was the way I felt as I boomeranged across the country and abroad, following the shadow of the man with multiple identities.

"I want to be very careful with this," Allen said, measuring his words. "As time went on and I was given additional information, I started to raise some suspicions about his true identity. As I came up with the different names, it did raise some concerns at the time."

"Some *concerns*?" I asked. But lying isn't a crime, Allen explained, unless it leads to a crime or is done in the aftermath of a crime; and a person can't be arrested for dodging the police when no crime appears to have been committed. "We couldn't issue a warrant, couldn't detain him," Allen said. "California had a missing couple, but there was nothing in their investigation that indicated any type of foul play or criminal activity. Legally, we couldn't detain him or force him to cooperate."

Allen seemed reluctant to get into deeper details. Either his memory had faded, or he felt it would be inappropriate for him to talk about the intricacies of his investigation. But I already had all of his records from the case, and they spelled out everything clearly. When Allen arrived at Kidder Peabody, he met Crowe's supervisor, Ralph Boynton, who told the detective essentially the same story he would relate to me twenty years later.

On their trip to Los Angeles, Crowe had discussed his family background with Boynton. "He talked about his parents' being in the secret service of some clandestine organization, and said that they were agents on the run," Boynton recalled. "He told me he had lived near the San Gabriel Mountains and was interested in going back to see that part of California. I let him talk. I got the impression that he had sort of a gray background, cloaked in espionage, and he was worried about his parents being apprehended by somebody."

Crowe declined to join Boynton on his flight back to New York, apparently opting to stay in California for a little while. According to credit card statements and other documents in my dossier, he stayed at the Biltmore Hotel in Los Angeles, then made a quick stop in his old hometown of San Marino, dropping in on a prayer session at the Church of Our Saviour on Halloween—the third anniversary of the wedding of John and Linda Sohus, as it happened. He stayed only long enough to have a quick supper and inform the parishioners that "he had been banking in Hong Kong and was in San Marino for the day, on his way to Oregon," according to a statement from one of them.

Crowe flew from San Diego to San Francisco, where he stayed at the St. Francis Hotel and dined at Ernie's, then one of the city's best restaurants.

Back in New York, Boynton was at home taking a nap when he was awakened by a telephone call. It was his old friend Richard Cook, a vice president at S. N. Phelps and Company.

"Do you know a guy named Christopher Crowe?" he asked.

"Yeah," said Boynton.

"I've heard bad things about him," said Cook. "I'd stay away from him."

"Gosh, I wish I'd known that before I went to California with him!" said Boynton.

By then, Crowe had apparently also returned to New York. As Cook later told police, before calling Boynton at home to warn him about his rogue salesman, he had tried Boynton at the office.

"Mr. Cook attempted to call Mr. Boynton at Kidder Peabody but was informed that Mr. Boynton was out of town until Friday," wrote Detective Allen. "Upon further speaking with the individual on the telephone, it was learned that it was Chris Crowe, the subject wanted in connection with this incident."

Boynton picked up the story. "A few hours later, I got a call from the Greenwich Police Department. The detective asked, 'What were you doing in California with Christopher Crowe?'"

Boynton explained that he and Crowe had been making sales calls for Kidder Peabody.

"The next thing he said was, 'Where is the pickup truck?' I said, 'I don't know anything about a pickup truck. I rented a Hertz car.' Then the detective said, 'Crowe's a person of interest in a missing persons case in California. Do you mind if we come in and interview him?'"

Boynton told Allen that of course he could come to Kidder Peabody's offices and interview Crowe. "Every morning for three days, at six in the morning, when I went to work at my office on Wall Street, the Greenwich police and the Connecticut state police were there, waiting for Christopher Crowe," Boynton said.

But Crowe never showed up. He must have caught wind of the investigation, because after calling in sick on the day of Detective Allen's first visit to Kidder Peabody, he placed another call to Boynton. He said he had to leave New York immediately to deal with an emergency concerning his mother and father. According to Boynton, "He said, 'My parents have been kidnapped! They're on the run or in harm's way!'"

Police reports elaborated:

Mr. Boynton contacted the investigator to relate that Chris Crowe was requesting a leave-of-absence from the company for a period of time to exceed two months in order to locate his parents, who were missing in Pakistan or Japan. That Mr. Crowe was making arrangements with the Pakistani Consulate and Japanese Consulate and would be leaving this country on an unknown date to further locate his parents.

The police asked Boynton to attempt to contact Crowe as soon as possible so that Allen could "interview him relative to Mr. and Mrs. Sohus and the vehicle wanted in connection with their disappearance." Crowe had told Boynton that he would come to the office and meet with him in order to wrap up the things he'd been working on, so Detective Allen went back to Kidder Peabody in the hope of intercepting Crowe there. However, as Allen later wrote in his report, "Crowe re-contacted Mr. Boynton . . . and related that, due to uncontrollable circumstances, he would not be able to meet there [at Kidder Peabody] but requested that Mr. Boynton meet him at a restaurant somewhere on Fifty-second Street."

Boynton was prepared to meet Crowe at the restaurant, he told me, "but the detectives said, 'We can't let you walk in there unprotected. This guy could be dangerous.'"

Crowe never showed up at the restaurant, but Allen finally managed to reach him by phone on November 18, 1988, at the home of a friend. Crowe agreed to meet with Allen at police headquarters three days later, on November 21, at 4:30 p.m. When that day came, however, Crowe called Allen to push back their meeting by two days, to November 23. He didn't appear, and the detective never heard from him again.

"I had taken the case as far as I could from the point of view of locating him and speaking with him," Allen told me. "I notified California that I hadn't been able to do so. I had other caseloads to deal with, and I went back to focusing on that."

There were eleven charges subsequent to November 21 on Crowe's credit card bill, all at New York City businesses: the bookstore of the high-end publisher Rizzoli, the Japanese bookstore Kinokuniya, Tower Records, Sam Goody Records, Raoul's Restaurant, the Oyster Bar in Grand Central Station, the Rhinelander restaurant, Zabar's delicatessen, J. Press (twice), and—the final entry, on December 6, 1988—the Japanese restaurant Hayato.

Then the man whose American Express card identified him as CCC Mountbatten disappeared—simply vanished—not merely from New York City and Greenwich, but seemingly off the face of the earth.

CHAPTER 9

Clark Rockefeller: New York, New York

From December 6, 1988, to sometime in 1992, Crowe wasn't seen by anyone from his former lives, at least no one who has come forward. Some believed he decamped for Tokyo or Delhi, owing to purchases of airline tickets to those Asian capitals that showed up on his American Express statements. In fact, investigators say, he was hiding in plain sight in New York City, living in an apartment with Rose Mina, the quiet, bright, well-educated Asian woman he had met when she provided translation services for Nikko Securities. He had a computer room set up in the closet of her apartment and would rarely venture out except to walk his dog. He spent his days watching *Star Trek* and fiddling with his computer, pondering his next move, while Rose Mina went to work, steadily rising up the ranks of the New York City financial community. Near the end of the two years, Mina decided that she had had enough of her strange boyfriend and wanted out, but found that it wasn't easy to extricate herself from the relationship. Finally, she left him in the apartment and moved into her own place.

The mystery man himself would later insist that during this four-year hiatus he was being mentored by a gentleman named Harry Copeland, who he said became his godfather. Later, some people would surmise that he was referring to the former habitué of the Belmont Park racetrack on Long Island. He was known as Harry the Horse for his prowess in predicting the ponies. But that Harry Copeland died in the late 1990s, and neither his daughter nor anyone else I could find knew of any ties he had with Christian Gerhartsreiter, Christopher Chichester, or Christopher Crowe.

Everyone agrees on one thing: if he had been ghostlike in his first decade in America, he became a real ghost for the next four years.

"He was *gone*," said Boston police deputy superintendent Thomas Lee. The veteran police officer had an almost encyclopedic knowledge of the immigrant's roller-coaster life, except for the period from 1988 to 1992. "We don't have good information about where he was during those missing years," said Lee.

"What do *you* think?" I asked.

"Again, he was someplace pretending to be somebody. I don't know who."

"Four years and not a single clue?" I asked.

"Not for sure, no," he said. "Nineteen ninety-two may be the first time we have him again, living in an apartment in New York."

He emerged then, as usual, in church.

St. Thomas Church, founded in 1823, is the epicenter of Episcopalianism in New York City, located on one of the most stellar stretches of Fifth Avenue. The church's French High Gothic building was completed in 1913, "of cathedral proportions, with the nave vault rising 95 feet above the floor," according to St. Thomas's visitor information. At the time of his arrival in the church, he would have seen many of the leaders of New York business, politics, and society, including Brooke Astor, who often attended with her friend Hope Preminger, the former fashion model who became the wife of film director Otto Preminger, as well as piano legend George Shearing and his wife, Ellie.

The church was a magnet for the then thirty-year-old expatriate, who had been driven underground for four years by what to him must have seemed like the uncivilized bleating of law enforcement officers. Its spires must have been a beacon of hope to the immigrant, now washing up as an entirely new person in New York City. "If you do not currently have a church home, or if you are new to New York City and have not yet found a church home, might you consider joining us?" asks one pamphlet.

The man who responded to that summons was no longer Christopher Crowe. When he entered the magnificent Gothic church, he had an equally magnificent name and a meticulously researched persona to go with it. "Hello," he greeted his fellow worshippers in his perfectly enunciated East Coast prep school accent, wearing a blue blazer and private-club necktie, which he would usually accent with khaki pants embroidered with tiny ducks, hounds, or bumblebees, worn always with Top-Sider boat shoes, *without* socks. His voice was as distinctive as his attire, a deep, hypnotic melody coming from the back of his throat, a voice that, to his mind and those who met him during this defining epoch, was the epitome of good breeding, vast wealth, and impeccable taste. "Clark," he said, "Clark Rockefeller."

Where, how, and when he conjured up the name may never be known, but in no time at all he had spread it far and wide, first at St. Thomas and throughout the city. He would later inflate it to James Frederick Mills Clark Rockefeller, but to those he met in the beginning he was just plain Clark Rockefeller, the reluctant scion of the family with the country's most famous name.

"In the late nineteenth century, St. Thomas was the church of the prominent but much newer money in New York—the Vanderbilt crowd, but not the sort of old Yankee New Yorkers," said a longtime member I'll call John Wells, who was one of the first to meet Clark Rockefeller when he arrived at St. Thomas sometime in early 1992, and who would eventually have close ties with him. We were sitting in one of New York's parks, and before Wells got to Clark, he felt it important to set the grand scene where the wily German debuted his greatest character. "The church has hundreds of millions of dollars in endowments," said Wells. "Their music program is second to none. Their choir is fantastic. Their main organist used to run the music at St. Paul's Cathedral in London. The rector, when I started going there, was John Andrew, who had been chaplain to one of the archbishops of Canterbury, and who had an affiliation with the Queen Mother. At the same time the church has attracted a lot of people who like to play at being New York society. The congregation ranged from people who actually *were* members of New York society to people who were totally playing the game."

It was a Saturday when Wells and I met, and I told him I would be up bright and early for services the next morning, so that I could experience the church where Clark Rockefeller struck gold. "You'll see tomorrow," he said. "The ushers wear morning suits every Sunday—you know, the striped trousers and gray jackets? On major Sundays they wear long cutaways, like a tuxedo. St. Thomas is the church around which the whole Easter Parade started. They would carry the altar flowers from St. Thomas Church to St. Luke's Hospital, when it was still on Fifth Avenue, and people would come out and see it." As Wells's oral history confirmed, this was a church where plenty of people pretended to be slightly more—or a lot more—than they actually were. "Back in my time, there was somebody lurking around calling himself a lord, who was nothing of the sort. He would come to church in hunting clothes and jodhpurs. It's a place where everybody is a little bit preposterous. Clark Rockefeller was just a little more preposterous than anyone else."

"There are plenty of perfectly nice people there as well; it's not as if the whole parish is caught up in some head game," Wells continued. "But there is definitely a certain element of people trying to live out their fantasies."

These were presumably the people the newly christened Clark Rockefeller intuitively knew would open their arms wide to him, hoping that some of the dynastic Rockefeller magic might rub off on them and raise them to a higher plane. John Wells would play a key role in connecting Rockefeller to some of the young, impressionable parishioners, who would in turn help him climb the ladder of social success.

"I remember meeting Clark at one of the coffee hours," he continued. "The coffee hour is just a reception after the Sunday service. They would have a long table with silver coffee urns and two ladies of the parish pouring coffee and that sort of thing. The church did theater well. Clark introduced himself, or I was introduced to him. I think I might have even asked, 'Are you one of the Rockefeller cousins?' His response was, 'No, I'm one of the cousins' cousins.'"

Wells took that to be a very subtle way of conveying, *Yes, I am a Rockefeller, but I don't take my famous family or myself too seriously.*

Rockefeller would soon take up with Wells's crowd of friends, who often socialized after church. Brunching with the young lions of St. Thomas Church, the newcomer had quite a tale to tell, one that would have been absolutely impossible to believe if a mere mortal were telling it, but coming from a Rockefeller it sounded not only wild and crazy but also improbably *true.*

"He intimated that he was from the Percy Rockefeller branch of the clan—not John D. ultra-rich, but plenty rich," continued Wells. "He even had an old painting that he said was Percy Rockefeller. He claimed to have grown up on Sutton Place," he said, indicating an East Side enclave of some of the grandest town houses and most prominent names in the city. "He said that he would see the steeples of Queens from his backyard, peeking out over his fence. He claimed to have gone to Yale at something like age fourteen. He had the Yale college scarf with the blue stripes on it. He said he had one of the J-boats from his grandparents—you know, the classic 1920s, 1930s sailing yachts."

He was referring to the big yachts built during the Great Depression for the likes of Vincent Astor and Cornelius Vanderbilt. "I wish I could summon his voice," Wells said, indicating that it reeked of being to the manor born. He told Wells that his J-boat was named *True Love,* and that the family was miffed that the producers of the 1940 film *The Philadelphia Story*, starring Cary Grant and Katharine Hepburn, had lifted the name to use for the yacht in the film.

"He said, 'The family was highly irritated,'" said Wells. But then Rockefeller added that he had recently sold *True Love* to the pop star Mariah Carey and her husband, Sony Music CEO Tommy Mottola, "who wanted it for a fancy yacht to watch the fireworks from." Wells recalled Rockefeller saying this with "utter disdain" for the nouveau riche couple. "And he was laughing at the idea of them using it as a pleasure boat, because, he said, 'A J-boat is a racing boat and not a proper place to host parties.'"

As always, the bonfire had begun with these tiny sparks, one or two well-placed individuals impressed by the friendly stranger with the colorful life. In the case of the newly minted persona of Clark Rockefeller, one of these was a fourteen-year-old girl walking her dog in Dag Hammarskjöld Plaza in affluent Midtown Manhattan. She was a student at Spence, the premier all-girls private school, her parents worked very long hours—her mother as a doctor, her father as a lawyer—and not one in a string of thirteen different nannies could succeed in keeping her cloistered inside her family's apartment at the prestigious United Nations Plaza.

Seeking companionship, she would escape to the park with her English pointer and her homework. It was here in early 1992 that she met the charming older man, then thirty-one, with the enormous eyeglasses walking a black-and-tan Gordon setter, the four-hundred-year-old breed favored in Great Britain for hunting pheasant, grouse, partridge, and woodcock, which he named Yates, after the obscure nineteenth-century British novelist and dramatist Edmund Hodgson Yates. They struck up a conversation, and the girl, whom I'll call Alice Johnson, was immediately taken. He was *so* friendly, so smart, and, best of all, he cared about *her*. Almost immediately, he was helping her with her homework and they were walking their dogs through the park together.

The day after she met him, Alice was in the park with her cousin, who, going through an inquisitive phase, just *had* to see what was in the stranger's wallet.

"You can't go through my wallet!" he said, which of course made the girls want to see its contents all the more.

"Are you a mob boss?" they began, trying to guess who he was and why he seemed so secretive.

"No . . ."

"Are you James Bond? A CIA agent?"

"No, no . . ."

Alice, who had been studying history, asked, "Are you the Lindbergh baby?"

Finally he relented, sheepishly opening his wallet to show them his identification, which bore the name CLARK ROCKEFELLER.

"A Rockefeller!" the girls shrieked, because they had studied the family at Spence. The revelation unleashed a torrent of information from Clark. He was worth *exactly* $450 million, he said. Because of his enormous wealth and his famous family name, he had to be extremely careful about security. "Normal for a Rockefeller, of course," he admitted. But it was no fun living in fear of being kidnapped and held "for millions" in ransom. However, there were perks, he added. Like having the keys to every door in Rockefeller Center. Maybe he would take Alice there to pull a prank one night: "We could turn off all the lights on the General Electric Building!" he said, referring to Rockefeller Center's art deco centerpiece. "That would be the coolest thing ever!" Alice exclaimed. Or perhaps they could run around the *Saturday Night Live* set in the building's NBC Studios, which Clark loved to do until his "Uncle David," meaning the philanthropist David Rockefeller, made him stop. He was in the middle of writing a book, *American Standard*, which would "educate the middle class on how to dress and how to act," and it was clear from his preppy clothing and perfect diction that Clark Rockefeller knew how to do all of that. He always wore khaki pants, a blood-red Yale baseball cap, and a Lacoste polo shirt, with the collar turned up. "He believed in the alligator," Alice would later say.

Everything about the man was special, important, and, to a fourteen-year-old girl, *magical*. Soon, Clark and Alice were running their dogs down the East River Drive jogging track, singing show tunes—Clark knew them *all*—from *Annie* to Cole Porter at the top of their lungs. They quickly abandoned the dog park for the city at large. They ate hot fudge sundaes at Rumpelmayer, the ice cream parlor inside the old St. Moritz Hotel, and bagels fresh out of the ovens at H&H Bagels on the Upper West Side. He took her to the Metropolitan Museum of Art, where he knew *everything* about every painting, and would always pause reverently for "a moment of silence" in the Met's Michael Clark Rockefeller Collection, named for his "cousin" who tragically disappeared in 1961 in New Guinea. Throughout every outing, he was constantly speaking into a radio, because, he explained, he had to regularly report his whereabouts to his security office. "See?" he would tell Alice, pointing at dark sedans in the street, which he said were forever following him to make sure he was safe.

Of course, she had to introduce him to her parents, and her mother was as entranced as Alice had been. Soon, they were all as close as kin. Alice began referring to him as her uncle or cousin (the monikers were sometimes mixed up)—while Clark introduced her as his "niece"—and her mother loved him so much that she told everyone he was her beloved "nephew." Mother and daughter visited him in his apartment at Dag Hammarskjöld Plaza on Second Avenue and East Forty-seventh Street, and while they thought the furnishings—lawn furniture, mainly—were a bit odd, they chalked it up to Rockefeller eccentricity. And when he would invite Alice's grandmother, a socially well-connected doyenne of the Upper East Side, to lunch, he would always hand her the bill at the end of the meal, saying he had been brought up to "never carry money." They chalked that up to Rockefeller eccentricity too.

Every Thanksgiving, he said, it was mandatory that he join the Rockefeller family for their traditional dinner at Kykuit, the historic home near Tarrytown, New York, that John D. Rockefeller had built in 1913, and that had been home to four generations of Rockefellers. Over the course of their friendship he would sometimes take Alice's dog along with his Gordon setter to the Thanksgiving event, returning to exclaim how glorious it had been to be with "Uncle David, Uncle Laurance, and Uncle Jay," leaving both Alice and her mother rapt with his descriptions of the vast estate, the endless servants, and the close family conviviality.

Yet despite his bloodline and everything that went along with it, there was something sad about Clark. He said he was all alone in the world—his parents had died tragically when he was very young, he explained—after they forced him to attend Yale at fourteen because of his "genius" IQ. Even his birthday was fraught with heartbreak: February 29, 1960, was a leap year, which meant he could celebrate it only every four years. "He told these stories with such emotion," Alice recalled, quite often accompanied by tears. What he did for work was important, complicated, high-level, and ultra-secretive—although he did share some details about that—but he always had time for the people he cared about. "I can't love anyone or anything unless they're special," he often said. And Alice and her mother felt privileged to be a part of his incredible orbit.

In time Clark became, with Alice's mother's blessings, a sort of surrogate parent. The 1994 New York debutante season was coming up, with Alice as part of it, and Clark would guide her through it. He even escorted her to a ball or two in his tuxedo, bow tie, and dress shoes, always worn without socks. "If I had to go back in time, I would do it again, because he was important to me and I was important to him," Alice later recalled. "I needed him then. He was my godfather, he was my uncle, my cousin. He was somebody I could turn to."

She and her mother, in turn, had provided Clark Rockefeller with two things he desperately needed: validation that his incredible new persona was believable and, equally important, a support system—a real family—in the upper echelons of New York City.

Thus the circle that Clark Rockefeller would soon command began to grow.

In his early days in New York he had arrived at St. Thomas Church in what would become a regular feature of his MO: a snit. He had fled his previous "church home," said John Wells, which was Fifth Avenue Presbyterian, on Fifth Avenue and West Fifty-fifth Street, a venerable house of worship that bills itself as offering "the personal touch of Jesus Christ amid the hustle and bustle of midtown Manhattan." He said he left that church because its elders had dared refuse to baptize the girl he was by then calling his niece, Alice Johnson. "Clark told us that he had been baptized at St. Thomas himself, that he wasn't a member but his parents had him baptized there in the sixties," said Wells. "So he claimed to have a long, sort of ancient family history there."

"He wanted to have Alice baptized, and her mother was very happy about it," said Alice Johnson's father, who explained that his wife (now ex) could be easily impressed—especially with a fancy name—and soon began vouching for her young friend who, she was convinced, was indeed a Rockefeller. He confirmed that Rockefeller had previously been a regular at Fifth Avenue Presbyterian, adding that he liked to point out that "the Rockefeller family had a home around the corner, where Nelson Rockefeller died. He died, as they say, in the saddle, with his secretary. He died happy." Clark Rockefeller knew all sorts of such Rockefeller family minutiae.

He was brilliant, John Wells added, casting himself as properly eccentric, and he told Wells exactly what he'd told the fourteen-year-old Alice Johnson: that he was "paranoid about security." "He would walk around with a radio device that he claimed was connected to a security office," Wells said. "He would carry it around and periodically check in—report where he was, who he was with, what direction he was going. He claimed it was some sort of extra-high-level security service, and he had to report in at all times."

Casting himself as obsessed with security was a clever means by which Rockefeller could deflect questions about his background. According to Wells, "In Clark World, you were always trying to find out how rich he was, because once he had established how maniacally private he was, he could take the position that he could decline questions that impinged on his privacy."

The morning after meeting John Wells I attended St. Thomas Church. The service was certainly impressive, with its tuxedoed ushers, its rectors marching paradelike through the pews with enormous candles, its regally attired worshippers. Like Rockefeller, I was there really for the reception held immediately after the service, in which the congregants retired to the church basement. Just as John Wells had described, it was good theater. Women served coffee from silver urns. Men poured wine from bottles with impressive labels. There were hors d'oeuvres and uninhibited conversation—a sense of welcome, fellowship, civility, and trust among those secure in the fact that no evil would dare darken one of God's grandest earthly homes.

Another early sighting of "Clark Rockefeller" came in February 1992.

By then, he had obviously deduced the credentials that are catnip to the cognoscenti. Paramount among them: a purebred dog; in Rockefeller's case, the Gordon setter named Yates. Nothing sparks a conversation between strangers faster than a walked dog, and soon Rockefeller was meeting any number of influential people, including, he insisted, Henry Kissinger.

One day, while walking Yates in the Tudor City neighborhood of New York, he met Sharlene Spingler, a young woman who had just downsized that day from a spacious 1905 brownstone to a one-bedroom apartment, having lost her home to her brothers in an estate battle. Sharlene was taking her black shar-pei and red-and-white English setter for a walk. Suddenly, "a short young blond man, looking to be somewhere in his early thirties," came bounding across the street to greet Sharlene, a stranger to him, and her two dogs.

"I love your dog, that English setter!" said the stranger. "I'll do anything for you! I'll walk your dog."

"I thought that was a little forward," Sharlene said, but at the same time there was something appealing about it.

We were sitting at a restaurant in Grand Central Station in New York when Sharlene, an extremely intelligent blonde with a rapier wit whose family had arrived in Manhattan in 1643, told me about the encounter. "It was my first day there," she said of her new apartment. "He just saw me in the street with the dogs. But dog people are like that. They'll just talk to each other."

That was, of course, the beauty of it for a striver like Clark. Connected by their dogs, they quickly became, well, if not friends, at least acquaintances. Then came what Sharlene called the infinite tales that the enigmatic young man began telling her. She related them to me one after the other, all improbable upon reflection, but seemingly plausible—for a Rockefeller—at the time: He said he was friends with Henry Kissinger. He said he would take a Learjet with his dog to London, where "the food is so terrible I just bring cereal." He said he regularly invited friends to run their dogs with him at the storied 3,400-acre Rockefeller estate in Pocantico Hills near Tarrytown. He said his profession was "advising foreign governments on how much money to print." Once, the socially well-connected Sharlene introduced him to some friends who suggested it would be nice to have a Rockefeller on the board of a satellite company they were launching and asked him what he would like in return. Rockefeller rose from his chair and said, "Gentlemen, there is nothing you can do for me, as I don't wish to jeopardize my tax status. I am tax exempt by an act of Congress, and Texas is my official residence." (He also told Sharlene about the various presidential inaugurations he had attended.) If that résumé wasn't enough, his clothing completed the portrait. "He was always in his bright green corduroy pants with ducks or something flying over them," said Spingler. "With a pink shirt. And a blue blazer. And a green bow tie. Looking like a typical Yalie." Soon he was helping her to configure her computer—he was a computer wizard,

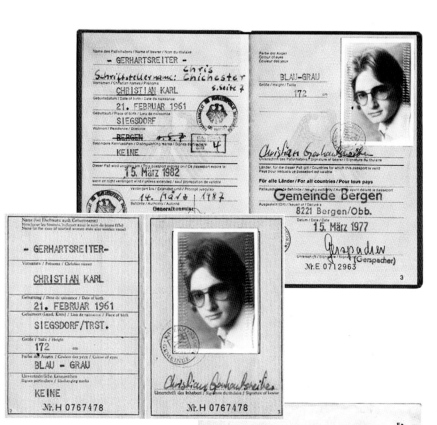

Christian Karl Gerhartsreiter, seventeen, arrived in Boston on December 16, 1978. Pictured here: his passport, his resident alien identification card, and his birth certificate. He told his parents that he had gotten a job as a disc jockey in New York City, and they agreed to send him money each month until he got settled. Once he obtained a tourist visa, he packed up his belongings and flew from Munich to Boston.

Gerhartstreiter stands front and center in a group communion photograph of nine-year-old third-grade boys in Bergen, West Germany. "That Christian stands in the front may be explained by his body size, or may be by coincidence, though he liked to play the role of a leader whenever possible," said a classmate.

Bergen looks like something out of a fairy tale, a picturesque hamlet nestled in a verdant valley of the majestic Bavarian Alps. The focal points of the town center are a church and a beer garden. The house where Gerhartsreiter grew up, at 19 Bahnhof (Train Station) Street, was almost the first house off the highway.

"He was always posing," said a woman who met him when he still lived in Germany. "In his mind, he had to be something someday," added her husband. "He wanted notoriety."

This U.S. Immigration and Naturalization Service photograph shows Gerhartsreiter on his 1978 arrival in the United States. After landing in Boston, he traveled to the small town in Connecticut that was home to a high school student who had met the friendly German on a train while traveling through Europe on a Eurail pass the summer before.

Gerhartsreiter arrived at his college dorm with a set of golf clubs and an aristocratic air. "Supposedly, his mother or father was an ambassador," said his college roommate. "He said he was from Boston." To buttress his Boston background, he would eat a Boston cream pie every single day, added another college acquaintance.

"He said to people he was from royalty in England and that his name was Christopher Chichester," said the Swedish cowboy hairdresser Jann of Sweden, shown here in his cowboy regalia. "Every time he meets a lady, he takes her hand and kisses it before he presents himself. These ladies were thinking Chichester was sent by God or something."

This clipping from the San Marino, California, newspaper shows Christopher Chichester as the producer of the local cable TV show *Inside San Marino*. Also pictured is the show's host, Peggy Ebright.

SACRAMENTO CONNECTION. Assemblyman Richard Mountjoy will be the featured guest on the May 29 edition of "Inside of San Marino," scheduled for 7 p.m. on American Cablevision Channel 6. Above, Mountjoy (center) discusses the program's format with producer Christopher Chichester and moderator Peggy Ebright. Mountjoy represents the 42nd District, which includes San Marino, and is one of the state's leading conservatives. On the cablecast, Mrs. Ebright asks him about reapportionment, legislative reform, the school finance bill and his grassroot political beginnings.

Christopher Chichester became a well-known presence in San Marino. Not only was he an in-demand man-about-town, popular with the city's wealthy widows, he also posed as an aspiring film student, telling some he was a teacher's assistant at the prestigious University of Southern California film school. Here, he's seen partying with friends.

Ruth Detrick "Didi" Sohus (top photo, far right) was a former debutante. She and her third husband adopted a son, John, who was something of a loner before he met the woman who would become his wife: the redheaded, part–Blackfoot Indian Linda Mayfield. Standing over six feet tall and weighing more than two hundred pounds, Linda dwarfed John, who stood five feet five. The couple are shown in the bottom photo, on the day of their wedding.

"I don't know why he came up here," said a local in Cornish, New Hampshire, where Rockefeller turned a historic home into a never-ending construction project. "I guess he wanted to be in the sticks. He said he was looking for a place he could do a lot of fixing up." The house was blocked off with a heavy chain and surrounded by signs reading KEEP OUT, CAUTION, and BEWARE OF DOGS.

"As I recall, he played Mars, and his daughter played a nymph," said a representative of the Saint-Gaudens Historic Site in Cornish. The god of war was an appropriate role for him, because by that time Rockefeller was fighting with many of the locals.

Above and on facing page: These snapshots were taken by Laura White, who became one of Rockefeller's best friends in Cornish, showing him at the White family dinner table. Also pictured is a page from White's diary with references to "Clark." At Clark's side is White's young son, Charlie. "He was the most exciting thing to happen around here in a long time," said White's mother.

"He hated to have his picture taken," recalled Laura White. In nearly every photograph Rockefeller was striking a pose that disguised him.

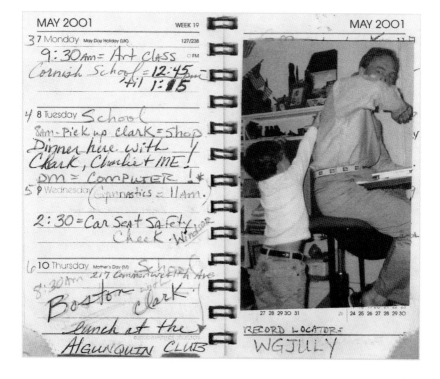

MAY 2001   WEEK 19   MAY 2001

3 7 Monday   May Day Holiday (UK)   127/238
9:30 AM = Art Class
Cornish School = 12:45
til 1:15

4 8 Tuesday   School
8Am - Pick up Clark = shop
Dinner here with
Clark, Charlie + ME!
DM = COMPUTER!*

5 9 Wednesday (Gymnastics = 11Am)
2:30 = Car Seat Safety
Check. Windsor

6 10 Thursday   Mother's Day (U)   School
8:30 Am   217 Commonwealth Ave
Boston with Clark.
lunch at the
ALGUNQUIN CLUB

27 28 29 30 31   28   24 25 26 27 28 29 30

RECORD LOCATOR =
WGJULY

Although Rockefeller wouldn't allow photographers to take his picture at most of the Boston social events he attended, he struck a pose here at an event at the Liberty Hotel, in a building that was formerly the venerable Charles Street Jail. It was prophetic that many of the guests, including Rockefeller, sported toy handcuffs, in keeping with the hotel's refurbished-jailhouse theme.

By the time of their arrival in Boston, Rockefeller said, his daughter, Reigh "Snooks" Rockefeller, was a proficient reader; she could read aloud from the scientific journal *Nature* when she was three. He said he had once read Tennyson's poem "The Daisy" to her twenty-five times in a single evening. She not only understood the poem, she loved it.

Los Angeles County
Sheriff's Department *Homicide Bureau*

INFORMATION **WANTED**

IN CUSTODY

Christian Karl Gerhartsreiter
1978 INS photo

Clark Rockefeller
2008 photo

Chris Chichester
1980's photo

Homicide Investigators are seeking the public's assistance in developing information regarding the 1985 disappearance of John & Linda Sohus of San Marino, California. The male depicted in this bulletin was a tenant at the Sohus residence, at the time of their disappearance. Anyone with information regarding this case or the male in the bulletin are urged to contact Los Angeles County Sheriff's Homicide Bureau Detectives.

File Number - 094-00061-3199-011

Attention: Sgt.s Bobby Taylor or Timothy Miley

LASD HOMICIDE (323) 890-5500

5747 Rickenbacker Road, Commerce California 90040

For investigators, the missing persons case had been fraught with witnesses dying, district attorneys leaving their jobs just as they had begun to make progress, and detectives becoming frustrated with the labyrinthine case and moving on, allowing the "person of interest" not just to remain free but to climb the social ladder in the shoes of a Rockefeller.

"Chip Smith," ship's captain, became a welcome regular presence in the offices of Obsidian Realty in Baltimore. Sure, he was a bit odd, in his salmon-colored pants and his boat shoes, always worn without socks. But he was a client, and at Obsidian the client is king. They let him use their computers. They even gave him his own key to the office. Eventually, they sold him a house at 618 Ploy Street. In the house, pictured at bottom, investigators would find the elements of his latest identity.

In the early days after his arrest, Rockefeller projected a sense of cool control, appearing unruffled in front of the cameras in two media interviews he granted, one to the *Today* show and the other, in this photograph, to the *Boston Globe*.

The lawyer Rockefeller first chose to represent him was the veteran Boston criminal attorney Stephen Hrones, pictured here. As the media storm grew, Hrones encouraged him to keep talking. "Fight fire with fire," Hrones later said. "We had to get out and tell his side of the story, emphasize the loving-father aspect. I pressed that at every point: how can you kidnap your own child?"

"He burst into the room smiling, with the cheerful demeanor of a host welcoming guests to a party," wrote a *Boston Globe* reporter. "'Clark Rockefeller,' he said, fixing his gaze on a visitor and extending a hand. His nails were manicured. He wore tasseled loafers with his jail-issued scrubs. He turned to another visitor and another, bowing slightly to each. 'Clark Rockefeller, Clark Rockefeller,' he said in a Brahmin accent. 'Nice to see you. How are you, everyone?'"

At Rockefeller's first court hearing in Boston for his arraignment on August 5, 2008, he still wore the preppy clothing he had always worn during his life as a Boston bon vivant. But the pressure of being on the run showed in his face and scruffy appearance.

S	YEAR	DR. HOWE	DR. ABLOW	DR. CHU
...arts Reiter	1979, Berlin, CT	"Not a Delusion"	"Probably Not a Delusion"	"Not a Delusion"
		"...ot a Delusion"	"Probably Not a Delusion"	"Not a Delusion"
	...5, Las ...as	"Not a Delusion"	"Probably Not a Delusion"	"Not a Delusion"
...Crowe	1985, Greenwich, CT	"Not a Delusion"	"Probably Not a Delusion"	"Not a Delusion"
...ntbatten	1985 Postal Offcls.	"Not a Delusion"	"Probably Not a Delusion"	"Not a Delusion"
...Rockefeller	1993-2008	"Delusion"	"Delusion"	"Not a Delusion"
...rles "Chip" Smith	2007-2008	"Probably Not a Delusion"	"Probably Not a Delusion"	"Not a Delusion"

COMM V CHRISTIAN KARL GERHARTSREITER

During the trial, the prosecutor, David Deakin, grilled witness after witness on Rockefeller's state of mind at the time of the kidnapping. Here, Deakin presents a chart showing the expert witnesses' findings about the defendant's mental state.

Throughout her testimony, Rockefeller's wife of twelve years, the extremely poised and ever-collected Sandra Boss, spelled out how she could have been duped by someone like Rockefeller, despite her being an undoubtedly highly intelligent career woman. "One can be brilliant and amazing in one area of one's life and really stupid in another," she said. Although repeatedly grilled by the defense on how she could believe the monstrous lies her ex-husband had told her, she held firm to her convictions while also making clear the pain she had endured after her daughter's kidnapping.

As his trial came to a close, the Clark Rockefeller who had greeted investigators and reporters as a gentleman of wealth and taste—holding forth as if he were hosting a party even while incarcerated—turned mute, pale, and ghostly in court. It was as if after a lifetime of lies, he had finally run out of stories to tell.

no doubt about that—and taking the computer to work on in what he said was his office, at the prestigious No. 5 Tudor City Place.

If he was indeed a human sponge, absorbing ideas, dreams, identities, and personas from everyone with whom he came in contact, what Rockefeller gleaned from Sharlene Spingler was something huge for what he would become in New York City. Through her, he learned how to gain entry to the portals of some of the world's most exclusive private clubs.

"He knew how to work the churches, so the obvious next step would be the private clubs," said Sharlene. "Back in 1993, you could join the India House, a private gentleman's club on Wall Street, for $850 to $1,200, for which you would get reciprocal memberships at"—and here she listed some of the premier private clubs in the city, among them the Lotos, one of America's oldest and most esteemed literary clubs and a preferred destination for Vanderbilts, Whitneys, Roosevelts, and Rockefellers since 1870; and the Metropolitan Club, founded by the leaders of New York City in 1891.

These were just the beginning of the bonanza of reciprocal private clubs that the India House membership would include. "He went through the back door," Sharlene patiently explained to me, just as she had explained to Clark.

Thus, with just a down payment of $850 to $1,200, Rockefeller was not only able to gain membership in the private clubs of the richest and most powerful citizens of East Coast society, but also to take an important first step in making their members think he was one of them.

Shortly after his 1992 reemergence, Clark Rockefeller moved into a one-bedroom apartment at 400 East Fifty-seventh Street, an imposing prewar white-brick art deco building. One day in 2008, I rode the elevator to the seventh floor, where I was greeted by a statuesque and effervescent brunette named Martha Henry, who runs Martha Henry Inc. Fine Art. She lived in 7L, the apartment adjacent to Rockefeller's. She showed me the door to his apartment, 7M, catty-corner to hers.

"I left mine ajar a lot," she said, explaining that she was a smoker and needed the cross-ventilation. "He introduced himself as Clark Rocke-feller. He never flaunted it or elaborated on it." He just let it lie there, having its hypnotic effect. "He told me his work was solving Third World debt, particularly on the Pacific Rim."

She laughed. The door to her apartment was open, and she stared at the door to his as if she could still see him standing there, togged out head to toe in his preppy casual daytime clothing, hair bleached with blond highlights. "When I heard the part about Third World debt I decided, you know, he's crazy. That's not a real job. But then I thought, okay, he's a Rockefeller, he's eccentric.

"He told me his parents had died when he was sixteen in a car crash, that he had grown up in Cambridge and Boston, that he went to Harvard. I said, 'If your parents died when you were sixteen, who took care of you?' And he said, 'I took care of myself and lived in the town house and went to school myself. But I graduated early.' And I thought, okay, he's a mathematical genius and therefore is solving these Third World debts."

He invited her over for a few of the parties he was soon hosting in his apartment, where young men were dressed just like Clark, "in their madras and khakis and drinking their gin and tonics." Once, she met his niece, Alice Johnson, whom he introduced as a debutante. As Henry got to know him, his "quirks and oddities and paranoias" multiplied.

"He told me once that he never ate in restaurants," she said. "So I said, "Clark, this is crazy! Why wouldn't you eat in a restaurant?' He said, 'Because you can't trust the kitchen. I only eat in private clubs.'

"He was *very* particular about his food," she continued. "He would only eat his little sandwiches—you know, the cucumber and watercress on white bread with the crusts cut off? He would only eat a certain Pep-peridge Farm cookie: the Nantucket. He would only drink Earl Grey tea. Oh, and what was his favorite food? Oh, my God. His favorite food was haggis."

"Haggis?" I asked.

"It's a Scottish dish," she said. "And his favorite drink was Harveys Bristol Cream."

Yet, she added, it all made sense in a strange sort of way, the pieces of the crazy puzzle the man of wealth, taste, and distinction presented to her, because it all was guaranteed sound by the famous name. She repeated, "You just think, 'Oh, well, he's a Rockefeller. He's eccentric!'"

One day Clark called to tell her he had inherited some paintings, and asked for her help in determining their value.

"Well, I've got a Jackson Pollock, a Mondrian, somebody named Rothko, and I think Twombly or something," said Rockefeller, mispronouncing the names of these masters of modern art. "I was literally almost on the floor!" said Henry. "A Rothko alone would have been eight million dollars back then. Today, Rothkos sell for thirty, forty million."

The art dealer cut Rockefeller short and rushed from her apartment to his, "doing the math" along the way. When she entered 7M, she was stunned by what she calculated to be a multimillion-dollar, irreplaceable, museum-quality collection of paintings, haphazardly hung on walls and sitting on the floor. She blurted out, "You need an insurance policy immediately, and you should probably get an alarm system! We're coming out of an art recession, but, Clark, these are very expensive paintings!" Then she asked him, "Where did you *get* all of this?"

"He said he had inherited them from his great-aunt Blanchette" (the Museum of Modern Art benefactor and widow of John D. Rockefeller III), who, Rockefeller threw in, "started that little old museum on Fifty-third Street." Henry was stunned.

"He then said, 'I'm really disappointed because I wanted to inherit the Bierstadt,'" meaning he wished his great-aunt had left him a work by the German-born nineteenth-century Western landscape painter Albert Bierstadt and not "all this modern stuff."

"It all made sense," said Henry. "I did a little research, and Blanchette Rockefeller indeed died in 1992, so there could have been an estate settled. And so I thought, 'He's a Rockefeller! What else could he be?' You don't go out onto Madison Avenue and pick up any of these paintings! You just can't do that in an afternoon!" The art had her convinced.

Next she got upset, not with Rockefeller but with herself for blowing what she felt had been a major opportunity. "I was living next door to somebody—right under my nose!—who had the means, being a Rockefeller, to purchase major works of art, and I had somehow missed this," she said. "I am an art dealer, so I was very upset about this."

She immediately reverted from neighbor to art dealer. She *had* to do a deal to stake her claim on Clark Rockefeller. This became immediately clear when she invited him to an opening in a gallery she had rented; as soon as his famous name floated through the air, the other dealers surrounded him like bees to honey. "He calls me the next day and says, 'I'm being bombarded by all of these art dealers!'" Martha Henry remembered. "I said, 'Well, you can't go to an art opening and tell everybody that you're Clark Rockefeller! If you want to keep a low profile, you need to leave that part out.'"

Henry had found him first, after all, and soon it was time for her to take him shopping for a major piece of art. First stop: Knoedler & Company, the esteemed Upper East Side gallery that had been in existence since the Civil War, and where John D. Rockefeller had been a client. Here, Henry showed him a work from the estate of Adolph Gottlieb, a historically significant painting from the 1950s. They agreed that, at $300,000 to $400,000, it would be an extremely prudent addition to his collection. "It's a perfect provenance for someone like Clark," Henry said. "The Gottlieb estate was allowing this picture out. They would not necessarily sell it to anyone. But to a Rockefeller they would do it."

Rockefeller kept returning to Knoedler, sometimes alone, to inspect the Gottlieb. I spoke to a woman who repeatedly showed him the painting. She had been chief of staff of the Whitney Museum of American Art, the preeminent museum for contemporary art on Madison Avenue in New York City. So she was an expert in contemporary art, and, she quickly discovered, Rockefeller was too. "He knew his art history," she remembered. "He talked about the other art in his collection." While debating whether or not to purchase the Gottlieb, he invited the woman from Knoedler to see his other pieces. Like everyone else, she was dazzled by the large and iconic works of the greats of American contemporary art. "Honestly, it never occurred to me for a second that those paintings weren't right," she said.

When it came to buying the Gottlieb, however, Rockefeller kept balking. Things came to a head one day in Knoedler when he studied the painting for the umpteenth time with his dealer, Martha Henry. They looked at the Gottlieb this way and that way, until the scion of the great family finally spoke. "That painting has *green* in it," he said. "I don't buy pictures with green in them."

"What are you talking about?" asked Henry.

"Well, Mondrian only painted in primary colors, and he would never have put green in a canvas," Rockefeller said huffily.

"'Oh, Clark, you've got to get past primary colors,'" Henry told him. "'We're not in kindergarten anymore.' But he would not budge, and we could not do the sale."

Meanwhile, strange things were always going on in 7M. Clark baked a loaf of fresh bread for a neighbor he barely knew, and Henry thought it odd. Most New Yorkers don't have time to toast bread, much less bake it. But Rockefeller seemed to have all the time in the world, especially for leisure pursuits. "Obviously he didn't work, but didn't seem to be broke," said Henry, who would occasionally go out to lunch with him. "He paid," she said, "in cash."

"One day he called and wanted to know if I knew any young men that could escort this teenage cousin of his to debutante balls," Henry continued. "He said, 'The family will pay for everything. Her date's dropped out.'" Henry pulled a little prank on him. She did know someone who had indeed just told her that he would *love* to go to a real New York City debutante ball. It was actually her own boyfriend, although she didn't tell Rockefeller that at first.

"Where did he go to school?" Rockefeller asked.

"St. Paul's," she said, referring to the prep school in New Hampshire.

"Oh, perfect."

When Henry said, "Oh, by the way, he's forty-three," Rockefeller said, "That's *not* funny, Martha."

Another person in his life during this period was Rose Mina, the investment firm star whom Clark had met while working at Nikko as Christopher Crowe. I found her name on the list of credit card charges Rockefeller made under his former alias: "October 14, 1988: Airline ticket for [MINA/R] via Pan American World Airways from JFK to London to Delhi purchased at Thomas Cook Travel." There was also a return ticket: "For [MINA/R] via United Airlines from Delhi to Tokyo Narita to JFK." In addition, he had purchased tickets for a Henry Mina with an equally complicated itinerary, from Pittsburgh to Delhi. That ticket had been refunded and reticketed.

Why was Crowe flying Rose and Henry Mina to Delhi and Tokyo? Later, Rose Mina would be identified in the media as his business partner and the trustee of his estate. But despite queries from the media—and dozens of e-mails and hand-delivered letters from me—Rose Mina has remained stoically silent on the subject of Clark Rockefeller.

Mina clearly played a role in his rise in New York City. "I've been trying to figure it out," Martha Henry told me, sitting in her apartment. "Because there was a time, when he lived here, that every night during the week somebody would come into that apartment, arriving between, let's say, eleven-thirty and one a.m. And every morning they would leave between, say, five-thirty and seven, something like that. I would hear the door open and close. If I was sleeping, it would wake me up. And it was very regular."

We stood up and looked through the peephole, which afforded an excellent view of the hallway. "At one point, I looked to see who was going in and out," she said. "It was an Asian woman. And she was dressed businesslike—a suit and a briefcase.

"At one point I said to him, 'Clark, you have a girlfriend!' He said, 'No, no, no! She's not my girlfriend. She manages my money.'"

Henry thought, "They're friends, and she's crashing on his sofa, because investment bankers really do work long hours." But she kept teasing Rockefeller about her, and he kept insisting that she was just his money manager. Then something strange happened. "She never stayed there again," said Henry.

Soon Clark Rockefeller was gone too. Approximately two years after he moved into the apartment adjacent to Henry's, he mentioned to her that he was looking for larger accommodations, and perhaps she could help. She called a friend specializing in residential real estate, who suggested Alwyn Court, the turn-of-the-century building on West Fifty-eighth Street with the most intricate terra-cotta façade in the city. "He said, 'Oh, I would never live there. That building is so dreary and depressing. The apartments are dark.' Blah, blah, blah." Besides, he added, he had to rent in a Cushman & Wakefield building. "Because those are the family buildings—the Rockefeller buildings—and I can get a very low rent."

He needed a spacious place, with plenty of room for his art collection, his Gordon setter, and—oh, yes—his bride. He was getting married, he told Henry. The lucky girl's name was Sandra Lynne Boss.

CHAPTER 10

Sandra

S he walked into the courtroom just as I imagined she had walked into all the phases of her life: confident, perfectly put together, seemingly in complete control. Tall, thin, elegant, and attractive, she was wearing a conservative navy blue suit. Her highlighted brown hair was cut in a chin-length bob, and her unblemished skin seemed to require very little makeup. Even in the confines of a courtroom, Sandra Lynne Boss, at forty-two, was clearly a star.

"My name is Sandy Boss, and my last name is spelled B-O-S-S," she told the prosecuting attorney in an authoritative voice, enunciating every syllable. She was living in London, where she worked as a director, or senior partner, at McKinsey & Company, the world's premier management consulting firm, which advises corporations, institutions, and governments on how to improve their operations.

She answered questions about her background succinctly. Born: "Seattle, Washington." Immediate family: "My dad's name is Bill and my mother's name is Verla. And I have a twin sister, whose name is Julia." Education: "Blanchet High School." College: "Stanford." Major: "American studies, and then I had what's called the secondary major in economics."

What Boss didn't say was that her life, like that of her ex-husband, had been a journey of reinvention. The daughter of a Boeing engineer, she came from an upper-middle-class family in Seattle and was raised in "a nice two-story Cape Cod house with a finished basement," according to a friend. Early on she developed what would become her defining trait. "She is one of the most competitive people I know," the friend told me, adding that Sandra competed most doggedly against her fraternal twin, Julia. As a 1985 article in the *Seattle Times* reported, "Julia and Sandra, seniors at Blanchet High, are the only sibling Merit Scholars from this area. They've never spent more than three days apart. . . . Nonetheless, when Julia announced, 'I want to go to Yale,' Sandra replied, 'Okay, I want to go to Stanford.'"

"Julia and Sandy used to play this crazy game that dates back to when they were growing up," said a friend of both. "They would find a point of competition, and they would confer on who won that particular round." In childhood, it was selling cookies; in high school and college, it was scholarship; in young adulthood, it was often material things. "If one of them had a Hermès scarf and the other one had Christian Louboutin shoes, they would have to figure out which one was better, because they both cost about the same." On the witness stand, Sandra said only, "Twins are very similar to each other and we get compared a lot, and so we had what I would describe as a normal twin relationship, which is we love each other and we compared how we were doing in life."

After attending a one-year master's program at Oxford University in England, Julia Boss received her Ph.D. in history at Yale and went to work as an editor at Algonquin Books in New York City. In 1994 she married Charles Knapp, a fellow Yalie, who also worked in the book publishing industry.

As Sandra moved through a series of impressive jobs, people found her smart but aloof, ambitious but intensely private. "We were a very collegial bunch," said someone who worked with Boss. "We did everything together—everyone except Sandy. Sandy did her own thing." But despite her shyness, the coworker added, "she was aspirational. She always wanted to be on the inside looking out, but she was on the outside looking in." Then she met her future husband.

After some preamble, the prosecutor, David Deakin, got to the pivotal question. He looked over at the defendant, who sat expressionless, staring straight ahead. "Do you know the individual seated at the counsel table?" Deakin asked the witness.

The second Boss looked over at Rockefeller, her expression turned stern and cold. Any trace of the smile that had lit up her face only a moment before disappeared.

"Yes, I do," she said stiffly.

"Were you once married to that individual?"

"Yes, I was."

"Under what name did you know him when you were married to him?"

"Clark Rockefeller."

"When did you first meet the defendant?"

She sat up in her chair and told a story that soon had the entire courtroom transfixed.

"In the spring of 1993," Boss began, "I was in New York, interviewing for a summer job." Then twenty-six, she was entering her final year at Harvard Business School that fall. "I spoke to him on the phone," she said. "He was a friend of my sister's through church . . . St. Thomas Episcopal, on Fifth Avenue. I don't know if she was formally a member, but she went every week."

Boss had been raised as an Episcopalian in Seattle, and during the grand jury hearing that would lead to Rockefeller's indictment on kidnapping charges, the prosecutor asked her to rank her family's level of commitment to the church on a scale of one to ten, from casual to devout.

"Eight or nine, in terms of, you know, church every Sunday, Bible study. I went to Christian schools."

"How important would it have been to you that the person [you married], or anybody you were seriously interested in, share your religious outlook?"

"It was important," she said. "I wasn't obsessed with it, but I wanted to be with somebody who had the same value system I did."

Thus Clark Rockefeller was vetted, in a sense, by his mere presence as a regular parishioner at St. Thomas Episcopal.

As for their first in-person meeting, Boss testified in court, "He was having a party, and he heard from my sister that I was in town, and he wanted to invite me to the party."

"What kind of party was it?"

"It was a Clue party, and everyone was supposed to be a character from Clue" (the board game in which players are guests at a mansion and try to determine which one of them killed Mr. Boddy, their millionaire host).

Rockefeller assigned each of his eight guests a character and instructed them to come in costume and tell his doorman that they were there to see Mr. Boddy. Rockefeller played the role of Professor Plum, a Harvard archaeologist who, appropriately enough, always becomes uncomfortable when asked about his past.

"I was supposed to be Miss Scarlet," Boss testified, referring to the game's femme fatale Hollywood actress, whose career is in shambles and whose desire to marry rich has brought her to Boddy Mansion.

Sandra arrived at the party with her sister and their host, dressed in purple slacks as Professor Plum, greeted them with a glass of sherry in his hand. She immediately liked what she saw. "He was blond, blue-eyed, preppy, clean-cut, fit," Boss said in her grand jury testimony. "He was very physically attentive and, you know, guys may or may not make an effort to make sure you're having a good time. He was very attentive."

"I'm pretty sure we played the game Clue," said Tom Rizer, who went as Mr. Green, the character whose sexual proclivities would cost him his job with the State Department should they become known.

"Obviously Clark arranged this to meet Sandy," Rizer continued.

"He had already taken an interest in Sandy's sister, Julia, but she was taken. So when he heard that she had a sister . . . Well, it seemed to me it was love at first sight for both of them. Sandy was overwhelmed with him. He was a very handsome man."

On the witness stand, Sandra said Rockefeller engaged mostly in small talk at the Clue party, but shortly after she returned to Boston he called and said he'd like to see her again. "I thought it would be nice," she testified. On her next trip to New York, they started "light dating," as she described it, although she wasn't eager to launch into a new relationship, especially not a long-distance one. She was on a career track.

None of Boss's previous relationships had worked out, she said, in part because most of the men she had dated were intimidated by her intelligence. Rockefeller was different. He "made a big deal of celebrating [it], as opposed to saying, 'You'd be nice if you weren't so smart,' which, you know, was appealing." In court she admitted to having been attracted by the simple fact that someone like Clark Rockefeller "was very enthusiastic about the idea of getting to know me and being romantically involved."

"How did that make you feel?" the prosecutor asked.

"Good, flattered. I liked him."

Boss continued in her grand jury testimony, "He said his father's name was George Percy Rockefeller, and that he was related to the William line [of the Rockefeller family]. His mother's name was Mary Roberts, and she was from Virginia. His father was an engineer and had done some design work for the Navy. His mother was, I guess you could use the expression, a stay-at-home mom, but he described her activities as being kind of charity stuff and shopping.

"He said they had a lot of money. He said that he grew up at number 19 Sutton Place, which was a large town house that he pointed out to me in New York." An old-money enclave spanning just six blocks along the East River, Sutton Place was a likely neighborhood for a Rockefeller to have lived.

"He said they had houses in Maine and in New Hope, Pennsylvania, and Pound Ridge. They had a big boat, that kind of stuff."

Yet despite his wealth and status, Rockefeller stressed that he was just an ordinary man, Boss said. "He took an interesting approach, which was to sort of let it all out in an 'I'm a really subtle guy' way."

His life of privilege had been fraught with considerable pain, he told Boss. When he was two or three, he had fallen down the stairs in his family's home on Sutton Place, and the accident "affected his speech so that he was perfectly smart in learning, but he didn't talk," she said. His being rendered mute prevented him from going to school (except for a one-day stint at the Collegiate School, a boys' day school on the Upper West Side that dates back to 1628) and necessitated home tutoring.

He was diagnosed as "aphasic," she added, meaning language-impaired, until he experienced a miraculous breakthrough: one day a neighbor brought his dog over to the Rockefellers' home—he had asked them to dog-sit while he was away. "And the dog was in the town house, and he saw the dog and said, 'Woofness,' and then after that began to talk."

Boss said all of this with a straight face. That single word, "woofness," magically broke the spell, and Clark began to perform phenomenally in school. He was chosen to attend Yale University at age fourteen.

"Did he explain how a fourteen-year-old could attend Yale?" the prosecutor asked in court.

"What he said was there was an early entrance program and that occasionally young students were accepted," Boss responded. He loved to talk about his cherished days at Yale, she said—the friends he made, his classes, and how he excelled in his major, mathematics. He even opened up to her about the tragedy that befell him during his senior year.

"He told me that his parents wanted to come up and visit him," she recounted. Clark wanted to stay on campus that weekend, however, so he persuaded them to take one of the family's sports cars instead of one of the sedans; that way there wouldn't be enough room for him to ride with them around New Haven. On their way to see him, he told Boss, his mother lost control of the sports car and both she and his father were killed, leaving behind their only child, then eighteen. "He told me that his father's family had attempted to assume custody of him, but that he had been able to resist that, because he was eighteen, and so he said that he lived on his own in the town house on Sutton Place."

"Did you have . . . any reason to doubt what [Rockefeller] was saying?" the prosecutor asked. The entire courtroom seemed to take a deep breath in anticipation of Boss's response.

"No," she said.

The prosecutor pressed her. Did she believe him to be so intellectually superior that he could enter Yale at fourteen?

"Yes," she said.

"Why?"

"Two reasons: one, he was very intelligent—he was one of the most intelligent people I had ever known; and because I myself had been asked as a young child to go to college early, I knew that it was possible for intelligent children to occasionally be taken into university early, even though I didn't do that."

Boss's relationship with Rockefeller progressed quickly, she told the grand jury. "He was well read. He had read a lot of classic literature, which I liked. He was quite interested and dedicated to the church. We had a lot of similar philanthropic values and aspirations. He was very attentive, very polite, very kind—very complimentary of me."

She said she loved the fact that he didn't seem concerned about material wealth—it didn't seem to bother him that the "fortune" he said his father had left him was "sadly" encumbered by a lawsuit. Rockefeller explained to her that his father was "perceived" to have embezzled money while employed by the Navy. She also loved that he shared "a lot of my values about kind of changing the world" and, according to what he told her, devoted his life to helping others.

"He told me he was doing debt renegotiation for small countries," Boss said in court, explaining that he helped developing nations reduce and renegotiate their debts to banks.

By the time she moved to New York in the summer of 1993, working in debt markets with Merrill Lynch ("pricing derivatives," she testified), "We were definitely seeing each other as boyfriend and girlfriend." And when the summer job was over and she returned to Massachusetts to begin her second year at Harvard Business School, the relationship continued long distance. Boss would drive down to New York at least twice a month to pick him up—"he said he did not have a driver's license" due to an eye issue.

Although they had known each other only a matter of months, Boss said, "It was already, you know, quite romantic, and so it was a continuation of that vein. . . . We were talking quite seriously about getting married."

He had his quirks, but what smart, wealthy, well-bred person didn't? "He really liked *Star Trek*," she told the grand jury, "and made sort of a big fuss about always seeing *Star Trek* at a special time on Sunday night or whenever it was. He was sort of a little bit of a Trekkie. He was very eccentric in what seemed like a cute and lovable way about his dog. You know, he'd cook for the dog, brush the dog's hair every day. He made a big deal about 'I can't go to that party or that event unless I can bring my dog.' It seemed kind of endearing, but it was also eccentric."

The endearing outweighed the eccentric, and Sandra Boss fell in love with Clark Rockefeller. In the spring of 1994, he took her to the island of Islesboro, off the coast of Maine, a secluded spot where many wealthy people have summer homes. He brought along a ring with three simple diamonds from Tiffany & Co., which he knew would fit Sandy because he had gone shopping for it at the flagship Tiffany store on Fifth Avenue with her twin sister, Julia, who had tried it on, Boss later learned. He would later contend that he spent "every last penny" he had on the engagement ring.

Clark proposed and Sandra accepted, and not long after that the couple flew out to Seattle so that Clark could ask Sandra's father for her hand in marriage. William Boss found that both old-fashioned and endearing, and of course he said yes. As for Sandra's meeting Rockefeller's family, there was hardly anyone to meet. He was an only child, and his parents were dead. There was the woman he called his aunt, and her daughter, Alice Johnson, whom he called his niece, and of course he had taken Sandra over to meet them in their apartment in the United Nations Plaza. And, of course, they fell all over Clark as if they were indeed family, which by then Alice and her mother felt as if they were. "This is my cousin Alice, and my aunt," Clark said, and Alice and her mother quickly came to love Sandra as deeply as they loved Clark. "This is the kind of woman I want to be: smart, beautiful, independent," Alice Johnson would later say, adding that when Sandra's mother and father met her family, they were also duly impressed and absolutely convinced that their daughter was indeed marrying a Rockefeller. "They were a constant fixture in our lives for a couple of years," Sandra Boss told the grand jury of the Johnson family.

None of this made Boss suspicious, but there were some warning signs that Rockefeller might not make an ideal husband. "For the two years before we got married, he was almost always the nice, sweet, smart person who I had met," she continued. "A couple of times, though, I saw that he could get very angry, which made me nervous. One time I even said, 'I see that temper and I'm not sure about this.' And he said, 'Well, you've already made a commitment, because I've already settled my lawsuit for you.'" He was referring to the supposed embezzlement claim that the U.S. Navy had filed against his late father; he told her that the settlement had cost him $50 million, his entire inheritance. "He chose to settle the lawsuit . . . rather than putting me at risk financially over this situation," said Boss. "He explicitly stated that love was more important than money, and that he wanted to protect me."

When asked how she could have swallowed such an obvious lie, Boss said during cross-examination in court, "There's a difference between intellectual intelligence and emotional intelligence. I thought it was a big gesture, and I didn't think that he needed to do it, and I told him so." When the prosecutor suggested that she might have had the "common sense" to see through such a blatant ruse, she replied, "Probably

so. I mean, I'm not saying that I made a very good choice of husband.
I mean, it's pretty obvious that I had a blind spot, and all I'm saying is
that one can be brilliant and amazing in one area of one's life and really
stupid in another."

After getting her MBA from Harvard, Boss went to work for McKinsey & Company as an associate, earning approximately $80,000 a year.

"What was Clark Rockefeller doing for work at that time?" she was
asked during her grand jury testimony.

"He surprised me by saying that he had quit his debt renegotiation
work, but that he was starting to do consulting for Third World countries that had economic problems."

"Before the two of you got married, did he discuss any other source
of income that he had besides the debt restructuring or the Third World
consulting?"

"No. He, in fact, made a point of saying that he had been cleaned out
in his assets settling the lawsuit. So he kind of said, 'Take me as I am.'"

And she did. Who he was, however—and what he had done before
entering Boss's upwardly mobile life—would remain a mystery to her, at
least for the time being, something she seemingly never thought about,
much less asked her fiancé about.

Sandra's sister, Julia, and Charles Knapp beat Clark and Sandra to
the altar by six months. They were married in an elaborate ceremony
in St. Thomas Church, with a reception afterward in the Great Hall.
Julia and Charles were graduates of Yale, class of 1990, and Charles was
a member of the Whiffenpoofs, the hallowed Yale tradition, started in
1909, in which fourteen Yale seniors are selected to comprise the world's
oldest and most famous collegiate a capella singing group. So, of course,
Charles's class of the "Whifs," as they were called, sang at the wedding.

Not to be outdone, Sandra and Clark held their engagement party
on the same day as Sandra's sister's wedding, so guests just moved from
St. Thomas Church to Clark's apartment. "It was a Stilton and sherry
party," remembered one of the guests. "And the dog, Yates, kept lick-
ing the cheese. They kept telling the dog, 'Yates! No face on the table.'"

By then, everyone knew Sandra's fiancé's quirks and eccentricities. Even his birthday was odd and rare, special unto him. "I hosted his thirty-second birthday, along with Charles Knapp, in a beautiful room on the second floor of the Landmark Tavern in New York," said Tom Rizer. "Clark's birthday comes only every leap year, because he was born on the twenty-ninth of February, at least that's what he claimed."

Actually, his birthday was February 21, 1961. But again, who cared, or dared, question him as he continued to create his own folklore? By then, he had become a master at making people believe whatever he told them. Even the crowd he fell in with in New York, intelligent, extremely well-educated people who had attended the same privileged East Coast prep schools and colleges that Rockefeller claimed to have attended, were convinced he was somebody. "We always assumed that Sandy knew the full story [of who he really was], and just wasn't telling us," said John Wells. Added someone else who knew Rockefeller well: "We thought he was someone's [meaning a Rockefeller] illegitimate son, whose mother had been paid off and then died, and he was seizing the family name of his birth father who wouldn't acknowledge him, out of spite. It was like a parlor game between us. Julia, Sandy's sister, would never be any part of this. She was very upset about it. She just didn't want to talk about it."

I asked the obvious question: "Do you think Sandy believed everything Clark told her?"

"I think she wanted to," said the friend. "I asked her about it once, and she got really offended. I was drunk and rude, and I said, 'How do you know that he's really Clark Rockefeller and not some axe murderer on the lam?' She said, 'I'm his fiancée. I'm going to be his wife. I would think that he would tell me more about his past than he would tell you!'"

But however suspicious they were of Clark's life, his friends told me, the truth would outstrip their wildest speculations.

The Boss-Rockefeller wedding was held on October 14, 1995, in the Quaker Meeting House on the island of Nantucket, Massachusetts, the summer getaway spot of choice for many of the wealthiest people in America. There were only seven guests—"my sister, her husband, my parents, and three people who were associated with the Nantucket [Quaker] Meeting House," Sandra testified—plus one dog, Clark's Gordon setter.

But Sandra and Clark were both devout Episcopalians. Why were they married as Quakers? It was the result of another of his soon-to-be-famous snits, and once again it concerned his "niece," Alice Johnson.

"He went to the vicar of St. Thomas to see if she [Alice] could be a member of the church and be confirmed without going to the confirmation class," recalled Rockefeller's friend Tom Rizer. "After all, she was a Rockefeller, Clark insisted—she shouldn't have to go through any of *that*. And they turned him down. He said he wouldn't even go to St. Thomas again, because they turned him down. And so he became a Quaker."

He told Sandra a different story. "He said that he was having increasing problems at St. Thomas with people pressuring him to make donations, which is plausible," she told the grand jury. "It's a rich church, and they do ask people for money. He was excited about the simplicity and purity of the Society of Friends. It was very democratic and it was kind of, each individual's spiritual life was the only thing that mattered."

The historic Quaker Meeting House on Nantucket couldn't provide Rockefeller with much in the way of social connections, but those he had already gotten from St. Thomas. What the Quakers did offer was the ideal wedding ceremony for someone desirous of keeping his name and personal information out of the public record.

"If you want to have a wedding where you don't have to deal with legal stuff, Quaker is the way to go," said John Wells. Before the wedding, Sandra said, she "signed all of the legal forms to be given to the town clerk" and entrusted her husband with the task of mailing them in to be filed "so that we could get the marriage license. He one hundred percent assured me that everything was done."

He never sent the forms to the town clerk. Thus they were married without a license, in a ceremony that was strange, to say the least. First, there was the matter of Rockefeller's family. His parents were dead. Other Rockefellers had been due to attend the nuptials, Clark said, but at the last minute a problem arose and he disinvited all of them. Not to worry, he assured Sandra, she would meet them in the future. In their place, Yates, the only guest on the groom's side, would serve as "Best Dog."

Then there was the ceremony itself, held in the simple, stark Quaker Meeting House, which was built in 1838 to house the congregation that had previously met at the home of early Quaker Mary Coffin Starbuck. Yates ambled down the aisle, drool dribbling from his mouth, and the seven guests sat on stiff wooden pews as Rockefeller and Boss stood silently facing each other. "In a Quaker wedding, you sit around until somebody says something," explained one of the wedding guests, adding that the bride and groom recite their own vows. As Sandra Boss said during her grand jury hearing, "The thing that's interesting about the Society of Friends is that there is no officiant. When you go to a Quaker service, everyone kind of speaks as moved." The guest with whom I spoke couldn't recall what Rockefeller and Boss said to each other, only that "it was all over pretty quick, and we went out to a restaurant and had dinner in Nantucket."

Then the newlyweds retired to the quaint little house they had rented to enjoy their first night as husband and wife. They honeymooned for a week on Nantucket before returning to their lives in New York City.

Part Two

CHAPTER 11

"San Marino Bones"

A t roughly the same time that Clark Rockefeller launched his new life as the husband of Sandra Boss in New York City, a sign from the long-missing couple John and Linda Sohus rose up from the grave. Until then, John and Linda had been mainly forgotten, their disappearance unsolved and unnoticed by the world at large. Two people of little importance, they were soon erased from the memory of even those who had known and worked with them.

Only one person refused to forget them, Linda's best friend, Sue Coffman. From the moment Linda and John went missing—with their cockamamie story about going to work for some top-secret government spy program and those subsequent bizarre postcards sent by Linda from Paris—Coffman knew in her heart that something wasn't right. There was, as she would tell anyone who cared to listen, "a big hole in my life, a big question mark in my head." At times she felt she was going crazy trying to answer the endless questions and piece together the puzzle of her friends' disappearance.

"I'd have dreams," she said as we sat in the living room of her house in Orange, California, not far from Disneyland. A thin, intense woman, a wife and the mother of two children, she was still very much on a mission to find her best friend, and she printed chronologies she'd assembled of the mysterious case on her computer while showing me pictures and paraphernalia of the disappearance she had spent almost thirty years attempting to crack.

Linda Sohus was always central to her dreams, Sue Coffman said, and I tried to imagine the big, redheaded artist and science-fiction fanatic flying through her friend's sleep like one of her fancifully drawn horses. "Linda would show up in my dreams and say, 'What are you worrying about? I'm right here.'"

"Why didn't you call me?" Coffman would ask her friend.

"Well, I was busy," is all Linda would say.

Coffman came to feel that her dreams were omens, directives urging her to keep pressuring the cops to find out what had happened to Linda. "I was so excited in my dreams, because I thought I wasn't dreaming. I felt like I was in the here and now."

Several times the police responded to her incessant calls by saying they were reopening what was by then a missing persons case. But nothing new ever turned up. Sue read me a note from one detective early in the case. "He said, 'She's twenty-one. She can leave if she wants and go where she wants. There's nothing to investigate.' He said, 'Don't worry about it. Stop looking for them.'

"His research claims that Linda and John live in France and never want to be involved with their old lives again," she told me, adding, "Did I believe it? No."

Even the discovery of John and Linda's pickup truck in Greenwich, where it was almost bought by a local minister's son from the mysterious Christopher Crowe—who the authorities knew was really Christopher Chichester and before that Christian Karl Gerhartsreiter—didn't give the cops enough dots to connect. But Coffman couldn't abandon her quest for answers.

"Dear Kathy," she wrote Linda's half sister on March 15, 1990, five years after Linda and John had gone missing.

Hope you remember me—Linda's old friend from ages back? How are you and have you heard anything new about Linda's disappearance? . . . Even though it's been 5 years now (can you believe it?) I still can't accept her disappearance. Sometimes weeks will go by that I don't think of her, and then all of a sudden I'll have a dream or remember stuff we used to do, and I'll get angry at myself for not doing more to find her.

The last time I talked to you I had a new angle on the case, with their pick up truck having been found back east somewhere with new registered owners. I was really looking forward to having some answers, but after 3 months went by and no one called me from the detective's office, I called them back. That was around March of last year. I found out then that the detective I had established a rapport with, no longer was in that department.

Coffman would run into such problems repeatedly. Detectives moved on to new posts and dropped unsolved cases. Relatives such as Linda's half sister eventually decided they had to move on with their lives. "Kathy—I sent you this letter last year and never got a reply," Sue Coffman wrote Linda's half sister almost two years after her first letter. "If you're not interested in the search anymore (I realize it's been almost 7 years now—I guess Linda's either on witness relocation or dead), I'll understand. But can you please let me know you received this letter. That way, I'll stop bugging you, this is still on my mind."

She was relentless. After reading a Dear Abby column "about the Salvation Army being able to locate lost relatives," she sent off for a packet of forms. She was told that only blood relatives could fill them out. Finally, as a desperate, last-ditch effort, she sent a letter to a show she had watched on television, *Unsolved Mysteries*, starring Robert Stack, which presented facts and restaged scenes with actors about unsolved and frequently forgotten cases. She didn't know anyone who worked on the program. She just sent it over the transom to the production company's Burbank, California, address.

"WHATEVER HAPPENED TO LINDA CHRISTINE HOPE BLACK-FOOT MAYFIELD SOHUS?" she began her letter of September 23, 1993. In three single-spaced typed pages, she laid out the whole, implausible story of Linda's life and disappearance. "I don't have the money or the wherewithal to hire a private detective, and the police seem to think that since she's an adult she has the right to disappear (and now that it's been over 7 years, they say the file is closed and she is 'dead'), but there are just too many idiosyncrasies in this whole story. Below is a list of items pertaining to her disappearance that just don't jive."

She listed each and every one: the murky government spy job, the six cats Linda left behind, the pickup truck they abandoned on Lorain Road, which the bank could never find to repossess, and which later turned up in Greenwich, Connecticut. Coffman even confessed that she felt the cops might be in on it. "It may just be coincidence, but each time in the years past that I have contacted the Police Department regarding the disappearance, a different detective has been assigned to the case. Each time they seem to be getting close to an answer, that detective is conveniently transferred," she told *Unsolved Mysteries*.

She asked them to consider the story "for a possible segment," explaining that her life "has one big hole in the middle of it because I just don't know where she is. I want to get on with my life. . . . If she's alive, I want desperately to see her again. If she's dead, then I can close that chapter in my life and go on. It's the not knowing that drives me crazy. I can't just shrug it off. . . . We were too close."

At the bottom of the letter, she addressed her friend directly: "Linda, I have so many things to tell you about!"

Unsolved Mysteries sent her a form letter thanking her but expressing apparent lack of interest. Eight months after Coffman wrote the letter to *Unsolved Mysteries*, however, Linda Sohus, in a sense, answered it herself, in a typically surreal way.

"Holy shit!" a neighbor remembered someone screaming, after Jose Perez, the Bobcat operator working on the crew of California Pools, unearthed something peculiar shortly after noon on May 5, 1994. He was digging a thirty-six-foot-long pit for a swimming pool in the yard behind 1920 Lorain Road in San Marino. Once the home of Didi Sohus, the property was currently occupied by Bob and Martha Parada and their three-year-old son. They had bought the house in 1986 from Didi, the lady who had moved to a trailer park after the mysterious disappearance of her son, John; her daughter-in-law, Linda; and her tenant, Christopher Chichester.

The new owners had replaced the dilapidated old house with a new two-story brick dwelling. They had left the guest quarters out back intact, however, and decided to put in a swimming pool. On that May morning in 1994, Perez was in a Bobcat bulldozer digging when his blade struck something hard four feet beneath the ground. He assumed it was trash because of its rank smell. Nothing unusual, Perez later told the *Pasadena Star-News*, "I've done 6,000 pools and found a car, a horse, and a dog."

As he hopped down off the Bobcat to move the trash out of the way, his father, Jose Perez Sr., who was also on the digging crew, went over to see why the work had stopped. It turned out that the Bobcat's blade had broken a fiberglass box in pieces. Inside the container, the crew members could see plastic bags. Jose Perez Sr. grabbed a metal pipe and started poking at the contents of the bags.

That's when Jose screamed, according to Bill Woods, who heard the shout at his home a few doors down on Lorain Road. One of the bags contained a human skull, "with some hair," Perez told the local newspaper. "He dropped it on the ground and saw what looked to be teeth and a jaw," read the police report about the incident. The newspaper added, "Perez said he saw other pieces of bone, including a forearm and a portion of a spine, near the bag."

The newspaper report went on, "The Parada family was trying to remain calm as investigators tried to figure out who buried the body." One police lieutenant commented, "It's definitely a whodunit."

The pool crew flagged down a passing police car. One of the first officers to arrive on the scene was Tricia Gough. I met Gough, a statuesque brunette wearing a long-sleeved black T-shirt with a biker insignia, at a Starbucks coffee shop fourteen years later. She was now teaching school instead of investigating homicides, but, like most others who found their way into this story that day, she had an indelible memory of it.

"The outline of the pool had been dug, and then, kind of over to the side, that's where the remains were," she said, "in plastic bags, the kind you would go to the store to get—like grocery bags. The body was all bundled up in these bags, completely clothed, in jeans and—if I remember—a plaid shirt. There were socks. When we took it to the coroner's office, they cut the materials off. There were toe bones in the socks. It was a body completely wrapped in plastic."

Was it John Sohus? The diminutive size of the skeleton fit, as did the jeans and flannel shirt, which were what Sohus wore practically every day. As far as concrete evidence went, though, there wasn't any: DNA tests weren't possible, because John was adopted and his biological parents couldn't be found. Dental records could have solved the problem, but Gough was told that John's dentist's old files had been lost.

The police then focused their attention on Christopher Chichester, of whom Gough said many people in San Marino had been enamored. "People really wanted him to be a part of their scene," she said. "But from the description, he came off as a phony, a pretender who wanted to be in with money. All those people didn't see that. His story was that he came from a family of rich industrialists. Well, if you're that rich, why are you living in a guesthouse behind a house that is beat-up, weedy, and in ill repair?"

After it came to light that Chichester was an impostor, she said, suddenly everybody acted as if they had known it all along. "Especially all the lovely ladies," said Gough, meaning the San Marino widows who had taken the young stranger in, ferried him to and from church, swallowed him hook, line, and sinker.

"Apparently he hung out in Alhambra a lot," she said, referring to a town that borders San Marino. Gough learned that Chichester would go to Alhambra with John and Linda Sohus, who had friends there. "He liked to read, and he got a connection with Linda Sohus through that," she added. "He is one of those people who will say whatever you want to hear to fit in. Like, 'You like books? Oh, I do too!' You don't have to have read a book in your life. You can get the other person to talk. Like a chameleon, a changeling, he becomes what he needs to become to fit in."

"Who do you think killed John Sohus?" I asked her.

"I felt like Chichester was involved, and still do," she said. "The only thing I never really had a strong feeling about was the wife, Linda. My gut feeling was that she was probably involved in some way. I don't think she is dead. I think she is probably out there somewhere."

Out there somewhere with her six cats—which were the dead giveaway for Gough. As everyone said, Linda's cats were her children, and that was why Gough was convinced Linda had sent someone to pick them up just before they were to be put down, someone who knew her whereabouts after John Sohus was dead, someone who most likely knew Christopher Chichester. "I don't believe in coincidences like that," she said.

In January 1995, ten months before Clark Rockefeller married Sandra Boss, John and Linda Sohus were suddenly national news. An *Unsolved Mysteries* segment titled "San Marino Bones" appeared on television screens across America, thanks to Sue Coffman's unrelenting pressure and the revived interest in the case after the skeleton believed to be that of John Sohus was dug up in his mother's backyard.

The episode begins with the swirling *Unsolved Mysteries* logo. "May 1994, San Marino, California, just north of Los Angeles," intones the host, actor Robert Stack. "Excavation for a backyard swimming pool came to an abrupt halt when workmen made a grim discovery: three plastic bags and a fiberglass box containing dismembered sections of a human skeleton."

There is a close-up of two members of the pool excavation crew unwrapping a plastic bag containing a decomposing human skull, with a voice-over of a detective: "We didn't know who this person was, and we were later told by uniformed officers from San Marino that in 1985 the people that lived in that house had reported two people missing."

Then the camera cuts to photographs of John and Linda Sohus on their wedding day, the runty computer geek in a gray suit and aviator glasses alongside his bride, a gargantuan gal with a white veil billowing around her face, her eyes unfocused and staring off into the distance. "The two missing persons were John Sohus and his wife, Linda, both in their late twenties," says Robert Stack. "Their sudden disappearance had mystified everyone who knew them. A grisly discovery was a macabre twist in a nearly ten-year-old mystery. It suddenly appeared that either John or Linda Sohus may have been the victim of foul play."

Stack walks toward the camera in a book-lined office. "Detectives probing the disappearance encountered a cast of characters that might have been dreamed up by a mystery writer. Though married for two years, John and Linda still lived with John's mother, Didi Sohus, by all accounts an alcoholic. However, the most intriguing character would prove to be a mysterious young man who went by the name of Christopher Chichester."

The screen fills with the picture of the bespectacled individual in question, wearing a suit and tie, his mouth agape in what appears to be his usual high-society lockjaw position.

The show then reenacts the life of the missing couple, their claustrophobic existence under the roof of Didi Sohus, leading up to "the break they had been hoping for"—an important, top-secret job with the government—and their disappearance. The show most dramatically recreates Didi's exchanges with the couple's friends and relatives, and ultimately the police, some of whom are portrayed by the real officers who investigated the case.

"Hello," the actress playing Didi slurs drunkenly after picking up a jangling telephone. She is wearing a ratty pink housecoat and holds an early-afternoon cocktail in her weathered hand.

"Is Linda back from her trip yet?" asks the actress playing Linda's half sister.

"I'm not supposed to tell you anything," Didi says defiantly. Then, after pause, she adds, "A mission!"

"A mission? *What* mission? What are you talking about?" asks the half sister.

Giving only scant details about the government job that John and Linda ran off to accept, Didi abruptly ends the conversation by announcing, "Well, that's all I can tell you," and returns to her drink.

"Didi refused to identify the person she called her source," says Robert Stack. "With no evidence of foul play, the authorities were powerless to investigate further."

The *Unsolved Mysteries* segment then recounts the facts of Didi's removal from San Marino and her death. "Nine months later, the case unexpectedly sprang to life," says Stack as the camera cuts from Didi's ravaged face to John and Linda's white pickup truck, cruising to a stop beside what appears to be a church. An actor resembling Christopher Chichester hops out of the truck and walks up to a young man holding a broom on the church steps—the minister's son.

The reenactment shows Chichester, who has now become Christopher Crowe, showing off the truck to the minister's son, explaining that he doesn't have the title and the buyer will need to get it himself from the California Department of Motor Vehicles. After sending off for the title—and being informed that there is an outstanding lien on the truck, due to an unpaid bank loan—the minister's son decides against purchasing the vehicle. But the title search has alerted the San Marino police that the truck belonging to the missing couple is in Greenwich, and eventually leads to Greenwich police detective Daniel Allen discovering that "Mr. Chichester and Mr. Crowe were the same individual."

The screen fills again with the image of Crowe/Chichester posing in a suit and tie.

"It was a stunning discovery," says Stack. "Crowe, Chichester—by any name, the enigmatic ex-tenant seemed to be the one person who might be able to shed light on the Sohuses' disappearance. But Christopher Crowe, alias Christopher Chichester, had vanished again. . . ."

Consequently, the investigation stalled again—until the dismembered skeleton was uncovered in May of 1994."

Forensic anthropologists showed that the remains were those of a slight young man, which was of course consistent with the physical description of John Sohus. But there were no dental records to prove that the body was actually his. Even more perplexing for the investigators was the state of the corpse—there were no bullet holes or other incriminating evidence to prove that the remains were the result of murder. But the bones, which were buried in three separate plastic bags, with the skull encased in a fourth, made the investigators suspect foul play.

Then another stunning discovery is revealed with the reenactment of a scene in which police detectives enter the guesthouse behind Didi's house. They spray the cement floor with a chemical called luminol, which, Stack explains, "will emit a distinctive glow when it comes into contact with blood, even when the stains were wiped away years before."

There was more about the luminol test in the documents I had pertaining to the case: the elderly woman who lived in the Sohus guesthouse before Christopher Chichester had sewn ticking—a decorative strip of cloth—along the bottom of the sofa. When Chichester left the guesthouse, he took the ticking with him, even though, the report noted, "It would only fit on that particular sofa." Two patches of carpeting were also missing.

When the detectives arrived at the guesthouse in 1994, they felt that because the ticking had been taken, perhaps it held some "incriminating evidence," meaning human blood. That was why they decided to test the floor with luminol. The report explained that the date of the luminol test—June 21, 1994—was the summer solstice, the longest day of the year. Luminol tests require total darkness so that any traces of blood will glow. The investigators had to wait until 2 a.m., when the moon had gone down. "Luminol was applied to the cement floors in the guesthouse on the former Sohus property," says Stack. "Within moments, it would become apparent if there was evidence of murder."

The detectives, wearing gas masks, turn off the lights and stare down dramatically at the floor, on which a large splotch lights up—"a copious amount of something put on that floor, and in our opinion that was blood," explains the San Marino police detective on the show.

"The telltale glow was unmistakable," says Stack. "But whose blood? Was John Sohus murdered in the guesthouse and buried in the back-yard? If so, what happened to Linda? Officially, both John and Linda Sohus are still missing, perhaps having the time of their lives gallivant-ing across Europe."

The segment ends with Robert Stack's voice-over with a picture of Christopher Chichester Crowe. "Authorities would like to speak to the young man known as Christopher Chichester. They now know that his real name is Christian Gerhartsreiter, a native of Germany. He speaks fluent English and has used the names Christopher Crowe and Chris-topher Mountbatten. Gerhartsreiter was born in 1961. He is five feet eight, 150 pounds, and has very thin, dark blond hair. While he is not a suspect, authorities hope he can shed some light on the disappearance of John and Linda Sohus. If you have any information about this case, please contact the Los Angeles County Sheriff's Department Homicide Bureau or call your local law enforcement agency."

The authorities now knew almost everything—their investigator had determined the impostor's real name, birth date, nationality, and description, even his last known whereabouts and assumed name in Greenwich, Connecticut.

And yet they really knew nothing, because he had already shed all traces of the man sought by the authorities and—thanks to *Unsolved Mysteries*—America's television audience. He was no longer known by any of the names in his past or in the public record. Now he was Clark Rockefeller, and at the time of the *Unsolved Mysteries* segment he was living a grand life on the Upper East Side of New York City, with his Harvard Business School fiancée, the smart, beautiful, and absolutely oblivious Sandra Boss.

CHAPTER 12

The Last Will and Testament of Didi Sohus

In hopes of getting to the bottom of what happened in San Marino, I arranged to speak with the lead investigator on the Linda and John Sohus case, Timothy Miley, a sergeant in the homicide bureau of the Los Angeles County Sheriff's Department. We met in a hotel bar, and Miley, who had worked hundreds of homicides, told me about perhaps the most twisted and daunting case of his career.

"This is like a thousand-piece jigsaw puzzle," he said. "There are going to be some gaps in it, but I think you're still going to see the picture and you'll be able to tell what it is."

He then told a story that seemed plucked from the reels of film noir that had so enamored the young immigrant through all the stages of his identity. Miley began by explaining how Christopher Chichester made his living in San Marino. "He was getting money here and there from a lot of the little old ladies. There were a whole bunch of little scams where he was trying to talk their husbands into $10,000 here and $15,000 there." Although no one was willing to admit to actually having given Chichester money, Miley felt sure that some of them had. "He had enough to live on, but he never had a job."

Miley continued, "I don't think he's brilliant; he's a manipulator. He finds people who are manipulable and he works that." In his alcoholic and dementia-stricken landlady, Miley suggested, Chichester saw the chance for a major score: Didi Sohus had a valuable home, plus antiques her mother had left her and sizable investments in stocks and bonds. He allegedly set about manipulating her into leaving him her estate.

Chichester's main obstacle would have been Didi's sole heir, John Sohus. She would have to disinherit her beloved son in order to make anyone else the beneficiary of her will. And that is exactly what Didi did after John took off on his "secret mission." Following John and Linda's disappearance, Didi revised her will to state, "I intentionally and with full knowledge of any consequences, specifically disinherit and omit any provisions for John Robert Sohus . . . in this will." In Miley's view, "To get her to change her will, he had to lead her to believe that John and Linda had abandoned her, didn't care about her anymore."

The investigator laid out his theory about what happened to John and Linda. First, Chichester convinced the couple that he had gotten them government jobs in New York. They were to fly east separately, John before Linda. The day of Linda's planned departure, however, she was seen crying in her pickup truck in Loma Linda, California, in front of the home of Elmer and Jean Kelln, the couple Chichester (then Gerhartsreiter) had met while hitchhiking in Germany. Chichester had gone to the Kellns' to pick up some boxes. John Sohus was likely dead by this time, killed by "blunt force trauma. A flat hard object across the back of the head," according to the coroner's criminalist, Miley said, but Linda could not have guessed that. She was likely crying because Chichester kept changing the plans on her. She was supposed to be on her way to New York, but instead she was still stuck in California. She was confused and scared, and perhaps beginning to suspect that Chichester had been lying to her and John all along.

I asked Miley if he thought Linda and Chichester were romantically involved or somehow in cahoots.

"I don't," he said. "Everyone else does."

"So what happened to Linda?" I asked.

"I think she's dead, buried somewhere out in the desert," said Miley. "I don't think she's alive in France and mailing postcards." To back up his contention that the postcards that Linda's friends and family received from her were phony, Miley noted, "She never had a passport, never entered or exited the country. She had no financial means of doing this . . . and she was not sophisticated enough to get a fake passport or a fake ID."

Chichester remained on Lorain Road for approximately four months after John and Linda vanished, "to continue whatever manipulation he had going on with Didi," Miley said. With the young couple gone, Chichester ruled the roost. "He had absolute run of the house. So one can insinuate that that means he was controlling Didi at that stage."

I knew a bit about the period Chichester had spent alone with Didi in her house after John and Linda's departure, both from the sheaf of documents I had been given during the trial in Boston and from my interviews with neighbors. One resident recalled that Chichester had come over to borrow a chainsaw, which the neighbor thought was odd, because Chichester was so slight that he seemed incapable of performing any serious manual labor. "He said he needed it to cut brush," the neighbor later told the police. A San Marino police report quoted another neighbor who said that around that same time Chichester was burning something in the fireplace at 1920 Lorain Road. The smell was "putrid, like nothing I've ever smelled before," the woman said.

In May 1985, Chichester invited his friend Dana Farrar, the film student at USC, over for a game of Trivial Pursuit. When she and another friend arrived, they discovered that Chichester wasn't in the guest dwelling out back but in the main house. Didi Sohus was nowhere to be seen. They sat on the patio, where Chichester had the game set up. Several times he went into the house for iced tea and other refreshments, acting as if he owned the place. "They're away. They won't mind," he said when Farrar asked him where his landlady and her children were.

At one point, Dana looked up from the game and noticed something strange. The backyard had been dug up, obviously very recently. It looked as if someone had made a big hole and then filled it in with fresh dirt.

"What's going on in the yard, Chris?" she asked.

"Oh, nothing, really," he said. "Just having some plumbing problems."

Tim Miley also spoke of Don and Linda Wetherbee, whom I had come across in my own research into the life of Didi Sohus. They lived twenty minutes from San Marino, in a trailer park in the city of La Puente, where they operated a business selling trailers, Linda's Mobile Homes.

Although they were a world away from the cosseted bubble of San Marino, the Wetherbees came to be Didi Sohus's closest friends in her final years, tending to her after she had been "abandoned" by her son. They handled the sale of Didi's house on Lorain Road after she supposedly became too ill and destitute to live there alone, and they sold her a mobile home practically next door to their own, in La Puente, becoming her sole caretakers. They also became the administrators and beneficiaries of her will. Don Wetherbee died in 2001, and Linda seven years later, but Tim Miley had tracked Linda down shortly before she died. She was old and frail, living in a nursing home, but her mind was still sharp, and she laid out what the sheriff's investigator called "the foundation for a confession."

"She talked very low in volume, real meekly," giving answers to "pointed questions," Miley said.

"How did you meet Didi?" was one of the first questions he asked.

"Through the guy in the guesthouse," she replied.

"The Wetherbees get introduced to Didi. They take over her life," Miley told me. "Upon selling her house, the Wetherbees borrow $40,000 from Didi. That's in her will, and that $40,000 loan is forgiven when the final will is executed."

"What happened to that $40,000?" Miley asked Linda Wetherbee.

"We gave it to him [Chichester]," she said, adding that it was part of the deal they had made with him—his fee for introducing them to Didi.

After Didi's death, Chichester was to receive another payment, perhaps as much as $100,000, which he and the Wetherbees figured would represent 50 percent of her estate—the proceeds from the sale of her house, her trailer home, her investments, and her personal possessions.

Did Chichester tell the Wetherbees the real story about Didi Sohus and her missing son and daughter-in-law? Trying to discover more, I contacted two of the Wetherbees' decendants. They weren't interested in talking. Didi Sohus's only living relative would not discuss the murder investigation but did say that when he visited her in 1986, Didi was in ill health, hard of hearing, and desperately lonely. "She wanted me to move out there and live with her," he said. (He declined.) As for Christopher Chichester, the attorneys who would represent him as Clark Rockefeller adamantly maintained that he had nothing whatsoever to do with the disappearance of John and Linda Sohus.

With Didi under the watchful eyes of Don and Linda Wetherbee, Chichester drove out of San Marino in mid-1985 in John and Linda Sohus's truck, and possibly with $40,000 of Didi's money—a sizable sum in those days—to launch his new life on the East Coast as Christopher Crowe. "It was his ante into the game, so he could go be somebody," said Miley. "Once Chichester inserts the Wetherbees into Didi's life, he disappears, because that's what he's supposed to do. That's the plan. Now they take over. Now she's distraught, because her adviser—which was him [Chichester]—is gone. So she puts all of her trust in the Wetherbees."

He didn't return to San Marino until November 1988. By that time he had become Christopher Crowe, and he visited his old home after having gone to California with Ralph Boynton to try out to be a bond salesman for Kidder Peabody. Reverting to the character of Christopher Chichester, he spent only one day in San Marino; Didi Sohus's estate had just been settled, and he was there to collect his share. He never got it, however, because the Wetherbees "double-crossed him," as Miley put it. "He shows up in '88 when they execute the will, and they tell him to go fuck himself. They've spent the money."

"We told him no, we couldn't give him any more money, we'd lost it all in bad investments," Linda Wetherbee said to Miley, adding that she and her husband felt that all of the proceeds from Didi's estate were rightfully theirs—fair compensation for the time they had spent with her before her death. "I took care of her for the rest of her life," Linda said. "I didn't just take the money. We drove her to her doctors' appointments, and we were her companions during those last two years."

At that point, a nurse entered Linda's room and insisted that Miley suspend his interview with her and come back another day. "The next time I went to talk to her, she was dead," the investigator said.

The whole damned case was like that, he lamented: witnesses dying, district attorneys leaving their jobs just as they had begun to make progress, detectives becoming frustrated with the labyrinthine case and moving on, allowing the "person of interest" not just to remain free, but to climb the social ladder in the shoes of a Rockefeller.

After Clark and Sandra's Quaker wedding in October 1995, something strange happened. The groom wanted everyone off Nantucket—Sandra's parents, sister, and brother-in-law—so that he could be alone with his wife. They complied with his wishes, taking the ferry back to the mainland. It was then clear to everyone that Rockefeller was calling the shots in the marriage.

"At the time of your marriage or within the next few weeks or months, did you detect any change in your relationship?" Sandra was asked on the witness stand in the Boston courtroom.

"Well, I would say that the defendant, then my husband, started to show more temper," she answered. "I had seen him be unhappy on a few occasions in the past and he always was very apologetic afterwards. He began to show temper more. And the second big change was he became much more directive about my movements."

He insisted on walking his wife to and from work every day, she testified, and began being "less supportive" of her personal activities, including trying to control the time she spent with her friends. He became increasingly critical in his comments, she said, telling her, "This person is, you know, stupid or tacky or something. You really shouldn't spend time with them."

They moved into an apartment at Fifty-fifth Street and Sixth Avenue in New York. Rockefeller was supposedly running Asterisk LLP, which, he told Sandra and others, advised Third World countries on their finances. "So that they would make good decisions about where to set interest rates and spending levels," Sandra explained. He didn't make any money in his job, because the nations that saw him as their financial savior were dirt-poor, and he felt that charging them a consulting fee would be "unconscionable."

It seemed completely plausible. While it is now clear that her husband's job was a sham, Sandra had a real career at McKinsey & Company. "We work for large institutions and we determine with them what their problems are that they're not solving themselves and then we help them structure work project plans to solve the problem. That's what I do," she told the court.

Despite her husband's increasingly controlling manner, she rose swiftly up the McKinsey corporate ladder—eventually leading the company's work for Senator Charles Schumer of New York and New York City mayor Michael Bloomberg—which Rockefeller would later say was partially owing to the unspoken influence of his name, "wherever it was to her advantage," as he put it in an interview. "She usually did so in a very understated way, calling special attention to it by keeping it extra quiet. Sort of the: *Psst, she is married to a Rockefeller.*" As a friend of Sandra's added, "Everybody knew she was married to a Rockefeller, and she could be all modest about it, like she didn't care. But she cared."

Her husband wielded his powerful name in much the same way: the less he said about it, the more it stood out. And no one had reason to doubt the authenticity of the name, just as no one had reason to doubt the authenticity of the art that hung on the walls of the newlyweds' apartment. The paintings gave credence to the name and vice versa.

So why couldn't he just sell a piece of art—which would certainly have fetched millions—to contribute financially to the marriage? Sandra replied that he told her the paintings were held in a family trust. "He said, 'It's a great inheritance and there's a limit on selling it. We can sell it in ten years.'"

Until then it was theirs to enjoy. "We celebrated our first art purchase, a large painting by Rothko, on a cold, wet New York City afternoon," read an article titled "The Spitting Image" in the magazine *ARTnews*, which was attributed to Sandra Boss but believed to have been written by her husband. "Our dealer and a Rothko expert had just arrived at our apartment when Yates, our 85-pound Gordon Setter, returned from his walk, jumped on his usual spot on the sofa, and shook his head. A four-inch swath of saliva emerged from his mouth." It landed on the Rothko, and Rockefeller nonchalantly wiped it off with a paper towel, which Sandra wrote was the proof of her husband's insistence that fine art and purebred dogs could live together harmoniously, despite their "slight incompatibilities."

Mr. and Mrs. Rockefeller were similarly different yet compatible, at least in the beginning. "They were both very stiff, very formal; she was very distant in some ways, equally awkward," said a friend who had gone to dinner with them on several occasions, which began with cocktails at one of Rockefeller's clubs, usually the Lotos, the tony literary club housed in a Vanderbilt mansion, where the staff always greeted Clark with a chorus of "Good evening, Mr. Rockefeller."

Once, they went to a club that had a splendid view of the skyline. Gazing out the window, the friend recalled, "I said, 'Look, Clark, you can see Rockefeller Center from here!' And he reached into his pocket and pulled out a key, and he said, 'Yes, I have the key right here!' That's really the first moment I smelled bullshit. I just thought, 'There's no fucking way there's one key to Rockefeller Center.' What did Sandra say? Probably nothing. I just remember the way she would say his name—absolutely two syllables: 'Oh, Cla-aaark!' And he would call her *Sohn*-dra."

Although the friend's husband, a respected professional with a recognizable name, was impressed, she wasn't. "I was repulsed by the name-dropping and the excessive wealth and the khaki pants and the polo shirt. Also, they weren't really people that you wanted to be around. They weren't warm. I found myself just kind of looking at the clock, thinking, 'Please, God, let this dinner be over.' I think other people were excited to be with a Rockefeller. It didn't matter how awkward it was to be with them. It was worth it, because they were Rockefellers."

The grandiose career, the silk ascots, and the museum-quality art collection (whose authenticity was never questioned) all gave credence to the con.

As her position at McKinsey grew, Sandra was away from her husband more and more, which left him with plenty of time to walk Yates in Central Park, where, he liked to say, "My dog was very much in love with Amelia, Henry Kissinger's dog." Broadway producer Jeffrey Richards crossed paths with Rockefeller while walking his dog through the park one day. They got to talking, and Richards told him he was producing a new play by David Ives, who had written *All in the Timing*. Rockefeller exclaimed, "I've seen that play *six times*!" He then hinted that he might like to become a backer of Ives's next play. It would look quite wonderful to have a Rockefeller on one's résumé, thought Richards, who arranged to introduce his new potential investor to Ives. Rockefeller offered to fly the playwright to the south of France on his jet, which he kept at Teterboro, the airport for private planes in New Jersey. However, neither the jet nor the investment ever materialized.

At home, Clark grew ever more focused on Sandra and her work. "Particularly in the early years, he was unhappy with the limited amount that I earned at my job and put a lot of pressure on me about it," she testified. "I observed that *he* could get a job that paid, and contribute, and he said that was what he was doing in this nonprofit advisory arena that was very important and would lead to big things."

What were those big things? "He said he was expecting that he might get an appointment of some kind as a result of the work he was doing," said Sandra.

In cross-examination, the defense attorney Jeffrey Denner suggested that Rockefeller's claims regarding high-level appointments—not to mention the $50 million he said he had paid to the U.S. Navy to settle his late father's embezzlement lawsuit—might have stretched a normal person's credulity.

"Now, you are an astute economist and business consultant, are you not?" the lawyer asked.

"At the time I was a twenty-six-year-old. I knew nothing about this kind of stuff," she replied.

Sandra's busy schedule at McKinsey gave Clark, who had no work of his own to do, even more time to engage in what was becoming his consuming occupation: walking his dog and collecting new friends. One was an artist named William Quigley, whose work was bought by politicians, entertainers, and business leaders. One day a friend informed him that she had been walking her dog in Central Park when a short man with a Gordon setter bumped into her.

"She said, 'Bill, this guy took me to his house, and his art collection is unbelievable!'" Quigley told me. We were sitting in his studio in SoHo, in lower Manhattan, where his large, bright canvases were scattered all around us. A somewhat stocky man with long hair and an amiable demeanor, he quickly warmed up about Rockefeller, pulling out letters and other mementos from the copious time he had spent with the purported connoisseur. He said that his friend, who was Canadian, had never heard of the Rockefeller family. But the art stunned her. "You have to see it!" she urged Quigley, who was living in Los Angeles at the time. To sweeten the pot, she told Quigley she had shown her new friend transparencies of his work, and the great collector was *impressed.* "He wants to meet you!" she exclaimed.

"And I said, 'Well, who is it?'"

The artist shot me a wry smile. "She said, 'I really don't know. He's got a really big name, from a big American family, and I just forget.'"

"And I was like, 'How can you not know? Is it Vanderbilt? Mellon?'"

"No, something longer," the friend said.

They went round and round, but she couldn't remember, until the next day, when she called Quigley and blurted out, "His name is Clark and he's a *Rockefeller*!"

Quigley almost dropped the phone.

His friend had been walking her dog with a Rockefeller? The artist was floored—even more so when his friend told him, "Yeah, and he's a really, really sweet guy. You've got to meet him."

Quigley flew to New York and his friend set up the meeting. Arriving in the lobby of the collector's apartment building, Quigley found a slight man dressed in what had become his daily uniform: baseball cap, polo shirt, blue blazer, khaki pants—the picture of preppydom. The man reeked of old money, good breeding, and impeccable taste. Immediately, Quigley knew he'd found Clark Rockefeller.

"Oh, you must be Quigley," Rockefeller said coolly, employing the single name he would use to address the artist from that point forward.

They went up to Rockefeller's apartment, where the great man offered the artist a glass of sherry, but he didn't show him the art. Not yet. He had learned the power of restraint by then, how not showing all of his cards at once only added to his mystique. He asked Quigley how long he would be in town.

"Three days," Quigley replied.

After some small talk, the artist took his leave. Two days passed, with no call from Rockefeller. Then, on the night before Quigley's departure, his phone rang. "Quigley, I would like you to come up to my apartment and see the art," said Rockefeller, instructing him to arrive at 10 p.m., when he would be taking his dog for his nightly walk.

They took the dog for a long walk around the park. Finally, Rockefeller said he was ready to return to the apartment and show his new friend his art collection. "We go into the apartment," Quigley remembered. "It's probably by this time ten-thirty, and I walk into this collection. I had been reading Lee Seldes's *The Legacy of Mark Rothko* at the time, one of the greatest books I've ever read. It really gives you an inside story of the business of the art world." Suddenly he saw on one wall *Black on Grey*, one of Rothko's late landmark works, a version of which would sell for $10 million at Christie's auction house in 2007. "That legitimized everything for me," said Quigley. "I was like, *Are you kidding?*

"Down the hallway I see another Rothko," Quigley continued. "Then I turned into the living room, a modest-sized room, which didn't have a lot of elaborate furniture. Two black sofas with a lot of dog hair on them, and a little coffee table. Light hardwood floors that were kind of worn. It wasn't anything that impressive."

But there on the wall was another canvas almost inconceivable for a residence. "A ten-foot Barnett Newman," he said, referring to the abstract expressionist pioneer who died in 1970. He added, "With a brown swipe on the bottom left-hand corner that he said his dog did. He was muddy one day and got brown dirt on the bottom of the painting, and Clark just left it."

So typical of an aristocrat, Quigley thought. But there was more. "Two Clyfford Still paintings—one of my favorite artists," he said. "*Large* paintings. And then a Robert Motherwell over his fireplace. And I remember there were either two or three Rothkos."

The value was incalculable, but that wasn't the main thing for the artist. The main thing was that all that art was right there under one roof, and not in a museum, which left him reeling. "I was very, very excited. Impressed. Not impressed like, 'Wow, I met a Rockefeller.' That was definitely part of the equation, but . . ." He seemed at a loss for words.

"I was really overwhelmed," he said. "I mean . . . *Mondrian.* And I was looking at them very closely. I never had any doubts that they were legitimate, never thought that they were reproductions or anything. I looked at them very closely and I thought, 'Wow, these are amazing paintings.' And I felt like I had a bit of a relationship with a lot of these artists. I knew a lot of their work. I was showing with Manny Silverman at the time, and Manny is the premier dealer for this type of work in the United States, maybe. These guys were my heroes. So I think that's what made Clark and me get along so easily in the beginning, because I actually knew the history of abstract expressionism. That was my forte."

Quigley and Clark spoke for about forty-five minutes. "I don't even think we sat down. I was so overwhelmed by the paintings. And then I petted the dog a little bit more, and then he said, 'Well, it's getting close to my bedtime, and it's getting late. So let's just stay in touch, and I'll communicate with you.'"

Quigley flew back to Los Angeles, and he and Rockefeller stayed in touch. Clark even helped him with his Web site, as he had done with so many friends. "Clark and I started to develop a friendship by e-mail and by phone."

Soon, however, Quigley moved to New York, where his affiliation with the important collector intensified. Later, when Rockefeller hit the headlines and Quigley was besieged by the media, he released a statement about his friendship with the supposed scion of the great family:

> It seemed he knew everyone in the art world, although he hated the idea of art for investment. He was a purist with impeccable taste, and we had a wonderful dialogue simply based on this. I would go to galleries where the dealer would pull out a whole collection of an artist's work because Clark made a phone call.
>
> Clark knew more about the history and aesthetics of art than most artists I meet. He was extremely well versed and schooled in art history and had very strong viewpoints on certain painters and artists. I was both complimented and excited about the romanticized, historic affiliation of being courted by a Rockefeller. Obviously, the family owned some of the greatest artists of the twentieth century. After seeing the collection I never doubted his identity. He took me to extravagant social clubs, where everyone referred to him as Mr. Rockefeller.

Although I have been fortunate to have met many great people who have supported my work from all walks of life, the dynamics of this particular relationship instilled additional confidence and faith that what I was pursuing in my paintings may have some historic merit.

In the back of his mind, Quigley hoped that his new friend might be interested in purchasing some of his art. But very soon what began as a business relationship developed into a friendship. Quigley became immersed in the great man's life. They settled into a routine of sorts, meeting at 3 p.m. sharp at one of Rockefeller's private clubs, usually the Lotos. "We'd sit in the little library and discuss the weekly events."

Everyone in the Lotos knew him. There was even a list of members posted in a window box at the entrance to the club. Quigley saw the name L. Rockefeller, which of course referred to the esteemed naturalist and philanthropist Laurance Rockefeller. And near that: C. Rockefeller.

"Quigley, if I made you a member here—and maybe I can get the yearly fee reduced for you—we could put a Q above R on the list, Quigley and then C. Rockefeller," said Clark, seeming to relish the idea of helping his friend gain entry into one of his clubs.

On rare occasions Sandy would join them, but most of the time she was working. At that time she was involved in a major McKinsey project in Toronto, which necessitated continual travel. That left the two men to traipse around New York City. Sometimes Rockefeller would invite a distinguished guest to join them, as he did once at the Metropolitan Club. "He was a professor from Harvard," said Quigley. "Very intellectual. And all they did was talk about quantum physics and literature, but mainly about Star Wars and quantum physics. I was in the middle of these two guys, and it was like Ping-Pong. I couldn't keep track of what they were talking about."

In the library of the Lotos Club, Rockefeller might enjoy a midafternoon Manhattan cocktail. On one of these cocktail hours, Quigley found his friend staring for an interminable time at the bookshelves that surrounded them. There were literally hundreds of books, but it seemed that one in particular had perturbed him. Finally, Rockefeller rose and plucked a volume from the shelf, turned it around, and put it back so that you couldn't see the title on the spine.

"I just couldn't look at *that* any longer," Clark said.

Quigley got up to look at the title: *Titan*, the biography of John D. Rockefeller by Ron Chernow.

From the library, they would retire to the club's dining room, where Clark would usually order the same things, which Quigley sensed were touchstones of his youth. "Oh, let's have the oysters Rockefeller!" he would exclaim as the waiters hovered and the eyes of the members were directed his way.

It quickly became a tradition: oysters Rockefeller with a Rockefeller. "Quigley, do you know why they call them oysters Rockefeller?" Clark asked on one occasion, after the dish of oysters baked in spinach arrived at their table. "Because they're *green*."

Clark also relished dining at the Seventh Regiment Mess, the restaurant in the Park Avenue Armory, which was something of a club for its well-heeled regulars. "We've been members for years," he told Quigley in the historic room where "Uncle David"—the only surviving grandchild of John D. Rockefeller—often ate. "Clark always used the word 'grand,'" Quigley remembered. "Everything we ate, or everything we talked about, he would say, 'Oh, isn't this *grand*!' I love that word. I just thought it was a real signature of Clark."

At the end of many a meal of the beef ribs and succotash that were the Seventh Regiment Mess's specialty, Rockefeller would fold his napkin and exclaim, "Isn't this just grand!" If it was an extra-grand evening, Quigley recalled, he would add, "'It's a peach melba night!' And then he would order peach melba, and there we were, two grown men, sitting there eating parfaits."

As for buying a piece of art by his friend, that enterprise had a less than grand end. Despite his promises, Rockefeller hesitated to purchase

a Quigley painting—they were then selling for approximately $10,000.
Still, he wanted to ensure that others did by enlisting one of the world's
great art dealers, Larry Gagosian, to represent the artist. "Some people
are after that guy, and he never calls back. With me, he calls too much,"
Rockefeller told Quigley.

He called the Gagosian Gallery and said he wanted to buy a Quigley.
One of Gagosian's associates immediately contacted the artist, and just
like that, Quigley was asked to send over transparencies of his work.
"Tomorrow, Sandy and I will go to Gagosian in New York and look at
your portfolio," Rockefeller wrote in an e-mail to Quigley on October
11, 1998. "We will take along a very important person from the Whitney Museum, and we will place an order for twelve paintings. . . . This
operation should impress Gagosian quite a bit."

Rockefeller repeatedly assured Quigley that price was no object
when it came to purchasing art. He wrote as much in a letter of recommendation for the artist:

> To Whom It May Concern:
>   Mr. Quigley asked me to provide references of his talent,
> the financial value of his works and his financial potential
> as an artist. I must consider any collector asking such a
> reference totally unfit to own art of any kind. In short, I
> consider Mr. Quigley one of the greatest talents of our time,
> and feel convinced that history will judge him so. I own one
> of the largest private collections of modern art and I strongly
> believe that Mr. Quigley's works will stand on equal footing
> with works by many of the greatest artists in my collection.
> I do not know about Mr. Quigley's prices or whether they
> represent value. For every work that I own, I've always paid
> with a blank check and asked my banker never to bother to
> tell me the amount. I consider this practice the only way to
> build trust between living artists and real collectors. The
> question of whether I consider Mr. Quigley's works a so-called

good investment, I can only reply that I truly loathe anyone
who buys art with no motives other than profit and greed. I
sincerely hope that so-called art investors will lose every last
cent on their purchases and beyond. Unfortunately, they would
not with a Quigley.

He signed the letter with only his last name, in imposing swirls and
downstrokes. Rockefeller later claimed that he had purchased a small
work of Quigley's, which, he said, made him the only living artist in his
collection.

Quigley, you will not believe it. I just bought one of your
paintings. I walked along Eighth Avenue in search of packing
tape when I looked in the window of a second-hand store
that sometimes has art. A friend of mine found a real Murillo
[Bartolomé Esteban Murillo, the Spanish Baroque-era painter,
1617–1682] there a few years ago worth probably more than
a million dollars. The store, owned by an antique dealer who
specializes in early American furniture, buys entire estates,
usually just to get antique furniture cheaply. They never have
any clue about their inventory and they often sell things
without knowing what they really have. An abstract in the
corner of their storefront window caught my eye and you
could not imagine the surprise when I saw the initials W.Q.
1991 in the lower right-hand corner. On the back, in typical
Quigley style, it said, "W.Q. 1991. Title: Abrupt Break.". . . I
bought it. . . . I love the little 12 x 16 piece. You have superb
talent. Did you get my message about Gagosian? Please let
me know your thoughts. I will meet with him next week and
pressure him.

But neither Rockefeller nor the Whitney Museum bought a Quigley
painting from Gagosian, or directly from Quigley.

Beneath his sunny façade, everything wasn't going swimmingly for Clark Rockefeller, especially at home.

To his friends, he'd say things like, "Sandy's coming in this weekend. We're going to have a delightful time. We may go up to Nantucket or we may go up to the Vineyard."

In actuality, Sandra was working extremely long hours and drifting further and further from her husband. His behavior was often irrational, especially when it came to going to Connecticut. While he delighted in telling friends of his sojourns on Nantucket and Martha's Vineyard, he drew the line when it came to Connecticut, where he had spent a past life as Christopher C. Crowe, and where he had eluded the state authorities while they were trying to question him in relation to the disappearance of John and Linda Sohus. "He wouldn't come to Connecticut," said his friend John Wells. "He claimed it was because his parents had their accident there. We had an apartment there with a lot of storage space. At one point Sandy drove up because Clark had a bunch of old issues of the *New Yorker* magazine that he wanted to store. Rockefeller Center publications were mixed into the stack."

"He had this crazy Connecticut neurosis," added another friend. He was so adamant about this that he once "threw a fit" when he realized that the car he was in was about to cross the state line. "Before we crossed the border into Connecticut, Clark made everybody stop and use the bathroom, because he wouldn't let us stop at all after that," said the friend. Once they crossed the Connecticut line, the friend added, Rockefeller turned up his collar, put on a hat, and hunkered down low in his seat. "The dog was bouncing all over the car and barking at everybody, and Clark was just—I mean, he really was acting like someone who didn't want to be seen. It was just over the top."

By the end of 1999, Sandra was about to be made a partner of McKinsey & Company, one of the youngest partners in the firm's history. She was now making major money, which was still controlled by her husband, who deposited her checks, paid the bills, and filed her taxes. The money wasn't the only thing he was controlling. "He cut off my contact with my friends," Sandra told the grand jury. "He cut off my contact with my family. He wouldn't let me make long-distance calls. He would scream at my friends. . . . He's, as I learned, capable of being an extremely scary and intimidating guy."

She didn't have to be asked to elaborate.

"He would scream at me and scream at me and scream at me until I couldn't resist," she continued. "He didn't hit me in the face because he knew that that was like the one thing in my upbringing—I was taught that you had to stay in your marriage unless you're hit in the face or he cheats. . . . Otherwise you have to work on your marriage, because that's the commitment you've made. So he didn't hit me in the face. I didn't know he was cheating until later."

"Let me ask you: did he hit you other places?" the prosecutor asked.

"At that time he used other techniques," she said, including sleep deprivation and sexual coercion. "Basically, just kind of proof of 'I'm master' kind of behavior."

"Why did you stay with him?"

"One, I was terrified," Sandra answered. "I could tell that he wasn't going to let me go. I didn't know why I had been picked for this situation, but I could tell that he was really strong, and I couldn't figure out how to get out. The other thing was that, you know, I had this upbringing, which is very much about duty and honor, and you're supposed to work on your marriage. My parents had a horrible marriage and stayed together thirty-five years. I was taught life is hard—suck it up."

She lived with her husband in New York from the autumn of 1994 until the end of 1998. Then, she testified, "Suddenly Clark, who had become quite unpleasant, but was otherwise generally functioning, suddenly he freaked out. I don't know how to explain it, but he claimed that he had had a nervous breakdown. He was getting more angry and more scary."

One incident, whether coincidental or not, seemed to have set off the nervous breakdown. He got into a fight with "some random bystander in Central Park," Sandra said, presumably while walking his dog. The fight was a loud one, and someone called the police. "The police had followed him in a car. I saw him walking back toward our apartment, and then I saw a police cruiser pull up, and he had a discussion with the officer."

He rushed into the apartment and told Sandra that he had had enough of New York. He was "overwhelmed" by the city, he told her. "His work was very stressful. That was right around the time of the Asian financial crisis [which began in July 1997, in Thailand, with the collapse of the baht, and then spread across Asia, raising fears of a worldwide economic meltdown]. And he said that some of his clients had run into severe problems."

The clients had the gall to be upset with him for the crisis, he said, as if he could somehow have protected them from the tsunami of financial problems a world away in Asia.

Sandra believed him, despite never having met a single "colleague, supervisor, underling," or anyone else who worked with him in his supposedly high-level financial advisory business. She believed him enough, in fact, to consent to his demand to move from New York to Nantucket, knowing that she would have to commute to her office in New York and live in a hotel during the workweek. "It seemed like it was going to make him happy, and that was good," she said.

At the end of 1998, Rockefeller sent out a mass e-mail to his growing circle of acquaintances, presumably from his office at Asterisk LLP:

First, I must tell you why you've not heard from me. While I'm in a meeting at the UN the Friday before Labor Day, I stared at some papers, a delegate handed it to me . . . then I remember nothing until I woke up at a New York hospital five hours later. The hospital discharged me shortly afterwards and the doctors told me that I suffered from severe exhaustion. In short, a quote "burnout." The obvious cause: too many 19-hour days. During June, July and August, I generated 1,085 billable hours, about 400 hours more than persons in comparable working situations. I've had other stressful situations last summer, including the unexpected retirement of my partner from Maine that almost ended up in a mid-air collision; and in all fairness, I must add Shelby [his other Gordon setter] to this list, too.

I love the little hound, but she adds quite a bit of work to my day, and her early-rising habits did not exactly help me get the extra sleep I so desperately needed. On the advice of my doctor, I have decided to change my lifestyle. My plan: I will take a sabbatical from my work and go to stay at my cousin's villa in Cap Ferrat, France, a small village on a peninsula between Nice and Monaco. Shelby and Yates will accompany me. How long I stay will depend on how I like it. I will return in six months or, if I feel like it, stay longer. If I continue my sabbatical through the summer of '99, I may either stay in France at a friend's summerhouse in the Brittany/Normandy region, or even visit Shelby's former home state, Montana.

Sandy also appreciates my mood. She can now stay in Toronto full time and no longer needs to commute on weekends just to see me. Sandy will take the time between Thanksgiving and New Year's as vacation and we will return to Cortina d'Ampezzo, in the Dolomites in Italy. We went there last year, and did absolutely nothing for one month and loved it. Yates had a good time there, too.

I should also tell you that my firm will close its New York office in March. Rising rents and a new landlord who did not renew our privilege to bring dogs in the building have forced us to follow through on our plan to, quote, "go virtual," sooner than we had intended. The main office of our firm will no longer meet at a physical location, but conduct our business electronically. We decided to invest almost five million in the creation of a private network in our Washington DC office.

He was not in Cap Ferrat or Cortina d'Ampezzo, but on Nantucket, usually alone, with his wife away at work at least four days a week. When the high season arrived and the rent quadrupled due to the tourists, the couple moved to Woodstock, Vermont, the summer home of Laurance Rockefeller. All this time Sandra was climbing higher and higher in McKinsey. Her layabout husband kept insisting that he was succeeding in business too, though Sandra couldn't see it in terms of any dollars and cents he brought in. He only put pressure on her to earn more.

By this point Rockefeller had been leading her to believe that he was expecting to be appointed to nothing less than a seat on the Federal Reserve Board, the seven-person committee that sets and governs monetary policy in the United States.

In his cross-examination, Clark's defense attorney asked why she couldn't see through such a monstrous fabrication. "The defendant was lying to me," she replied, explaining that she was still young and naïve in her private life, even though she was smart and savvy in her professional life. Although it wasn't immediately clear what he was driving at, the defense attorney kept hammering away at all the lies Clark had told Sandra. At some point, shouldn't she have realized that she had married an absolute figment of his own imagination, whose only tenuous connection to reality was the woman who was now testifying against him on the witness stand?

The defense attorney addressed her as "Ms. Boss" and referred to her first job in New York City. "Did you find it coincidental that you had just gotten a job at Merrill Lynch, working in their debt markets, and that this man that's pursuing you is also working in debt markets?"

"No, debt is a very, very broad concept, and there is nothing remotely similar between what I was doing, structuring municipal derivatives, and what he was doing in trying to renegotiate debt for Third World countries."

"Let's talk about credit cards. Have you ever seen him with a credit card?"

"Yes . . . when I met him he had a credit card that had his name on it."

"Do you know that he had a bank account?"

"I do not know that he had a bank account."

"Did you ever see him with a checkbook?"

"Mine."

That brought a loud laugh from the spectators in the courtroom.

"I'm sure that's true," said the defense attorney. "Other than your checkbook, did you ever see him with a checkbook of his own?"

"No, just credit cards."

She had never actually seen him writing a check from his own account, and while she had no evidence that he had a checking account or a savings account, she assumed that he did. Because most people have them. And it wasn't a question she felt she needed to ask.

The defense attorney seemed determined to make Sandra break, or show some emotion, but it was clear that she was unbreakable.

"You were married to this man for over twelve years, and you were together for a period of fifteen years," the defense attorney continued. "You are an economist. You are a major consultant for one of the highest-end business consulting entities in the world. You had no idea if he had bank account, and in terms of your joint finances it never came up?"

"I think consistently you're making a connection between business intelligence and personal intelligence. I mean, I came from a place where people don't jaywalk—it's a very honest place. It never in my entire life occurred to me that I could be living with someone who was lying about such basic stuff."

The jackhammer questioning continued. Had she ever seen him with a car registration? "Many car registrations, yes," she said. (This was odd, since her husband didn't drive.) Were they in his name? "No, they were in the name of the trust that owned the cars." And who funded the trust that owned the cars? She did, Sandra said. In the fifteen years they were together, did she ever see an investment or stock market account in her husband's name? "No, I can confidently tell you that no matter how many different questions about legal documents with his name on it that you ask me, the answer will be no."

The questions continued, and she calmly and intelligently answered each and every one. She hadn't seen baby pictures, but he had shown her pictures of himself when he was a youngster. She had seen pictures of people he said were his parents, who were killed in the car accident when he was eighteen. She had never gone to a Rockefeller gathering, although, she said, her husband had told her that invitations to these events had been made. She was asked if she had actually ever seen an invitation. "I didn't," she said. She had been interwoven so deeply into the life of the man with whom she had lived for fifteen years, twelve as his wife, that she couldn't see him for what he was.

When his questions were exhausted, the defense attorney said, "No further questions, Your Honor," and the court shortly went into recess.

CHAPTER 13

The Country Squire

To his friends and acquaintances, Clark Rockefeller was a prince. He was so friendly, so attentive, so eager to please. He cared about people and seemed genuinely interested in them. He was a man others sought to know and befriend, an in-demand dinner guest, an aristocrat who tossed off bons mots and society lingo— "Quite so!" "Oh, dear!" and "Good heavens!" were among his favorite expressions—and made frequent, not-so-subtle allusions to his famous family.

To his wife, however, he was a completely different person—glum, territorial, tempestuous, and, especially after the altercation in Central Park that had led to a run-in with the police, paranoid. The handsome young man who had showered Sandra with attention and gifts was gone.

Moving from New York to Nantucket, and then to Woodstock, Vermont, hadn't been enough to snap Clark out of the malaise that had been brought on by his supposed nervous breakdown. By late 1999 he wanted to go somewhere even more remote, and he insisted to Sandra that they move to Cornish, New Hampshire.

Cornish was described by the *New York Times* in February 2010 as "a town of about 1,700 on the banks of the Connecticut River, [with] two general stores, a post office, a church and miles of pines, oaks, farmland and rolling hills." It was made famous by Augustus Saint-Gaudens, the great late-nineteenth-century sculptor, who helped turn it into a popular summer colony for artists, including the painters Maxfield Parrish and John White Alexander. President Woodrow Wilson even spent a few summers there, making the home of the writer Winston Churchill (no relation to the British prime minister) his summer White House.

The Cornish art colony fizzled out in the years after World War I, and in early 2000, when Clark Rockefeller used $750,000 of his wife's money to buy Doveridge, the former estate of the renowned jurist Learned Hand, Cornish had just one famous citizen: the ultra-reclusive novelist J. D. Salinger. Some said the presence of Salinger, whose 1951 masterpiece *The Catcher in the Rye* stands as the ultimate depiction of teenage angst and alienation, was what attracted Rockefeller to Cornish.

The story of Rockefeller's arrival in town is best told from the perspective of Peter Burling, a former state senator and longtime member of the New Hampshire legislature, who grew up in the Cornish area and received his undergraduate and law degrees from Harvard. We met at a café a few miles from Cornish, and I asked Burling why he felt Rockefeller had chosen to live there.

"I think it had something to do with the artist colony history," he said. "It's quiet. It's remote. It's small. If you're a great pretender, Cornish is a good place to ply your skills.

"I heard about him before I saw him," Burling continued. "I heard there was a Clark Rockefeller who bought property in town. We were introduced to Clark at one of the community events for him. The hosts were Jim and Judy Brown. He's a trial lawyer and she's a constitutional law professor at Northeastern. They are very, very astute judges of character—great friends and very smart."

"So why would they give a party for Clark Rockefeller?" I asked.

Burling looked at me as if I had asked a glaringly obvious question.

"New neighbors," he explained. "That is what we do. He was new to town, and Jim and Judy wanted to introduce him around."

I asked Burling what his expectations were before meeting him.

"I didn't have any expectations. There are Rockefellers in Woodstock, and I went to school with a Rockefeller at Milton," he said, meaning Milton Academy, the Boston-area prep school whose notable alumni include T. S. Eliot and Robert and Ted Kennedy.

Burling and Clark Rockefeller got off on the wrong foot, however, at the welcoming party the Browns gave for the new arrival, which was attended by about thirty people. He walked up to Burling's wife, Jean, a superior court judge, and asked her, "Do you know what abstract expressionism is?"

The senator shook his head. "Of course she did," he said. "But it was asked in an utterly rude and humiliating way to indicate his view that she was a doofus and a rube—not a great thing to do. It cued her to the notion that this guy had an investment in putting people down and setting himself up above everybody else. I think the phrase was, 'I gave him my usual twenty seconds.' She has spent twenty-eight years on the bench, so she has developed her sense of what is bullshit and what's not. She stopped having anything to do with him at that point."

Burling took a sip of coffee. "When somebody new arrives in any small community like Cornish, they are the subject of conversation for the next twenty or thirty days. I dismissed him as not being real. I started telling people, 'He's not a real Rockefeller.' They would ask me, 'How do you know?' I'd say, 'Well, all of the Rockefellers I know— and Woodstock has quite a few of them—were born in the U.S. This guy's not from America. His adjectives and adverbs are from a different place.' Someone said to me, 'It's the prep school accent!' I said, 'I grew up in Newport, Rhode Island, and that isn't a prep school accent.'"

Given Burling's mistrust and dislike of Rockefeller, he was dismayed when the newcomer got close to, and, in Burling's opinion, took advantage of, one of his most cherished Cornish friends, Don MacLeay. Burling said he once described Donnie MacLeay in a newspaper article as "Michelangelo with a Caterpillar tractor." I told Burling that I was going to meet MacLeay later that day. "He's going to take me to Doveridge," I said.

"Do please be careful if you get near it," he said—a bizarre warning, but one that I would understand soon enough.

As I walked up to Don MacLeay's house in Plainfield, New Hampshire, a small town that abuts Cornish, I noticed a sign he had plastered to his pickup truck:

DON MACLEAY

BULLDOZING, DITCH DIGGING, TRACKING, LAND CLEARING,
BRUSH CLIPPING, GRADING, PLAINFIELD—
AND IF IT AIN'T COUNTRY, IT AIN'T MUSIC.

He was a reed of a man who looked to be in his late seventies, weathered by decades of work and harsh New England winters. He motioned for me to come inside the house, which he had built by hand. He settled into a chair, folded his spindly legs, and began to tell me his story.

MacLeay had been on his tractor when he was introduced to Rockefeller, and, work being more important to him than meeting new people, he told the neighbor making the introduction, "Let me finish what I'm doing here, and I'll be with you in a minute."

"I don't catch names very good," MacLeay continued. "I got off the tractor and said to him, 'So, you're Chris Rockefeller.' And he kind of jumped, a little irritated, because I called him by the wrong name."

As MacLeay and I drove to Doveridge in his truck, he told me, "I don't know why he came up here. I guess he wanted to be in the sticks. He said he was looking for a place he could do a lot of fixing up."

He pulled over, parked in a grassy area off the main road, and walked me up to the twenty-five-acre property. "Well, here it is," he said when we got to the driveway, which was blocked off with a heavy chain and surrounded by signs reading KEEP OUT, CAUTION, and BEWARE OF DOGS.

I gasped. The place was a dump. The grounds were overgrown, and the house was hoisted up on jacks and appeared uninhabitable. The signs were there not to ward off thieves, MacLeay told me, but because parts of the house, stripped down to the studs, could literally come crashing down. At the time of my visit, all attempts to sell it had come to naught.

I couldn't imagine a successful career woman like Sandra Boss living there, and apparently she couldn't either. She was away on business in the months after purchasing Doveridge (although Rockefeller made the arrangements, the deed was in Boss's name).

Rockefeller wanted MacLeay to oversee all of his home improvements, but MacLeay told him up front, "I do excavation; I'm not a contractor." When MacLeay asked what he was going to do with the expansive estate, Rockefeller replied, "Sell honey and hard cider." He wasn't much better at that enterprise than he was at renovation, said MacLeay: he ordered apple-grinding machinery, but not all of it arrived before winter. So the truckload of apples he'd also ordered quickly froze.

As we ducked under the chain and walked around the property, MacLeay explained to me Rockefeller's habit of hiring and firing people at a furious pace. "Construction folks," he said. "He had fourteen different masoners. He'd get in an argument and fire one, then go find somebody else."

He suggested we walk away from the old house and get back to the main road before something fell off the building or we slipped and fell into a trench. I asked about the gaping hole that had been dug beneath the house.

MacLeay sighed. "The guy that raised the house jacked it up so Clark could put a foundation under it," he said, adding that Rockefeller paid $25,000 for cement alone. "He wanted to put in a basement as a place to keep his cars. He was kind of a nut for old cars."

True, he didn't have a driver's license, but in Cornish he bought not just one car but a fleet, most of them antiques. One, said MacLeay, was a limousine, custom-fitted with seats that revolved to face each other so passengers could do business while being chauffeured, that he insisted had belonged to the Rockefellers in Woodstock.

"What did you buy *that* for?" MacLeay asked Rockefeller.

"Well, our trust is set up where we can buy anything we want, but we can't sell anything unless it's to a family member." Rockefeller added that he snapped it up for a song, just so it wouldn't end up on the scrap heap.

"I thought, 'Rich people are kind of odd,'" MacLeay said.

Before long Rockefeller's car collection numbered twenty-three—vehicles of all vintages and makes, some so old that they wouldn't run or be good for anything but show. He kept them scattered around the property, because the garage beneath the house was never filled in, much less finished.

"I'm going to put a pool in," Rockefeller said one day, to which his excavator and by then close friend Don MacLeay responded, 'Geez, why don't you finish *something* first?"

The pool was going to cost $50,000. As with many of his projects, the only stage of it that was completed was the digging of a hole. Clark and the pool company didn't get along. It seemed that Rockefeller was desperately trying to fit in with Cornish—while also defiantly trying to stand out. Either way, it was extremely odd behavior. It was one thing to want to dupe the strivers in a bustling city like New York, where one can flit from place to place and person to person without gossip and innuendo trailing close behind. But in an insular small town like Cornish, where everyone knows everybody? Perhaps he had indeed had a nervous breakdown, as he had claimed. Or perhaps Cornish was just another lark, to see how far he could push things before being unmasked.

"I don't know," MacLeay said, marveling at Rockefeller's various failed undertakings at Doveridge. "I think he was trying to see how fast he could spend her money," he said, referring to Boss. The citizens of Cornish rarely saw her, but they spoke about her often. No one could have suspected, however, that she was the one who made Rockefeller's big show in Cornish (and in Nantucket and Woodstock before that) possible—or that he was dangerously close to losing her.

Sandra was commuting between her broken-down house on Blow-Me-Down Brook in Cornish and her high-powered job with McKinsey in New York. Sometimes she would fly to work from New Hampshire, and sometimes she would have to drive, but either way it was grueling, and she spent much of her time in hotels in New York or on the road.

"In the summer of 2000," she told the grand jury, "I had been spending enough time away from [Clark] that the torture and the bad stuff was less a part of my daily life, and I was getting stronger. I decided to leave him. I took a small apartment in New York. I just said, 'I need to figure things out.'"

After a while, she later testified, "I started to finally come to the conclusion that I needed to change my marital status. I said I wanted to spend more weekends in New York to sort of think things through. I wasn't happy in the marriage at that time, and, you know, was talking about the possibility of leaving."

With that, Rockefeller shot back to New York. No longer the dark, moody, isolated curmudgeon, he reverted to being the man Sandra had fallen in love with. He was once again on her doorstep bearing gifts, flowers, and jewelry, and lavishing compliments and attention on her.

"The old Clark was back," Boss told the grand jury, "being incredibly personally attentive, being romantic again. Incidents like borrowing expensive jewelry from the [Rockefeller] family that he had me wear to a party. Later I found out, or surmised, that it was actually borrowed from a friend, but he claimed that he had borrowed it from the family. He introduced a new friend who had known him since childhood, who was vouching for him again. There's a lot of stuff like that."

She admitted in court that she reveled in the attention. "I was receptive to it, I liked it, but I wasn't decisive about it. I still went along with my plans to separate."

But then, one night during this period of "re-romancing," as Boss called it, her husband, with his suave manner, his grace and charm, took Sandra to bed. "We used condoms for birth control, which meant that he had the ability to alter them, which is, I think, what he did," she told the grand jury. "Things got a lot wetter, and I wasn't thinking that my husband was—I mean, you don't really think that someone is trying to get you pregnant in that kind of context."

"When did you become pregnant?" she was asked.

"Early September of 2000."

With that, she launched into a litany of despair:

"He was creating a cloud of paranoia around family and friends, trying to make me very nervous about how I could only depend on him.

"I was feeling, you know, the psychological effect of being pregnant, which is you feel disoriented and unsettled.

"My parents were getting divorced right at that time.

"I felt like I was too weak to figure out how to leave him at that time.

"I was also influenced by the belief that a family should be together, and that the child should be with its father, and that kind of thing." She repeated the same sentiment during the trial: "I was raised to believe that you're supposed to work on your marriage. It was very hard for me to leave to begin with, and to be leaving pregnant felt somehow like I wasn't doing my duty. . . . I just felt that the burden for leaving a marriage was very high, and I was very uncomfortable leaving a marriage just for my own happiness. And the idea of doing it when there was another person involved"—her unborn child—"it was very difficult. I just didn't feel strong enough to do that."

"What did you decide to do?" the lawyer asked.

"I decided to stay. . . . I said to my then husband, you know, that I thought that we should make a go of it."

Her husband, in the game he was playing with her for control, made a seemingly odd but in retrospect quite cunning move. "For a while he wasn't sure," Boss testified. "He said, 'Well, I need to think about it, and don't come home for a while.' So there was a phase of uncertainty."

Sandra went home to Cornish for Christmas of 2000, and things were looking up for the couple. Not only were they reunited with a baby on the way, but also, Clark told Sandra, he was engaged in a very exciting start-up company called Jet Propulsion Physics. He had acquired a patent in the jet propulsion field at a cheap price, virtually free, really, and he would be working with some of his academic colleagues to develop the patent for commercial use. Although she never saw evidence of the patent, she had no reason to disbelieve him. After all, he had told her about equal or even grander achievements: that he helped friends manage oil wells in Texas; that he had very close connections with Michael Heseltine, deputy prime minister of Great Britain; that he was a member of the Trilateral Commission, the private coalition of world leaders established by David Rockefeller in 1973 to foster relations between the United States, Europe, and Japan. He casually referred to the powerful organization as "The Group," and intimated, when questioned about whether or not there might be money forthcoming, that it would be below a Rockefeller to ask for a salary. None of these things was questioned, much less challenged.

It was clear that Clark Rockefeller was again holding all of the cards.

CHAPTER 14

Snooks

On May 24, 2001, Reigh Storrow Mills Rockefeller, the daughter of Clark Rockefeller and Sandra Lynne Boss, was born in Dartmouth Hitchcock Medical Center in Lebanon, New Hampshire. The child's first name was chosen by Rockefeller, after the Cornish town clerk, Reigh Helen Sweetser, merely because he heard and liked the name while standing at the clerk's window in town hall one day.

When Reigh was born, however, Rockefeller was nowhere to be found. He wasn't at the hospital. His wife didn't even know his whereabouts. It wasn't until eighteen hours after Reigh's birth that Rockefeller finally paid a visit to his wife and newborn child. Where was he during that pivotal time? As always, he was interacting with the locals of Cornish, which he continued to do for the first three months of his daughter's life.

He had the freedom to do this because Sandra, who had taken a three-month maternity leave from McKinsey, was initially the child's exclusive caretaker. "We were inseparable," she would later testify, adding that her husband spent very little time with their daughter. "I think he was like many fathers, which was he thought she was cute, but he didn't engage a lot with her at that time."

Down the road from Doveridge, in one of Cornish's grand homes, the White family, longtime stalwarts of the Cornish community, invited me over to talk about Clark. Laura White was his best friend for the first five years after his arrival in Cornish. A vivacious blonde, she was a single mother who worked as a flight attendant. Because she was often flying, she lived in her childhood home with her mother and father and her young son, Charlie.

Laura drove Clark to the hospital after his daughter was born, although she wasn't clear about how long after the birth they arrived, "just that it was in the middle of the night." She drove him in one of his growing collection of cars. For the auspicious occasion, he selected a Roadmaster, those large highway cruisers Buick introduced in the 1930s, instead of his bulletproof Cadillac limo.

He told Laura White that he needed her to drive him to the hospital because his regular driver, a fireman from the nearby community of Claremont, was unavailable. After checking on the condition of his wife and child, he instructed Laura to drive him back home, because, he said, "I have a phobia about hospitals."

We were sitting on the Whites' patio, looking across a summer vista of blazing green, an idyllic setting that, I sensed, had turned a bit banal in the absence of the famous man who so enlivened the little town with his oversized and outlandish antics. "When he would go over the covered bridge in one of his cars, people would say, 'Wow!'" Laura said, referring to the National Historic Landmark bridge that spans the Connecticut River and connects Cornish, New Hampshire, to Windsor, Vermont.

She looked over at her young son, Charlie, who had joined us on the patio, and asked the boy if he wanted to tell me what he and his friends always called Clark.

"We called him Purple Pants," said Charlie.

"Because he always wore purple pants," Laura explained.

He would stop by to visit Laura and her family almost daily, especially around mealtimes, never bothering to knock on the door, just walking in. They were that close. And when the family had intimate parties—for birthdays and such—Clark was often included.

"He hated to have his picture taken," recalled Laura, pulling out a stack of photographs of Rockefeller with the White family. What was remarkable was that in each and every one, Rockefeller was striking a pose that disguised him. In one of him at a birthday party, his eyes were deliberately closed. In another he screwed his face into a mask and stuck out his tongue. In another he was shielding his face with his hands. I suggested that he seemed to be attempting to leave no clear photographic record of his time in Cornish. "I gave up taking pictures of him because he would ruin the ambience" is all Laura would say.

She pulled out a diary she had kept during Rockefeller's time in Cornish. "I wrote Helmut Kohl," she said, referring to the former chancellor of Germany, "because he told me Helmut Kohl had come to visit him in Cornish. Here's one with Mom," she said of a diary entry regarding her mother: "Clark Rockefeller takes us to Boston with his chauffeured Cadillac."

The diary sparked more memories. "Oh, God! He told us he went helicopter skiing in Canada! And skiing in Italy. And that he had an apartment in Paris he was trying to sell. And when he graduated from Harvard, he traveled around the world for years. And that he had a cousin in Cap Ferrat."

She stopped to think back for a moment. "Oh! He told me a good one! He said, 'Did you know Britney Spears is a physicist?' I said, 'No, Clark, she's not a physicist.' But he said she was, and he said, 'I've had my people call her people, and she's supposed to be coming up this weekend!' The weekend happened, and I said, 'Clark, did Britney Spears come?'"

She moved on to another tall tale. "He said he was in touch with [radio host] Garrison Keillor. He said, 'My people are talking with Garrison Keillor, and Garrison is coming to the house to do a performance when the house is completed.'" Garrison Keillor never came to Doveridge, and Doveridge was never finished. Still, Clark Rockefeller came to win over many in Cornish. While he might have seemed odd, and more than a little "off," he was still somehow, as always, let in. He had created perhaps his biggest, brashest, loudest, and frequently angriest character yet, a country squire in a historic house with a seemingly bottomless bank account.

It's not hard to imagine that this welcoming community would find room for someone with all of these quirks, because, of course, New Englanders are known for their eccentricities. This was, after all, a very small town, whose famous covered bridge still bore the ancient sign WALK YOUR HORSES, beneath which was stated the penalty for those who trotted across the bridge: TWO DOLLAR FINE.

As Laura's mother said, "He was the most exciting thing to happen around here for a long while."

Many locals recalled him sailing down Platt Road, which runs in front of Doveridge, on his Segway, the two-wheeled gyroscopically balanced "personal transporter" on which the rider stands erect behind handlebars. The Segway was invented by another New Englander, Dean Kamen, who lived in a hexagonally shaped house of his own design just outside of Manchester, New Hampshire. And while a New Englander created the Segway, no one in Cornish seemed to embrace the newfangled gadget, aside from Rockefeller. "It wasn't something the ordinary person in Cornish was going to be seen going out to the barn with," recalled Senator Peter Burling. "But at some point, I was literally in the barnyard watering the horses, and up Platt Road comes Clark. In his Yale baseball cap. On a Segway."

Burling recalled, "I think I must have said, 'Oh, my God, look at this!' In twenty-twenty hindsight, there were so many visual hints that it was all wrong, and all phony, and just plain stupid." But back then, the senator added, the man in the Segway was big news in Cornish, and all doors were open to him.

He was a regular presence in the Cornish Town Offices, a red-brick building in what comprises Cornish's town center. BINGO EVERY

TUESDAY, read a sign out front. At her desk in the office was Merilynn Bourne, chairwoman of the Cornish Board of Selectmen, who essentially ran the town. A busy, no-nonsense blonde with a New England accent, she was known as Clark Rockefeller's fiercest critic during the time he lived in Cornish. She flew into a nonstop rant the moment I said his name.

"Everything he did was to aggrandize his position," she began. "It was to be bigger and better. He was not a very big guy if you looked at him. So everything he did was to puff himself up, just like the cock of the walk. Wearing his boat shoes in the middle of winter without socks, his yachting pants, his blue blazer, his white shirt. His chauffeur! He didn't have a license, and every now and then he would be driving himself and I would remind him, 'You don't have a license, Clark.'"

He had total disdain for local laws, and when Bourne ever called him out for driving without a license, he would just "sneer." She often questioned his identity, telling him that she had friends who knew the actual Rockefellers in Woodstock, Vermont, and those friends said the real Rockefellers had never heard of him.

"Why is that, Clark?" she would ask.

"Because I don't use my real first name," he replied, adding that he had changed his first name "for anonymity," which of course Merilynn thought odd, because if he wanted anonymity he would have changed his last name. Someone less skeptical might have accepted this explanation, but Merilynn said she didn't.

"A lot of people bought it, and when they would say to me, 'I don't understand. Why do you keep doubting him?' I would say, 'I don't understand why you believe a word that comes out of his mouth. Don't you recognize a phony when you see one? It is like the emperor in *The Emperor's New Clothes*: Don't you see he is standing naked in front of you?' And they would go, 'You don't know that.' I said, 'Well, I haven't been to outer space to see that the earth is round, but I'm pretty sure it is, and no, I can't do DNA research on him, but I know he is not who he purports to be. I know a phony when I see one. That is not a prep school accent, and it is not a high Boston accent. That is an Eastern European accent—I'd put money on it.' I wish I'd bet."

As he did with Sandra Boss, he told Merilynn Bourne about his new business venture, Jet Propulsion Laboratories. But when she asked for his company Web site, the site he directed her to had nothing but the name JET PROPULSION LABORATORIES and a box into which the user had to enter a code, which Rockefeller never divulged.

In addition to frequent visits from Rockefeller, Bourne said, she also had Cornish-area officials he had contacted show up in her office, offering grand gestures of his largesse. She related several scenes involving people in positions of power who were snowed by the supposed philanthropy of Clark Rockefeller.

"Clark has offered to buy the Highway Department a backhoe!" exclaimed the county road agent one day, meaning Rockefeller was going to give a piece of road equipment to the town that the town couldn't afford to give itself. "Stop talking to Clark!" Merilynn Bourne would admonish. "You can only get yourself into hot water. It is never good for anyone. He is not giving us anything, because he doesn't give *anybody* anything."

A week later, Rockefeller was in her office in a snit, saying, "I understand from the road agent that you are not willing to accept my gift. I don't understand."

"Well, Clark, I have this assumption that if the town were to accept your gift, you would probably ask us in a short period of time to do something with your gift for you, for free. Would I be right in that assumption?"

"Well, yes, of course."

"I said, 'Well, then, it is not a gift, is it?'"

He was equally generous with the police chief, telling him, "I am willing to get you this or that for your police car," after which the chief would also be in Merilynn's office, saying, "You know, I was talking to Clark—"

And Merilynn Bourne would erupt: "Every time someone comes in here and says they were talking to Clark, it just makes my hackles come up! Why would you talk to the man? He is a liar. You can't trust a thing he says. Stop talking to him!"

"Well, he wants to get me a piece of equipment for the car," said the chief.

"The answer is no," said Merilynn. "We are not entertaining the idea."

"So, because we wouldn't entertain the idea, he gave money to the town of Plainfield," she explained. "Then anonymously he actually wrote a letter to the editor of the *Valley News*, signed it with the name of someone who didn't exist, saying, 'Gee, it's too bad Cornish is so backward that they wouldn't take advantage of the generosity of a man like Clark Rockefeller.' I'm thinking, 'If they only knew.'"

"'I don't understand you people,'" Merilynn remembered Rockefeller telling her. "He'd just look at you with this hooded-cobra look and sneer at you and say, 'I've got important things to do.'"

I asked her how he could have so successfully duped almost everyone in such a sophisticated place as Cornish. "Two things: Cornish, the artist colony, has some history, some panache and sophistication," she replied. "It has class. And [Clark thought], 'It is filled with a bunch of little country bumpkins, and I can impress the heck out of them.' Absolutely, that is all he tried to do. Who the hell who lives in Cornish comes to a town meeting in March with Top-Siders and no socks? His sweater was draped over his shoulders and tied around his neck. It was *The Preppy Handbook*. I grew up in Newport, Rhode Island. I've been there, done that, seen it. I have one friend who still puts his sweater over his shoulders, and I tell him all the time, 'You know, you are like sixty-two years old. Don't you think it's time to put that sweater routine away?'

"So, yes, I think he duped the town, and it was a shame," she continued. "I wish the town had been a little smarter. Not everybody can see through people like Clark. You heard what Sandra said on the witness stand: 'I can be brilliant and amazing in one area and very stupid in another area.' I think people like Clark look for people like Sandra, who have low self-esteem when it comes to personal relationships. I think that's where he was able to take advantage of her. She's actually a very quiet, reserved, conservative female. She may work in an area of high finance, but she's a consultant. She is not the CEO running the company. And someone like Clark was able to spot the weak one in the herd and think, 'This is where I'll focus my attention—build up her self-confidence, make myself important to her.' He's sitting home all day long being the preppy while she goes to work."

After her three-month maternity leave, Sandra had to return to work in New York, leaving her baby in the care of a nanny. Sandra would return home midweek and stay through the weekend to be with her daughter. Soon, however, the first nanny quit, and another was hired, and then babysitters replaced the nannies, working shorter and shorter hours, until Clark became convinced that he was the best person to care for Reigh.

"He did not want to hire any more nannies," Sandra testified. "He said he thought he could do a better job."

Clark and Reigh bonded over books. She was only a little over two when she began reading, and reading—which was the route Clark Rockefeller took to discover America—was what made him initially connect with his daughter. "He liked being able to engage with her intellectually," Sandra Boss said.

For the next few years, Clark took charge of Reigh. Sandra was traveling all week much of the time, leaving her husband in full control of their daughter, their house, and her checkbook. She argued that living in Cornish had become intolerable for her, but Clark would not budge.

"The defendant wanted to live in the country and was not willing to entertain discussions of moving," she testified. She said Rockefeller even preferred for her not to come home midweek. He seemed to want to keep his life in Cornish—and his daughter—to himself.

"Reigh is very smart," Sandra told the grand jury. "She learned the alphabet when she was very young, and she learned to read very young. When she became intellectually interesting, he got interested in wanting to basically control her—he would have used the word 'guide' her. He told me he had made the unilateral decision that he was going to be Reigh's primary caretaker. Because I was working and he felt he wasn't contributing enough, and he wanted to take care of her. I disagreed with him, but he said he wasn't terribly interested in my opinion."

Her husband "really dominated the situation" with their daughter, she said. As the child grew, he "was unable" to grasp her emotional needs. "And so he obsessed on her intellectual development, pressured her to learn very quickly. He became very routinized about what she would eat, what she would wear. . . . I didn't mention before, he used to tell me how to dress. He would insist that I wear certain things. He started doing that with her."

Merilynn Bourne had a clear memory of that. "He dressed her exactly the way he dressed himself. She wore the same little Izod or Lacoste shirts with the alligator and the same khaki pants and the same L.L. Bean lobster belt and the same Top-Siders, boat shoes without socks, and the little pageboy haircut. I said, 'She's simply an extension of himself. It's self-love; it's not parental love.' He made her quote lines, scripture, and then pranced her out and made her perform."

"She was going to be the ultimate proof, the ultimate vindication, of his talent," the prosecutor David Deakin would later say of Rockefeller's obsession with his daughter, whom he soon began calling Snooks, probably after the small daughter of the Savio family in Berlin, Connecticut, with whom he had lived shortly after arriving in America. "I think it's clear that he found in Reigh the ability to accomplish something real. She was going to legitimize him. He was going to give her the opportunities that he didn't have. She would become someone extraordinary. In raising Reigh Rockefeller, the winner of the Nobel Prize in Physics, or Reigh Rockefeller, the Pulitzer Prize–winning novelist, or Reigh Rockefeller, the president of Stanford University, he would be known as the father of Reigh Rockefeller. And that was a real accomplishment in his mind."

The child would have a profound effect on Clark Rockefeller. As she grew in years and intelligence, he came to love her and be absolutely devoted to her. And with that love and devotion, the man who so successfully was able to flee all remnants of his past had at long last acquired an anchor, the one person he couldn't cheat, con, or escape. "The one real thing in his life was his daughter, and his love for his daughter," said Boston deputy police superintendent Thomas Lee. "Everything else has been a fraud."

CHAPTER 15

The God of War

Down the road from Doveridge was the Saint-Gaudens National Historic Site, the 365-acre former home of Augustus Saint-Gaudens, who came to the area in 1885 in search of "Lincoln-like men" to use as models for his soon-to-be-famous sculptures of the American president and other heroic figures. In 1905, to celebrate the twentieth anniversary of Saint-Gaudens's arrival, the members of the Cornish art colony—which by then included rich New Yorkers who had followed the artist to the bucolic hamlet—performed a masque, a play based on classical drama.

In 2005, the staff of the historic site marked the centennial of that seminal Cornish event by restaging the masque, called *The Gods and the Golden Bowl*. As he had done in San Marino twenty years earlier, Clark Rockefeller found his way into the cast.

"As I recall, he played Mars, and his daughter played a nymph," said Gregory Schwarz, the director of visitor services at the Saint-Gaudens Historic Site. A photograph shows Rockefeller in a golden suit of armor and matching golden headpiece, his jaw clenched, holding a spear. The god of war was an appropriate role for him, because by that time Rockefeller was fighting with many of the locals.

The unpleasantness had begun in the summer of 2001, when two Cornish women, Nancy Nash-Cummings and Dr. Sylvie Rudolph, decided to go for a swim. State senator Peter Burling said of them, "Nancy is a hugely accomplished and wonderful woman. To say she is completely well read, educated, and part of the arts community is to understate by a factor of twelve. Sylvie Rudolph is a profoundly trusted and beloved physician who works at the emergency room up here. She is trained as a lawyer as well."

Burling suggested I call Nash-Cummings and get the facts from her, so I did. When I asked how she was, she exclaimed, "I'm dandy!" then launched into her Clark Rockefeller story.

"It was such an *unpleasant* encounter," she began. "My friend Sylvie Rudolph and I do a lot of walking, and there was a property that adjoined Clark's. We stopped for a swim and our lunch. There was a big pump going in Blow-Me-Down Brook, and it was very loud, and we didn't think they had a permit to be pumping water. So we went on Clark's land and turned off the pump. Within seconds, a caretaker came down and asked us what we'd done. We said we'd just turned off the pump, that it was loud and noisy, and we wondered if Clark had the right to be pumping water. That afternoon, Clark began trying to figure out who we were. The first fax he sent was saying that he was going to file charges!"

Technically, they may have indeed been trespassing. But the property lines get hazy in Cornish, and the two women assumed that everything could be explained and resolved in a friendly conversation, which is of course how things would typically happen in a small, close-knit town. Nancy showed me the fax, which Rockefeller had sent to an intermediary, a local man named Max Blumberg, telling him to notify the two women of its contents regarding the bizarre incident:

Dear Max,
They did it!
For me to stop Melissa [Rockefeller's lawyer] from filing charges, I will need

a written apology for
- trespassing
- tampering with my pump

and **a promise**

> **not ever to go anywhere near the swimming hole again.**

Must receive written apology and promise by tomorrow, 10 AM, **signed and dated by both persons,** and stuffed into my blue Union Leader [a local newspaper] mailbox.

If not received by 10 AM, <u>with a copy mailed to Melissa Martin at [address witheld] Lebanon, NH 03766</u>, postmarked August 2, Melissa will

> **file a complaint with Cornish Police**
> **AND WE WILL PRESS CHARGES**

for

> **criminal trespass**
> **tampering of my power equipment**

In case they do not know what that means:

- They will have to go to the Cornish Police Station
- They will have to undergo arraignment in criminal court
- They will need to hire a lawyer or multiple lawyers
- They will have their names published in police logs in newspapers and public court records
- After conviction, I will pursue civil charges, which will cost them even more

Their choice. Let me know what they want to do. You might also want to let them know that I do not bluff.

"Now, I pooh-poohed this at first and said, 'He sounds like a nut, I'm not going to do all this stuff,'" Nash-Cummings told me. "My husband was furious, because he said I *had* trespassed and I *had* tampered. And a lawyer with whom we spoke said we should write the letter of apology, because he really could take us to court, and it would be expensive, blah, blah, blah. It took me hours to craft this pathetic apology. We delivered it on time the next day, and we felt, 'Well, this is the end of it.' Then a month later he sent us some honey with an apology—said he didn't realize we were women of such standing in the community or some stupid phrase like that."

She sent me a copy of the letter, which was typed on stationery with the word DOVERIDGE at the top. Rockefeller wrote that his ire had been sparked because some other culprit had been tampering with his pump: disconnecting its hose couplings, filling its gas tank with sugar, even stealing it. "We have avoided reporting the incidents to the Cornish Police because we don't want to involve them without a definite suspect," he wrote. "We have now installed a wireless motion-activated night-vision camera, monitored by Tasco Security, in a tree near the pump's location and hope it will help catch the perpetrator."

He ended the letter on a cordial note: "Please accept the enclosed jars . . . of honey, produced by our bees—the first of the season. Let us not speak again of our differences from a few weeks past and let us hope we can catch the responsible person soon." He signed it simply "Rockefeller."

The incident was typical of the face Rockefeller presented to Cornish. His obsession with security bordered on the fanatical. At the entrance to his home he parked an old police car, which he had purchased at auction, with the words DOVERIDGE SECURITY stenciled on its side. When he wasn't riding his Segway—which always caused a stir—he was chauffeured about town in his armored Cadillac.

The god of war, secure in his fortress, was ready to do battle in Cornish.

One of his early enemies was Alma Gilbert-Smith, the founder of the Cornish Colony Museum, a shrine to the artists who had inhabited the town in its cultural heyday. The artists were long gone, but their art endured—much of it was in Gilbert-Smith's home, which formerly belonged to Maxfield Parrish, whose colorful, romantic, sometimes whimsical works made him the most frequently reproduced painter of his era. The magnificent fifty-acre estate, called The Oaks, was where Parrish created many of his greatest works.

"Parrish built this house following the curve of the hill," said Gilbert-Smith, a dark-haired, diminutive woman with a slight Spanish accent she had picked up during her years living in Mexico City and South Texas. As she took me around the estate, she asked, "Do you smell the lilacs and the apple blossoms?"

There was a pool out back overlooking an extraordinary view of Mount Ascutney, across the Connecticut River in Vermont. "Parrish and the other artists of the Cornish Colony built what they called moon pools, to reflect the moon," Gilbert-Smith said.

She motioned to an adjacent house. "That building over there was Parrish's fifteen-room studio. And these," she said, indicating a patch of pink flowers, "are Lydia Parrish's original peonies" (often depicted in the artist's work). Among the Cornish Colony artworks inside my hostess's house were Daniel Chester French's sculpture *The First Minutemen in Concord*; Saint-Gaudens's giant gilded sculpture *Diana of the Tower* ("the Saint-Gaudens Historic Site has the same Diana in bronze, and I kind of tease them, 'You guys scored a bronze; I scored gold as part of my collection'"); and her most prized piece, Parrish's *North Wall*, the largest single-panel mural he ever created, a five-by-eighteen-foot extravaganza of color and light.

As we continued our tour of her property, Gilbert-Smith told me a story. "I had a fire on February 24, 1979," she said. "One of the worst fires in New England history. At night. We had no water. All we could do was throw snow at it."

We were in her backyard garden, and she gestured toward a very high second-story window. "My husband actually jumped from the second story, carrying a big Parrish. He's a Whitney, [from a family] who had the good fortune of collecting Cornish Colony artists when the artists were still alive." She added that her husband was a descendant of "Colonel Barrett, who led the Minutemen," and General Benjamin Lincoln, "who took Lord Charles Cornwallis's sword of surrender."

The implication was clear: this was the home of *real* American blue-bloods, and they would do anything, including risking life and limb, to honor and protect the legacy of the Cornish Colony artists.

We went back inside for tea, and Gilbert-Smith told me, "Parrish entertained often here. President and Mrs. Woodrow Wilson, Teddy Roosevelt, Zelda and F. Scott Fitzgerald, and [the writer] Winston Churchill visited and praised the beauty of the property and the artist's gardens. And Isadora Duncan danced in the music room."

Finally we got down to the reason for my visit: Clark Rockefeller, whom she referred to as "the defendant," owing to the fact that he was on trial in Boston at the time.

"The defendant was very dismissive of the Cornish Colony," she said, and I could tell that the wounds he had inflicted on her by his artistic arrogance were still very fresh. "It shows how much of an art historian he was. He said to me, 'Who cares about these obscure nineteenth-century artists?'

"Well, *excuse* me," she said, indignant at the memory of the carpet-bagger who would so casually put down the artists to whom she had devoted much of her life. "They were the core members of the golden era of the United States: Augustus Saint-Gaudens, Thomas and Maria Dewing, Frederick MacMonnies, Frederic Remington. Right now this obscure nineteenth-century art—as the defendant put it—is still being bought by real Rockefellers, and by people like the Whitneys, the Vanderbilts, the Astors."

She added that the two great intellectuals who had called Cornish home in recent years—J. D. Salinger and the controversial Indian-British novelist Salman Rushdie—also admired the work of the Cornish Colony artists. "Both Salinger and Rushdie asked me to open the museum on days when there would be no one here," she said, "so they wouldn't see people. And I opened the museum so they could go through."

"Did Rockefeller visit the museum?" I asked.

"No, he never did."

Which led us to the story of her unfortunate encounter with him. "Let me bring the book," she said. She left the room and returned with a copy of *A Place of Beauty: The Artists and Gardens of the Cornish Colony*, by Alma M. Gilbert and Judith B. Tankard, a teacher at Radcliffe College. "Judith Tankard is the preeminent authority on gardens, and I am considered the preeminent authority in the world on Maxfield Parrish," she explained. The book focused on the artists and gardens of the Cornish Colony, both back in the area's heyday and today. "Maria Dewing had one of the great gardens of Cornish," Alma Gilbert-Smith explained. I knew that Maria and Thomas Dewing—whose painting *Roses* had recently "sold for several million," Gilbert-Smith noted—were the longtime owners of Doveridge.

Clark Rockefeller "completely demolished" the gardens after he purchased Doveridge, Gilbert-Smith said, "so I wanted to use Maria Dewing's photographs of the gardens in the book, because they were very famous. I had originally asked the previous owner of Doveridge if they would allow us to have some photographs, and she said, 'Yes, of course.' Then she sold the property to Sandra Boss. I found out there was a new owner, so I approached them.

"I understand you recently acquired the Doveridge property, and welcome to the area," she recalled telling Rockefeller. She felt sure there would be no problem whatsoever getting his permission to use photographs of the gardens of Doveridge, both historical and current. "Knowing the Rockefellers of Woodstock, I knew that they were very generous, very art-oriented individuals."

In her first phone call, she cheerily explained that she was in the process of writing a book on the major properties of the Cornish Colony, where the artists lived. And of course she had received permission from the former owner to photograph whatever was left of Maria Dewing's extraordinary gardens. At this, the Cornish art historian's face darkened and her voice deepened in imitation of the inconceivable reply she received on the telephone that day.

"He said, '*Well*, you don't have *my* permission.' And I said, 'No, sir, that is why I am calling.' And he said, 'Well, *no*. I am a very famous person.' As soon as I heard that, I said, 'Excuse me, there are a lot of famous persons here.' He said, 'I don't want anyone to know where I live.' I said, 'I think it's public knowledge that you live here. I mean, I read in the paper that a Rockefeller was moving to the area.' And he said, 'Yes, but they don't know *where*. I wouldn't let them know where I live, and I *forbid* you to take *any* photographs.'"

I could sense her anger simmering. "I said, 'This is one of the very important gardens. If you don't want me to take photographs, I will not take photographs. I'll have to use vintage, historical photos of the home.' He said, 'No. I won't allow you to do that.' I said, 'You don't have a choice. There are historical photos, and you cannot prevent me from putting them in my book.' He said, 'Excuse me, I can not only *prevent* you from putting them in your book, I can prevent that book from coming out. I can put an injunction on your little book!'"

She let the words "little book" hang in the air for a moment, then continued.

"You know, I'm processing that, the 'little book.'" She went on to say that she had written *fourteen* books. She flashed a defiant little smile. "So I said, 'Well, this book is going through.' He said, 'No, I'm putting an injunction on it. I am a very famous person, and I don't want anybody to know that I'm here.'"

That's when Gilbert-Smith let him have it. "I said, 'Well, Mr. Rockefeller, if you don't want anybody to know that you are here, how long do you think it would take for it to come out in the press [that a Rockefeller was suing to stop publication of a respectable coffee-table book]?' I said, 'I am a media darling, and I can make an awful lot of noise.' Then I said, 'My publisher in California,' and he said, '*What did you say?*' I said, 'My publisher in California, Ten Speed Press, will probably be very annoyed and will do a little publicity on their own if you try to place an injunction on our book.' He said, 'I'll think about it and talk to my attorneys.'"

"You see?" Gilbert-Smith asked, and of course I knew what she was driving at. She couldn't have known the significance of it at the time, but in retrospect she realized that that one word, "California," must have had quite an effect on Rockefeller, since he was a "person of interest" there in the disappearance of John and Linda Sohus. She heard from Rockefeller's attorney very quickly: his client wouldn't allow new pictures to be taken of Doveridge, but he wouldn't place an injunction on the book. "So you see that the only color images in that section of the book are the paintings [of the gardens] by Thomas and Maria Dewing," she said.

Rockefeller's caustic encounter with Alma Gilbert-Smith and his broadside against the women who turned off his pump at Blow-Me-Down Brook were merely preludes to his biggest conflict: the battle over Trinity Church.

His main antagonist was Peter Burling, and before waging war over the church they had engaged in several preliminary skirmishes. "It embarrasses me to talk about this, but at some point Clark decided he would take on parts of my persona," Burling told me over breakfast. The senator had once owned a 1937 GMC pumper fire engine, which he had purchased for $200 in the mid-1970s to protect his horses in the event of a fire. He had long since abandoned it, but Rockefeller managed to scoop it up, and it became part of the growing collection of vehicles scattered around Doveridge.

"Clark, what are you going to do with a fire truck?" the locals in Cornish would ask.

"I'm going to drive it in parades and give kids rides," he would reply.

Next, Rockefeller and Burling clashed over a small house that had belonged to Rosie Leclaire, beloved caretaker for Burling's grandfather, who was a close friend of the famed jurist and Doveridge resident Learned Hand. ("One of the things I cherish most in my grandfather's papers is a note that he sent to Judge Hand: 'To walk in the Cornish woods with you is one of the high points of my life,'" Burling said.) When Leclaire died, Burling was named executor of her will. Her only significant asset was her house, and Burling was determined to sell it for the best possible price and give the money to her heirs.

Enter Rockefeller, who put in an insultingly low bid for the property. "I got the suspicion early on that Clark was dampening interest in the house, letting people know that there was no chance that they were going to get it, because he, Clark Rockefeller, would make sure that he got it, so nobody else need bother. So I decided I would throw a bid in; I wasn't going to let him be the only bid. This is Rosie! She would have expected me to defend her interests."

Burling's exasperation was evident. "I got this phone call from Clark: 'You are trying to force me to pay more money! You don't want this house! I'm going to take it! It's *my* house!'"

He shook his head. "Please. It was just fucking insane—sorry for the French. But that's what it was. I'm standing there listening to the shouting, and I said, 'Clark, we're going to make sure there is a fair price paid for the property.' So I threw in another bid, and he went nuts and raised his bid. Of course, who knew at the time he was spending Sandra's money? I think that might be the moment that he really decided that I was the enemy. But it's clear that on some level his ego really needed to challenge me. He focused on me as the big boy that needed to be knocked down or replaced."

From what Burling heard, Rockefeller bad-mouthed him all over town. "From time to time, I was the subject of some pretty deprecating things that Clark had to say."

In Cornish, as was his pattern, Rockefeller gravitated to a church—specifically Trinity Church, the 1808 wooden structure that Walker Evans had photographed and that the National Register of Historic Places had listed as critical to preserve. "It's a gorgeous, wood-framed church, the second-oldest Episcopal church in the state," said Burling. "I had purchased it in 1984 with a promise that I would give it to the town."

"The church was like his child, his baby," Cornish selectwoman Merilynn Bourne told me of the state senator's devotion to the place, which he spent twenty years lovingly restoring. By 2004 it was in immaculate repair, and Burling decided to make good on his promise. It should have been his shining moment.

"But Clark, who had other plans, scurried around quite a bit, stirring up virulent opposition to the town accepting the donation of the church," Burling said.

What rationale could Rockefeller possibly have provided against Cornish's accepting such a generous gift?

"The church is a wreck," Burling quoted Rockefeller as saying to anyone who would listen. "It's not properly restored. The town shouldn't take this on."

"Goodness knows what else he said to people. He obviously had the ability to convince almost anybody that it was snowing in August," Burling said.

The stage was thus set for what came to be called "the famous town meeting of March 2004." Burling was the moderator, and the first order of business was whether Cornish should raise $110,000 to build a new satellite police station as an annex to the fire station. "I opened the discussion on that warrant article, and the first thing I see is Clark, in the front row, putting up his hand to be recognized. I said, 'Yes, Clark, you have the floor.'"

Burling recounted what happened next like a boxer recalling a fight, his wounds still smarting. "His hand went into his pocket. He pulled out what appeared to be a check. He said, 'I have here a check for $110,000. If the town will accept Burling's donation of the church and sell it to me for one dollar, I will donate the money to build the police station.'"

He let out a long sigh. "It was a breathtaking performance. New England communities find it very difficult to see public demonstrations of wealth like that. You could hear the sound of teeth hitting the floor and see four hundred and ten mouths hanging open. I swallowed hard. He was putting me in a box. One of the selectmen said he was watching my face and the first thing that crossed his mind was, 'The fucker has put Burling into an impossible situation.'"

Rockefeller's cunning gambit paid off. He gave Cornish $110,000 of Sandra Boss's money to build the new police station, and the town sold him the church for one dollar. He could claim to be more generous and to care more about Cornish than Burling, and furthermore, he could try to fill the church with a congregation of his choosing—one that, Burling said, would help Rockefeller mount a campaign against Gene Robinson, who had recently been appointed bishop of the New Hampshire diocese. Robinson, whom Burling called "one of the most wonderful men you will ever meet," was the first openly gay, noncelibate person to become a bishop in the Episcopal Church, and many conservative church members were opposed to him.

Even after the town meeting, Burling was not quite prepared to accept defeat. "I must admit I got a little naughty at this point," he said. "The deal was, I gave the church to the town. No mention was ever made of the contents."

I asked Burling what was inside the church he had so lovingly saved, only to lose it to the man who by then had become his nemesis. "A granite baptismal font, some furniture that I had made for the back of the church, a portrait of Philander Chase—one of the most important Episcopalians from Cornish and the first bishop of Ohio—plus the usual collection of hymnals. There were these wonderful organs from the mid-1870s, and more."

He continued, "So I call Clark up and say, 'Clark, I'm glad you got the church. I'm going to give the contents to the historical society. You might want to acquire this stuff from them or make a donation.' He went just through the roof, saying, 'You dirty bastard! How dare you! That stuff is included in the deal!' I said, 'Clark, this is property that was not part of the purchase of the church.'"

The senator clearly relished his brief victory. "So I gave this stuff to the historical society, and, very sadly, I realize I never should have done it. Clark just turned his guns on them. He threatened them," Burling said, "telling them, 'That is my property, and if you try to take it out, my lawyers will be in touch with you.' It was a horrible performance. The people of the Cornish Historical Society are salt-of-the-earth, wonderful folks, and they were just crushed. He literally bullied the historical society into giving him all of the stuff. They were shaken. They just kind of folded, like a leaf in the wind. They had no idea what they were dealing with. At that point, none of us had any idea who we were dealing with."

"Who did you think Clark Rockefeller really was at that point?" I asked.

"I don't know. I didn't think he was a Rockefeller, but I had no idea who he was."

The battle over Trinity Church caught the attention of the *Valley News*, a daily newspaper covering parts of New Hampshire and Vermont. On July 3, 2004, reporter John Gregg wrote about Clark Rockefeller's plans for the church, adding that he "declined repeatedly" to say whether he was related to the John D. Rockefeller family. "Maybe I am, maybe I'm not," Rockefeller told the newspaper. "It's not something I would confirm or deny."

Rockefeller's warlike spirit also manifested itself at home. At Doveridge, where his art collection was stored in tubes to protect it from the nonstop construction, Rockefeller exerted complete power over his child, his wife, and her finances. "The defendant controlled all the money," Sandra Boss testified. "The defendant spent all of the money. There were no savings. I didn't control the checkbook. He looked at the bank accounts all the time. I didn't know what the online passwords were. It was very challenging to get money without asking for it."

When Reigh was three or four, the age when most children of privilege are enrolled in preschool, Rockefeller made a decision: "He wouldn't let her go," said Boss. He rarely allowed her even to associate with other children, let alone spend several hours a day in a schoolroom with them. "I wanted her to be engaged in more formal activities, so she would have more social activity," said Boss.

"And why didn't that happen?" she was asked.

"The defendant did not like the available options and thought he could do a better job."

Rockefeller controlled both the heat and the food supply at Doveridge, usually leaving Sandra—who was by then earning $2 million a year—hungry and cold in her own home. "When I was in New Hampshire, the defendant declined to provide me with enough to eat," she testified. "I woke up hungry most nights."

"Was there any heat in the house?" she was asked.

"Honestly, very little," she said. "In the main house there was often not enough heat, except in the part where he was sleeping." Which indicated that by then the two were sleeping apart. She was trapped, she said, and afraid. She was asked in court if she ever tried to assert herself. "I asserted myself, [but] the abuse was pretty rough," she said. "There was a very angry response, a lot of yelling."

She wanted to leave him and escape the horror show that Doveridge had become, but she couldn't figure out a way to do it without losing her daughter in the process. She was asked, yet again, why alarms didn't ring in her head after she failed to see "all the regular indicia of somebody who has a real life, an ascertainable, identifiable person," in the words of Rockefeller's defense attorney.

"I was focusing on things like getting enough to eat and getting enough time with my daughter," she said. "I didn't have a lot of energy for this topic" of her husband's nebulous identity, which at that point she still had not seriously questioned.

"So you're waking up cold and hungry, he's incredibly abusive to you . . . You're telling us that even though you're the person making $40,000 a week, you don't change the situation?" asked the defense attorney.

"I was afraid," she said at one point.

"You were afraid that if you went to a lawyer you would lose custody of your child?"

"The defendant, on one occasion when I told him that I was strongly considering getting a divorce, screamed at me in front of Reigh that if we did [divorce] he would manage to get full custody of her."

The isolation of Cornish added to the haze in which Sandra found herself. "I needed witnesses," she said. "This is a person who had established a somewhat credible reputation in the world. It was going to be very difficult for me to get out."

The defense attorney asked her with whom Rockefeller had established a credible reputation.

"As far as I knew, he had good contacts with many of the neighbors, who thought he was a very nice guy."

Finally, she insisted that they make a change, at least in their residence. "I began to threaten him that I would leave him if the situation did not change dramatically. As the situation got unacceptable, I pressured for the move to Boston."

She was already working in McKinsey's Boston office. "I wanted to get closer so I could spend more time with Reigh. I said, 'We *have* to move to Boston. We have to put her into a school.'" Rockefeller conceded to give it a try. "Reigh and the defendant started spending more time in Boston, attending events and just generally getting into the city."

At long last, Sandra said, her husband "acquiesced." He would move from Cornish to Boston. Of course, he would require suitable accommodations, which he and Sandra found on Beacon Hill—one of Boston's oldest and most expensive neighborhoods—in a five-story, ivy-covered town house at 68 Pinckney Street. The price: $2.7 million.

Clark Rockefeller moved to Boston with his wife and five-year-old daughter in September 2006, leaving behind in Cornish his unfinished house, his historic church, and many unanswered questions.

CHAPTER 16

The Boston Brahmin

For almost a month during Rockefeller's trial, I stayed in Boston, at the Taj Boston, the historic hotel just outside the Beacon Hill neighborhood where Rockefeller had lived with Sandra and Snooks. Shortly after I arrived in the city, I walked to Beacon Hill, and from the moment I set foot there, I knew why Clark Rockefeller had acquiesced to move from Cornish to Boston in 2006.

According to the Web site Beacon Hill Online, "Beacon Hill is a 19th-century Boston residential neighborhood situated directly north of the Boston Common [the city's lush and sprawling park] and the Boston Public Garden [America's first botanical garden, created in 1837]. Most people think of city living as anonymous and isolating. But this cozy enclave, filled with nearly 10,000 people, is more like a village than an anonymous city. It has a rich community life, with neighbors knowing neighbors and everyone meeting on the Hill's commercial streets and at its myriad activities." John Hancock had lived on Beacon Hill, in a "country house," when the area was pastureland, the Web site noted, and by the 1800s the area was home to Boston's wealthiest families, known as Boston Brahmins, the name taken from the highest caste of Hindu society.

I walked up Charles Street, the neighborhood's main thoroughfare, and then took a right on Pinckney, continuing to number 68, where Sandra, Clark, and Reigh had lived. It was a charming, elegant ivy-covered house, with gaslights burning out front. Senator John Kerry, I learned, had a house right around the corner. Here the German immigrant had found the address of privilege he had always been looking for.

It was a quiet morning, and the street was empty. Then a man approached, walking a dog. I stopped him and introduced myself, and the moment I mentioned Clark Rockefeller, he smiled and said he lived practically next door to him. He gave me his telephone number and said, "Call my wife. She can tell you everything you need to know."

A few hours later, I was sitting in the living room of a house rich with history, civility, and good taste, listening to a friendly, erudite woman tell about the arrival of the stranger who had taken her neighborhood by storm. "The whole Hill was fascinated and obsessed with Rockefeller," she said after she had served me coffee. "We knew him as a wonderful father. 'Mr. Mom,' we called him. They lived here for a year and a half to two years, and we saw his wife one time. Seriously. Supposedly she had the little girl on weekends, but we never saw her." She recalled that she had met Clark on the street. "He said, 'Clark Rockefeller. And this is Snooks.' We never knew her name was Reigh. He always called her Snooks."

She described him as having "sort of the ruffled New Hampshire look—you know, the Birkenstock sandals." She added that he always wore an Izod shirt, a blue one or a red one, with the collar turned up, preppy style, with either red pants or his khaki pants, and always Top-Siders, without socks. "In the wintertime, I know he had to have had on more than that, but he always looked pretty much the same."

As for employment, the woman said he didn't seem to have any. He didn't need to work, she assumed, because he undoubtedly had a sizable trust fund. His main role in life was caring for his daughter, and the neighbors had a clear recollection of Snooks. "We sit on our stoops here—we're friendly. The dogs are out," she said, trying to help me understand the Hill. "There's one fellow, Phil Short, he's everywhere, all over the Hill, and he looks like the ballet dancer Alexander Godunov. One day we're sitting there," she said, meaning on Short's doorstep, "and Clark comes up with Snooks, and Snooks sits right on Phil's lap and starts messing up his hair. We said, 'Phil, you have a new friend!' And Phil said, 'First time I've ever met her.' Oh, yes, she was very precocious.

"She always said to me, 'I want to come in and see your house!' When she said that to the lady at number 58, she told her, 'Well, Snooks, this isn't a good time. But maybe you can come for a play date.' Snooks said, 'Oh, no, I don't do play dates. Play dates are for children, and I'm not a child.' She was five or six at the time. He was so proud of her, and she was so smart."

I interrupted her to ask if she had been to Rockefeller's house. Yes, she said, he had invited her over shortly after they met. "He was really never settled," the lady continued. There were still boxes around a year after Rockefeller moved in, probably, everyone surmised, because he was so busy taking care of Snooks. "He'd come out in the morning and take her to school. And then he'd be running back in, because she forgot a sock or something. He was always the one who would take her to the school bus—take her everywhere."

She paused. "You could tell he spent lots of time with her, because she really was very bright. The first time she met one of the neighbors, she said, 'What's your name?' And he said, 'Well, my name's Elwood Headley.' And Snooks said, 'Hmm, let's see. E-L-W-O-O-D H-E-A-D-L-E-Y.' She *spelled* his name! And she was five! There was a picture of her on the front page of the *Beacon Hill Times*."

She was referring to a photograph of Snooks standing beside a diagram she had drawn in chalk on the sidewalk: the *entire* periodic table of the elements on the corner of Charles and Beacon streets. "I said to Clark, 'Does she know what it means?' And he said, 'Oh, yes.' I never learned the periodic table in *high school*, and here she is five or six at this point."

Having seemingly left behind all the aggressiveness and unpleasant-ness he displayed in Cornish, Clark, accompanied by Snooks, soon became a familiar sight on Beacon Hill, the two playing and dining together. They spent a lot of time in the Boston Athenaeum, one of the oldest and most exclusive libraries in America. "Predating all American public libraries, the Boston Athenaeum was founded in 1807 by a group of gentlemen who wished to provide themselves with a reading room, a library, a museum and a laboratory," reads the visitors' pamphlet. "Past members of the Athenaeum include John Quincy Adams, Ralph Waldo Emerson, Amy Lowell, Henry Wadsworth Longfellow, Daniel Webster, and Lydia Maria Child."

On Sunday mornings, Clark would read to a group of children in the Athenaeum's children's library. "He was an excellent reader, who could perform in a number of accents," said someone who had witnessed him reading at the Athenaeum. "I heard him recite Robert Burns—long pieces from memory—in a flawless Scottish brogue." By the time of their arrival in Boston, Rockefeller later said, Snooks was a proficient reader; she could read aloud from the scientific journal *Nature* when she was three. He said he once read Tennyson's poem "The Daisy" to her twenty-five times in a single evening. She not only understood the poem, she loved it. The seemingly carefree, towheaded child, whose fa-vorite book and movie was *The Little Princess*, was so good-natured that she seemed to hop or skip every fifth step. And the adoring father was always beside her. "I love you too much, Daddy," Snooks would often say.

"He was so devoted to that little girl," said John Winthrop Sears, the Harvard Law graduate, former Suffolk County sheriff, and highly re-spected Beacon Hill Brahmin who lived in a historic carriage house on Acorn Street, just a short distance from Rockefeller's house. Sears had helped Clark get a membership in the Athenaeum library. I visited him in his house at the end of a charming cobblestone street. The white-haired seventy-eight-year-old gentleman, who stood six feet four, led me into a living room that was spilling over with books. They lined the walls and littered the floor, and huge mesas of magazines and newspapers—including what he identified as a collection of forty years of the *New York Times* alone—rose in columns along the walls of every room.

"You're admiring my pile of junk," he said. The books had stacked up over the course of his thirty-five years living in the carriage house, he said. "Some of them are brand-new *Economist*s like the ones you're sitting on at the moment, but most of them are relics of a very active life in local politics. Things I wanted to read. The high pile of stuff beside you is the history of my father," Sears said. "I was the family historian. Where I went wrong was not studying the history of the *Rockefeller* family until it was clear that there was something amiss."

He handed me a two-page résumé of his extraordinary life. He was a Rhodes Scholar, a veteran of several venerable Wall Street firms, a member of private clubs, a philanthropist involved in numerous charities, and a politician of considerable renown. Yet he admitted that he had been completely captivated by the charming new arrival with the adorable little daughter.

"I got a call from a friend, who I would say is highly respected," Sears began after making cocktails for us. The friend was a physician from the Los Angeles area. "He said, 'You have a brand-new neighbor. And I knew him from out west in California. Would you be nice to him?' He described some conversations he'd had with Clark about his curiosity and his scientific bent." Sears took a sip of rum and Coke. "This happens to me every now and again," he continued. "So it wasn't difficult for me to contact my neighbor, Clark, and he came into this house maybe a half dozen times with the little girl."

As a lifelong Boston resident, Sears knew the area's accents intimately. So I asked him to describe Clark Rockefeller's. "His accent was dead-on for a privileged young person on the East Coast of America," he said. "He was very plausible. Clark had the same tones I heard in a good New England prep school. Or the nice clubs I'm allowed to belong to here. Clark was suited perfectly to the neighborhood." He mentioned Senator John Kerry, adding that he certainly wasn't the only famous person living on Beacon Hill. "There's Nan Ellis, sister of the old President Bush, and the novelist Robin Cook. If we can't impress you with a senator and the sister of a president, what can we do?"

Early after their arrival in Boston, Rockefeller and his wife, Sandra, invited Sears to an event for McKinsey & Company. "And I sat with them at what turned out to be a grand table, because the chairman of McKinsey was at the table," right alongside Clark and Sandra, who was of course, as a partner in the Boston office, seated next to the head of the powerful global consulting corporation. "And Sandy and Clark were still a couple at that time, and it looked like a perfectly ordinary family situation."

He recalled Clark and Sandra making something of a debut in Boston society on November 30, 2006, when they attended a black-tie benefit for the Mount, the grand and storied fifty-acre Lenox, Massachusetts, estate turned museum of the late novelist Edith Wharton, author of such classics as *The Age of Innocence*, for which she became in 1921 the first woman to win the Pulitzer Prize. Her tormented marriage and eventual divorce from the well-bred but conscienceless cad Teddy Wharton shared similarities with Sandra and Clark's relationship. "Both men spent a lot of their wives' money," said someone familiar with both women. "Neither were what they seemed to be." The benefit, held at the Back Bay mansion of a Boston philanthropist, was to raise funds to save the debt-ridden Mount from possible foreclosure. As the young, bright McKinsey partner, Sandra had accepted the board's invitation to ply her business acumen as a trustee to help save the Mount. According to *Boston* magazine, as she and her husband entered the grand home where the wealthy crowd had gathered for the event—Sandra young, slim, and beautiful in her evening dress, Clark perfectly dapper in his dinner jacket—Boston society photographer Bill Brett raised his camera, just as he had done for the other glamorous couples entering the event. "You will *not* take my picture," Rockefeller was quoted in *Boston* magazine as huffing as he led his wife swiftly away.

He was not at all like the other Rockefellers who had inhabited and enriched Boston with their acts of kindness, charity, and philanthropy. First of all, Clark Rockefeller didn't really know anybody. With the help of John Sears, that would soon change.

"Since Clark was brand-new to Boston," Sears said, he tried to give him a "bit of navigation legs," including entry into the Athenaeum. "Yes, I was the prime mover; I opened the door for them there. I got them reader's tickets. I paid for them too. I remember the first flush of excitement at doing something for a Rockefeller. And then, if they use the library reasonably and responsibly, the library will invite them to be readers without a host."

Which the highly educated and erudite staff of the Athenaeum would have done, Rockefeller or not, Sears insisted. "That is not a place where a Rockefeller takes the place by storm. They are pretty accustomed to grand folks." He went on to name several Rockefellers he had known who had lived in Boston and become his friends. "Nelson Rockefeller had a function for me when I was running for mayor of Boston in '67. These are not novelties. We weren't exactly bowled over, but it was sort of fun having Clark."

As the conversation stretched on, I could see that Rockefeller had moved yet another step up the social ladder, entrancing the longtime Boston business leader and politician (and former sheriff!), his highly educated Beacon Hill neighbors, and the extremely astute staff at one of America's most prestigious libraries. Sears said that a pleasant two-year friendship ensued, as the proper Bostonian would bump into Clark and Snooks on the street and later entertain them in his book-filled house.

Sears smiled slyly and said, "He gave me a book on the Rockefeller family."

"I'd love to see it," I said.

"And so you shall."

He rose to fetch the volume, *David Rockefeller: Memoirs*. The cover had a black-and-white photograph of the famous scion in profile, which actually looked a little like Clark. I read the front flap copy: "The youngest child of John D. Rockefeller, Junior, one of the richest men in the

United States, and the great patron of modern art Abby Aldrich Rockefeller. He graduated from Harvard College in the depths of the Depression and studied at the London School of Economics and the University
of Chicago, where he earned a Ph.D."

John Sears told me to turn to the title page. There was Clark Rockefeller's flamboyant handwriting, familiar to me by then, in an inscrip-
tion dated 12/26/06:

Although I have not seen him since the late eighties or the early
nineties, DR did send me (perhaps by mistake) two copies of his
Memoirs. Signed. One of these shall now belong to you and I hope
you enjoy it. I feel so privileged to have met you this year—Thank
you for all your kindness. Your neighbor, Clark Rockefeller

The book was also signed by David Rockefeller. I asked Sears if he
thought the author's signature was authentic, or if he thought Clark had
forged it. "I have no idea," he replied. "I knew Nelson Rockefeller, but I
never knew David."

Sears said he had gone to Rockefeller's house, around the corner, a
couple of times. "A Mondrian painting was laid out on the floor," he
said. "He told me how much he paid for it, at least a million dollars."

With that we took our drinks and walked up spindly stairs to the
terrace on the top floor of his carriage house. From there I could see
the spires of Boston. Down below was another, more recent landmark,
which Sears pointed out. On the corner of Beacon and Brimmer streets
was a bar called Cheers, which inspired the hit 1980s television series.

"Snooks got into Southfield," said Sears, referring to the Southfield
School for Girls, which shares a campus with Sears's own alma mater,
Dexter, where John F. Kennedy was also educated. "It's a very special
school. They taught me Latin at eleven. A different teacher drives the
school bus every day. I think that very well-run school was as badly
fooled as any of us. But, then, I don't think it mattered to them that that
little girl's dad was called Rockefeller."

Every morning Clark would take Snooks to the bus stop on the corner of Beacon and Brimmer, and every afternoon he would be waiting there to pick her up. "All of the people who had children in Dexter or Southfield got to know Clark and Snooks," said Sears. "He got to know all of the young parents who lived in the neighborhood."

If I wanted to know more about Clark's time on Beacon Hill, Sears suggested, I should show up at the bus stop around 7:30 the next morning.

There were Porsches and backpacks all around as the resident parents engaged in the early-morning ritual of getting their kids off to school, the boys in their Dexter caps, the girls in their crisp Southfield uniforms. By 7:30 a large and chatty group was gathered in front of Cheers, waiting for the arrival of the buses. Once the children were safely aboard, the parents stood there waving as they shouted, "Bye, Daddy! Bye, Mommy!" The parents did not move from the corner until the buses were out of sight.

The moment I uttered the name Clark Rockefeller, they shot daggers at me and began to disperse rapidly. Most were unwilling to talk. However, one or two eventually acquiesced. Some merely wanted to talk about the man who had brought notoriety down on them; others felt compelled to do so, so that the truth about the real Clark Rockefeller would be told.

"He told me he'd sold his jet propulsion company to Boeing for a billion dollars, and that was the last time he worked," said one Southfield father with whom I soon became friendly. Rockefeller had taken him to the Harvard Club in Boston, presumably to discuss a play date for their daughters. "He told other people that he worked for the Pentagon or the CIA or the Department of Defense. Then Snooks was born, and he cashed out with the sale to Boeing."

The father was putty in Rockefeller's hands, in the beginning at least. "Later, I heard his wife, Sandy, was paying the bills. But he led me to believe the opposite. He said, 'Oh, she only makes $300,000 to $400,000 a year.' And judging from what they had"—Rockefeller showed him his collection of abstract expressionist art and some Rockefeller memorabilia—"I thought he had a lot of his own money. I mean, he talked about donating a planetarium for our daughters' school."

Until he made the donation to Southfield, however, he seemed content to work as a volunteer at the school's Clay Center for Science and Technology. The school's state-of-the-art observatory is "better than the one they have at Harvard," said the Southfield parent.

"I'm a portfolio manager, and I asked him, 'How are you positioned?'" the parent continued.

"Exclusively in treasuries," Rockefeller replied, and his new friend had no reason to doubt him, since many fellow Southfield parents were positioned the same way.

The father invited me to visit him and his family at their home in the Boston suburbs. There, I found a picture-perfect house, a smart and attractive young wife, and a little girl who had gone to school with Snooks—the whole family bubbling over with enthusiasm about the doting father and the peculiar little girl who arrived at the Southfield School for the 2006 semester.

One day, the phone in the family's house rang. On the line was a fellow Southfield father, who said his name was Clark Rockefeller, suggesting that since their daughters were the same age, "How about arranging a play date?"

Over the phone, he asked the mother what her daughter liked to do. "And I said, 'Just little-kid things,'" recalled the mother. "She likes to play house, play teacher, play baby and mommy.' And Clark was totally on foreign ground. He was like, 'Does she like to go to the MFA [the Boston Museum of Fine Arts]?' And I said, 'She doesn't really read. No, she's never been to the MFA.'

"We went to the MFA together," the mother continued. "Snooks knew every single painting, every artist, the dates. She knew odd facts. Like we would walk around the city and Clark would say, 'Snooks, what does this stamp stand for?' Just the abbreviations around Boston. She would know it was the Boston Public Waterworks. She knew things that no one else knew. Especially a little girl like that."

I asked the daughter, a girl wearing tennis whites who came to be friends with Snooks, what she thought of her. "No one else was like her," she said. "She was the only one who knew how to read words and every time we didn't know a word we would go to her. Like if we didn't know the word 'decide,' we'd go to her and she'd tell us. She was the smartest one."

The little girl was equally close with Snooks's father, whom she called "Uncle Clark." "He was nice. He taught me how to read and all of that. Uncle Clark taught me a lot of things."

Despite Snooks's superior intelligence, though, the administrators of the Southfield School chose to detain her in pre-kindergarten, instead of placing her in the actual kindergarten class where a child her age should have been. The reason for the setback: the girl was severely socially handicapped from the years she'd spent sequestered away from other children, something that the family I visited had witnessed. "You'd go to birthday parties and she would refuse to play with the other children," said the mother. "She wouldn't join in any group. If they wanted to take a group picture, she wouldn't. Everybody would line up for pizza and cake; she wouldn't. She wouldn't join in. She was always doing something, a game by herself. She talked to herself, always asking things like, 'What do people eat in Africa?' She lived in a whole other world."

They recalled ice-skating outings with their daughter, Snooks, and her father. "Remember how they had to carry her off the ice?" asked the mother.

"She would just start babbling," said the father.

"Screeching and screaming," said the mother. "Temper tantrums."

"Saying, 'Reigh is good, Reigh is good,'" said the daughter. "We'd be sitting there and she would be, 'Reigh is good, Reigh is good, Reigh is GOOD!'"

Despite all of this, Rockefeller was determined that in the following year his daughter be reinstated from the pre-kindergarten to what he believed should have been by now her rightful place in the first grade. He went on a crusade to make this happen, promising the school that he would make a major donation.

"Clark had told us that he was planning on putting in a planetarium, and I think he threatened the school with different things," the father said. "In our conversations, he gave me the impression that he would repeatedly use the idea that he was going to put in a planetarium and possibly more than that as sort of a threat to the school that they should be more attentive to his child, forgiving. They had to put up with a lot of BS. It was amazing what they put up with. He was just not accepting of the fact that they made her go to pre-K. He was very offended that she was put down. And I suppose as a parent I can understand that."

So the implication was the planetarium in exchange for moving his daughter out of pre-kindergarten and into the appropriate class for her age group?

"Totally," said the mother.

Clark Rockefeller not only snowed the school with his famous family name and promised munificence, he snowed the parents in the living room, they both had to admit, so much that they were comfortable leaving their daughter with him at times. "He would watch the girls," said the mother.

"Is Uncle Clark a genius?" asked the daughter.

"Perhaps," said the father. "I don't know. But he's a bright guy, I'll tell you that. He knew how to push people's buttons, what to say, to get their attention. John D. Rockefeller's first company was Clark and Rockefeller. He was a produce vendor. His partner's last name was Clark. I mean, that's obscure. Clark just *knew*."

Although parents are discouraged from visiting the school during classroom hours, they are invited for special occasions, like parents' night and the Christmas pageant. Rockefeller showed up at these events, of course, rarely, if ever, with his wife, but, as always, totally in character. In this instance, he was the generous philanthropist from the famous family who was going to donate a planetarium to the school. "Bow tie, navy jacket, khakis, sometimes loafers, sometimes Top-Siders," said the mother.

"I forgot to add something," said the daughter. "I remember that Uncle Clark never wore socks."

In the fall of 2006, Sandra Boss brought up the subject of money with Clark. She recalled in court that her husband had told her that he could not sell his art collection, which was held in a family trust, for ten years. He had said this when Sandra first met him in 1996, however, so the ten-year limit would presumably be up, she felt. Surely he would finally sell a piece of art and contribute some money to the marriage.

The art collection was the only tangible proof that he really was a Rockefeller, Sandra explained. "It was lovely, and it was one of the ways that seemed convincing about having some connection with his family, that he had this great modern art," she said, adding that art authorities far more knowledgeable than she had deemed it authentic. When I heard this statement in her testimony, I called former New York art dealer Sheldon Fish, who saw Rockefeller's art collection many times before he decamped to Peru. "I must say the quality of the art was extremely high," said Fish. "Very convincing! I even offered him $800,000 for his Rothko in 1999 and he turned me down saying, 'Prices have gone up.'" If Rockefeller's paintings had been forgeries, Fish noted, they would have had to have been painted by a phenomenal expert, "able to copy different styles so exactly! One giveaway with new copies of modern art is checking the drying of the paint. It takes at least twenty years for paint to 'dry.'" Fish didn't bother to give Rockefeller's paintings the fingernail test—if you stick your nail into a dry painting, it won't penetrate, he explained—because he was certain the paintings were real. "I saw him unpacking a Mondrian that he said he bought in Japan. He told me he spent ten million a year on art."

"Lots of people from museums came in and looked at it; they thought it was great, so I thought it was real," Sandra Boss continued.

"At random one day, in probably October or November of 2006, he said, 'Wow, I've been following the prices, and I think it's worth over a billion dollars now.'"

She was questioned as to whether she had ever asked her husband directly if he might not consider "selling off a painting" and perhaps "put a couple million dollars away." Of course, she had asked him to sell a painting many times, she replied. "I was pretty shocked when, after he spent all of our money and refused to save any of it, that he then suddenly said, 'No, we're not going to sell a painting.'"

Still, she stayed with him, steadfastly attempting to hold her family together in the waning months of 2006. She had gotten him to move to Boston, and Snooks was happily enrolled in school—no longer in pre-kindergarten but, thanks to her father's influence, in first grade. "He said he would stop micromanaging her and we would share in her care, that he would basically let her have friends, that he would act like a normal human being," Sandra said. "But that was not true."

CHAPTER 17

Peach Melba Nights

Once Snooks was safely on the school bus, Rockefeller would stroll east on Beacon Street to the Starbucks on the corner, where he soon attached himself to a group consisting of lawyers, researchers, businesspeople, and a local architect who got together for coffee on their way to work. They had a name for themselves: Cafe Society. I went to that Starbucks one morning, and the group was easy to spot—a convivial bunch of men and women in the middle of the store. When I introduced myself, they seemed quite ready to speak about the man who had become a Beacon Hill fixture as easily as he had obtained a new e-mail address (Clark@Beacon-Hill.net).

One morning, they recalled, the aristocrat in the Izod shirt had been out of breath when he arrived, having stopped at his house on Pinckney Street after dropping off Snooks at the bus. According to Bob Skorupa, a lawyer, "He said, 'I'm exhausted. I've just pushed an armoire up to the fifth floor of my house.' That's how he integrated himself. You immediately knew he had a five-story house."

With Snooks on his shoulders, they said, Clark was soon a familiar sight in the neighborhood, heading home or to church, or to karate classes, or to lunch at the Algonquin Club. If Snooks was given the kids' menu, the little girl would snap, much to her father's clear approval, "We are adults. We would like *adult* menus."

As the Starbucks group got to know him, they came to like him and accept his eccentricities, because, after all, he was a Rockefeller. He told the coffee klatch that he had been the inspiration for the smart, effete character Dr. Niles Crane on the TV series *Frasier*. When the other Starbucks regulars rushed off to work, Clark would linger, because he really had no place to go.

Patrick Hickox, with his degree from the Yale School of Architecture, was known for designing homes and buildings on the East Coast. He wore his hair long, dressed in a boldly striped jacket, and spoke with a Yankee flourish. Of his friend Clark, he told me, "He said he was extremely good at thinking through processes and problems. He described himself as having been involved with the military, essentially as a contractor, and said he had benefited financially from the two Iraq wars. I never got too deeply into it, although on a couple of occasions we talked about projects he had worked on. Clark was not one to boast about his accomplishments."

Bob Skorupa, the attorney, added, "One day he said there was a sled or a rocket out in New Mexico, on some military base, and it had blown up and somebody died. He said, 'I designed that.' I hadn't read anything about it, but afterwards I went and looked, and buried deep in Google was a story about some accident with a rocket. Some guy had died. So that really happened."

John Greene, a dark-haired, blunt-talking businessman, picked up the thread. "Once, he was going to New York, and he said he could catch a ride on a CIA or Navy transport plane." Greene smiled. "Cool. He had those kinds of connections."

One reason they believed him was that he was a member of the Algonquin Club, a refuge of the upper classes since 1886. It stood imposingly on 217 Commonwealth Avenue, just a short stroll from the Starbucks, and Rockefeller somehow let it slip that he was not merely a member, but a *director*, of the club. On several occasions he invited his newfound friends to join him there. "It was quite splendid," said Hickox, "and as far as I could discern, the people there were very fond of him. He was a bit eccentric, but rather modestly so. Clark was cordial and amusing to the staff, and they were clearly affectionate."

I asked him if he recalled any specific instances of Rockefeller's interacting with other members at the club. "My understanding is that he gave an introduction to the German consul general—introduced him in a speech . . . in *German*," said Hickox. "Clark was a lively, very compelling conversationalist."

They all agreed that the aristos at the Algonquin, a number of them related to *real* Rockefellers, never questioned his identity. "He invited Bob and me to go the Algonquin," said Greene. "His name was up on the wall—as an *officer*. You think he would pay for breakfast, since non-members can't pay. But the next day, he asked us for the money."

"Yankee thrift—that would be typical of the Rockefellers," Hickox explained. "John D. was famous for his thrift, and Clark was very, very reluctant to go out and have an expensive dinner." When they did go out for drinks, Hickox said, "Clark would often just get a soda water, because that would not even appear on the charge. It made him very uncomfortable to spend money."

"When you walked into this fancy-schmancy club, there in the hall was the board of directors, officers of the club, and his name was up there prominently. I saw John Silber there," said Greene, referring to the noted author, philosopher, and academic who was president of Boston University for twenty-five years. "I admired the guy, and Clark said, 'I can have you introduced.' And he tapped the shoulder of a big shot, an officer of the club, who took me over and introduced me to John Silber! He went in there and established himself. At a club like that, people get a hard-on over the name Rockefeller."

Clark invited the Starbucks group to join him for the Algonquin's New Year's party in 2006, complete with ballroom dancing, a multi-course dinner, champagne, and a midnight rendition of "Auld Lang

Syne." Rockefeller's table was front and center, filled with his friends from Starbucks, as well as other members of the Algonquin—the king and his growing court.

I asked Thomas Lee, the Boston police superintendent, about Rockefeller's reputation at the Algonquin Club. He said he had interviewed many of the club's members and came away absolutely certain that they had been duped.

"He was well accepted," Lee replied. "Now, of course, the people there have said, 'Oh, yeah, we knew he wasn't this or that.' But believe me, he had them fooled."

"How did he do it?" I asked.

"A con man gets by because you want to believe what he's telling you. That's how a con works. People already have their preconceptions, and he just plays into what they're thinking."

The more I talked with people, the more I knew I had to see the Algonquin Club for myself. But my social contacts in Boston, which were not at all shabby, just shook their heads when I asked them to pull strings or make introductions. In the end, I decided to gain entry the same way Rockefeller had: through a reciprocal membership in another private club. The only club I belonged to was a spa in Colorado, with absolutely no reciprocal benefits, called the Aspen Club and Spa. I asked the concierge at my hotel to call the Algonquin and reserve a table for one for dinner that night.

"Tell them that I am a reciprocal member from the Aspen Club," I said, leaving off the last part of the name. The concierge called the Algonquin, then cupped the phone and told me, "She said they'd love to have you, but you'll have to pay for dinner and drinks by credit card." I nodded agreement. "Then eight p.m. for one," the concierge told the person on the other end of the line.

It was a vast gray multistory building with valet car parkers and gaslights blazing out front, as they had been blazing for a century and more. I walked into a small lobby, where a woman sat behind a desk.

There was a board with the names of the directors on it, and I noticed that Clark Rockefeller's name had been removed.

"Good evening, Mr. Seal! And how are things at the Aspen Club?" asked the receptionist.

"Quite fine," I said. "Can you direct me to the bar?"

As I walked across the lobby toward the bar, I took a quick detour through the private dining rooms, named for members—the Calvin Coolidge Room, the Daniel Webster Room. There were paintings of yachts and portraits of the men for whom the rooms were named. I soon realized that the eyes of the Algonquin were on me. No one seemed to question that I was anything less than an equal, starting with the older couple having cocktails in the Marlboro Lounge, where a waiter brought me a drink and I nibbled cheese from a silver tray and wiled away an hour making light cocktail conversation. "Mr. Rockefeller would eat here or in the dining room," a waiter in the Members' Bar told me. When I asked if they all assumed he was a real Rockefeller, the waiter replied, "He was a *member*. So nobody asked."

I walked upstairs to the dining room, a huge space with paneled walls, paintings, pewter chandeliers, four fireplaces, and massive picture windows. A waiter in a tuxedo approached my table, and I asked what Clark Rockefeller usually ordered for dinner.

"The smoked salmon appetizer and, sometimes, the Dover sole."

"I'll have it," I replied.

As the efficient waiters and busboys served me, I asked them about Rockefeller. Though he had been a director of the club, they said, he had eventually let his membership lapse. "He was here on a reciprocal, just like you," one of them said. How he got to be a member, no one knew. "You're either sponsored or you just come in and fill out an application. We knew he was a member of a prominent family," the server went on. "He was always Clark Rockefeller! Everyone seemed to like him. Nobody questioned anything."

I returned to the Algonquin another evening. That night, a younger crowd showed up. Men in preppy clothes with their wives or girlfriends were seated in the dining room. A few business types played billiards in the Members' Bar. As they cavorted and conversed, they were all secure in the knowledge that they were among their own kind.

It wasn't just men who fell into Rockefeller's growing sphere of influence and entertainment in Boston. Women were soon jumping onto the joyride as well. Another member of the early-morning Starbucks coffee group, a woman named Amy Patt, testified to the grand jury about Rockefeller's irresistible gravitational pull. She was at the Southfield bus stop one morning, her infant in a stroller while she took her daughter to the school bus, when a well-dressed stranger came bounding up from the park across the street. "Don't you look pretty today!" he exclaimed, introducing himself as Clark Rockefeller.

After seeing each other twice a day with their daughters at the bus stop, Clark and Amy became friends. They began meeting for a post–bus stop coffee at Starbucks and soon various other places around town, including the Algonquin. According to *Boston* magazine, they decided to "merge" their respective creative talents by writing what would quickly evolve into an eighteen-episode script for a sitcom based on the Starbucks coffee club, which Rockefeller entitled *Less Than Proper*. Of course, he planned to star in the TV series; to prepare for his television debut, he began taking classes at a local comedy center.

As the pair wrote the sitcom, it was clear that Rockefeller wanted their friendship to deepen. "He would say silly things like, 'Oh, Amy, Amy, Amy, we should have children together,'" she recalled. "'You're so smart and our children would be so brilliant!'"

As for his wife, Sandra Boss, who always seemed to be away on business, Rockefeller had only disparaging comments. So Amy presumed his marriage was over, and that he was the one who wanted out. Of course, he gave her his standard New York City/Yale blue-blooded bio, only with some specially tailored embellishments. "He said he went to school with the writers of the Frasier character on the sitcom," Amy said, referring to the persnickety Dr. Frasier Winslow Crane, played by

Kelsey Grammer. "And said he was involved in weaponry of some sort; ballistics and things."

She had no reason to disbelieve him. And while their relationship didn't go any deeper than friendship, she looked forward to their time together. "He was really energetic and flirty and just sort of fun to be around," she said.

To hear more about Rockefeller's sway over young women, I called the architect Patrick Hickox. One night he picked me up at the hotel in his convertible BMW and took me to dinner at B&G Oysters, where, he explained, he and Clark had often dined together.

"Clark has a tremendous, passionate eye for beautiful women," the architect said on the way to the restaurant. "And he seeks them out with great skill and charm."

That was how the two men met. "It was a large black-tie event." Hickox was there with his wife and "a very beautiful employee, whom I imagine Clark must have spotted at a considerable distance." Immaculately attired in his J. Press tuxedo, Rockefeller introduced himself, and the threesome quickly became a foursome. After the gala they retired to the bar in the Boston Ritz—now the Taj Boston—where, entertained by Rockefeller's endless anecdotes, they partied until five in the morning.

"Then we walked over—my employee was still there—to Clark's house on Beacon Hill. It was remarkably spare—hardly any furnishings at all—but with an extraordinary abundance of paintings, most of them not exhibited, but in enormous tubes."

"Did you believe the paintings were real?" I asked.

"I had no reason to think otherwise. They were by major people— Rothko and, I believe, Motherwell. It was quite a fantastic collection," said Hickox.

A close friendship ensued. "At one point, some people were questioning his identity and being derogatory about it. I said, 'Clark, I wouldn't pay that any mind. You are your last great story, your most recent trenchant analysis, the witticism you let float in the air. That's who you are.'"

Once we were seated in B&G Oysters and the wine was ordered, Hickox commented on Rockefeller's good points: his volunteer work in the community, helping people and nonprofit organizations by setting up and servicing their computers. Rockefeller was so proficient with computers he almost had "telepathy" with them, Hickox said. He never paid by credit card, only cash. The architect said he chalked it up to being "an ideological thing," that the man from the famous family had been taught to distrust credit. After all, he seemed finely attuned to the stock market, even e-mailing Hickox in the spring of 2008, before the American financial meltdown began that fall, "There is tremendous danger in the market. Get out of the stock market and go into commodities, into gold."

As Hickox ordered two oysters each of six varieties, I asked him how Rockefeller had fit in with the Starbucks group. "Oh, he was lovely, provocative," he said. "On occasion we'd talk very seriously about business, invention, and technology. But fundamentally this was a *divertissement*, for amusement. We talked about cars, anything. Clark has a profound love of music, ranging from torch singers to great opera, to opéra bouffe—the light opera of nineteenth-century France. We had a little group of two, where we would whistle in very complex harmonies. We named our group the Whistlepoofs, after the Whiffenpoofs of Yale. I lent him recordings of all of the Whiffenpoofs of the entire twentieth century, which he then put into digital form and returned the CDs."

Taking a sip of Chablis, he said, "Clark *adored* the music of Cole Porter."

"Which songs?" I asked.

"Oh, I can tell you one he especially loved—'From This Moment On,' which is a very beautiful song, really the embodiment of the quintessential brilliance of Cole Porter: to take a line, a little phrase, a particle of speech, and create a small universe of it. Clark loved diction, language."

We sipped more wine and hummed a few bars of the Cole Porter classic, about a world that turns on a dime on account of a beautiful woman. "One night, Clark came over and he had *nine* versions of the song," Hickox said. "We listened to them all, and he tested us on them as to who the singers were. Tough test."

It wasn't just American music; Rockefeller had a broad range in tastes, stretching to the obscure. "He's the only person I know who could play the didgeridoo, which is an extraordinary Aboriginal wind instrument. A long, long horn. One night—God knows why—I asked him if he played this instrument, and he got up, ran over to his house, and within minutes came back with an eight-foot-long horn, which he then played with extraordinary resonance and power."

Hickox was just warming up. "On Saturday mornings, even when we'd been out late the night before, he'd make it a practice to read to children at the Athenaeum. He was an excellent reader. He was a true connoisseur."

"And a true con," I said.

"I actually don't like the word 'con,'" said Hickox. "I mean, you are allowed to use that word, but it is not a word I would use. There is no question that this person over time presented a variety of personalities, but I never thought of him as being a person of multiple personalities or any of that."

The oysters arrived on a bed of ice on a tin tray. "I think there's a concept of this person as not being real," Hickcox said. "But there's no doubt that this was somebody who was loving and caring. And I'm sure that other people have described the care and attention that he had for his little girl. Not in an obsessive way. There's little doubt for me that he was a caring father. His love for his daughter was moving. I think the love for his daughter was the most central reality in his life."

"Maybe the only reality," I said.

"I wouldn't say that, because I think many, many things were real for Clark. And I hesitate to say this, but it may be that to some extent, for Clark, things that are imaginary were very, very real. That's why the con man description may be really off. This was somebody who might be involved with changing the world intellectually."

I raised a skeptical eyebrow, but he continued. "I'm an architect. You know what I do for a living? I hallucinate. I hallucinate things and they become real. I have an office. I attach dollars and cents to this. But it may be that all of us in varying degrees do this because otherwise we would be completely stuck with a preexisting reality."

He looked at me and drove his point deeper. "You're involved in a voyage of discovery," he said of my mission to capture the riddle of Clark Rockefeller on paper. "You don't know where it's going to end. To some extent you pose to yourself and to the various people you interview what *might* be a reality, and then you test for that, and as time goes on a vision is becoming clearer and clearer. So something that's really very imaginary and fictional gains greater and greater materiality."

He was saying that all realities exist because of ideas and visions that come from our imagination. If you look at it that way, I thought, we're all posers. Rockefeller, however, clearly took his ability to construct assumed and exaggerated realities to extremes. Hickox compared his friend's American odyssey to something out of the novel *Tom Jones*, or a book by Joseph Conrad. "There is a phrase of Truman Capote's: 'a genuine fraud,'" he continued. "Not that the person is a complete fraud. Quite the reverse. It's a person who actually may be genuine, but built upon a fictional armature. I think all Americans are our own inventions. That's part of the allure of this country. And in some ways one has to see Clark as an archetypal immigrant who constructs a new life and a new persona, free of the constraints of the country he left behind."

"How do you think he learned so much to construct this new persona?" I asked.

"Prodigious reading," said Hickox.

"And Clark Rockefeller was his greatest creation," I said.

At that moment, Hickox turned his attention to the oysters. "So, at the risk of being pompous, I am going to show you how I eat oysters," he said.

This was exactly what he had done with Clark, he said, picking up an oyster.

"I brought Clark here and started describing the aspects of the oysters, and Clark turned to somebody he had been chatting with and said, 'Look, really, an oyster is an oyster,' in his rather peremptory and aristocratic way. I said, 'Just wait.' So then I ordered carefully, and as we had the oysters—we had two of each variety, just as we're doing tonight—I described each of them."

He did so again, differentiating the Wellfleet from the Malpeque and the Pemaquid and instructing me to raise the shell to my mouth and drink the oyster whole. As I did this, he described the various tastes, which he called low tide, medium tide, and ocean. "Very similar to wine, oysters are conditioned by their *terroir*"—meaning the region they are from. Rockefeller became instantly attuned to the complexities, the salinity versus the vegetable nature. In Hickox's words, "Some have sea breeze and some have a kind of earthiness rather like seaweed. Within minutes Clark was thinking along those lines. And that's how Clark was with art, with literature, with conversations, with wit."

He mentioned martinis. "He was not very fond of wine. He would drink an excellent wine if one offered it to him." Hickox motioned to the bottle in the ice bucket. "He enjoyed this very Chablis." But when Hickox made him a perfect vodka martini, "so icy that you could see turbulence in it," another new world opened. "He said it was the best martini he ever had."

"He was a sponge," I said.

"Well, if a sponge could also be analytical, then he was a sponge. He learned things very fast. He was not rigid."

After dinner, Hickox took me to the Beehive, a nightclub across the street from the restaurant. "I thought this would be useful for you to see," he said. The place was loud, lively, and filled with attractive young women.

"Clark charmed women," he continued. "Much like a cat delivering mice and dropping them in one's shoe, Clark would bring over women and say, 'This is Patrick Hickox, not just one of the greatest architects in this area, but anywhere.' And I would immediately find an enthusiastic crowd about me, wishing to hear my insights about art, architecture, and the future of civilization."

He said he and Clark "went to all sorts of water spots to play among the demimonde of the nightlife of Boston." He said that Clark would lure women by employing "the reverse of a pickup line. Within seconds he would have them engaged and following his every word. Then he would lead them away enchanted."

"And would he say, 'I'm Clark Rockefeller'? That was the best aphrodisiac," I said.

Hickox nodded his agreement. "One day he mentioned that he liked a certain woman because she didn't like to dance, and he said he hated dancing," he continued. "A couple of weeks after that, I said, 'Clark, I ran into your dancing teacher . . . and she said that you are a very fine dancer.'"

He had caught his friend in a little white lie, but the architect didn't dwell on it. He preferred to recall the nights when the two of them would also frequent the bar in the Liberty Hotel, the former Charles Street Jail, which had been transformed into trendy lodgings. The main bar, for instance, was called the Clink. "Yes, that was definitely a favorite," said Hickox. "A couple of other places I might have really liked he would reject, saying they were overly gerontological."

"Gerontological?" I asked.

"Rather rudely suggesting that the people were not young enough," he said.

Oysters. Martinis. Young women. Dancing teachers. Where was Sandra Boss during all of this nocturnal merrymaking?

"Did he ever talk about how he fell in love with his wife?" I asked the architect.

"Not a peep," he said.

Despite the high life he was living in one end of Boston, Clark Rockefeller was sinking in another, as best illustrated by an episode that unfolded in the waters of Boston's Back Bay. After meeting a couple who were fellow parents at Southfield at the Boston Sailing Center one day, he gave them the usual buildup, saying that his father had sold his company to the U.S. Navy for a fortune, and that he himself worked for the Department of Defense. But he always had time in his insanely busy schedule to indulge in his love of sailing. He had just returned from a sojourn in France, sailing for the America's Cup team. So when he invited the couple to go sailing with him on what he described as his "yacht," they were of course extremely excited.

When the couple arrived at the Boston Sailing Center for their day at sea, Rockefeller was waiting with his daughter, Snooks. However, his yacht was in the shop, he explained, so they would have to go out on one of the sailing club's considerably smaller boats. "We were a little disappointed not to be going on a Rockefeller's yacht," the husband remembered.

The man was even more disappointed when they got out to sea in the little borrowed sailboat, and the America's Cup sailor didn't seem to know what he was doing. Other boats were flying past them, as the sailboat seemed to flounder in the gusty wind. The boat was flopping around in the water, practically sideways, and Rockefeller had absolutely no control over it. Things got so desperate that Rockefeller even turned the boat over to his daughter to sail, which made the couple on board even more nervous. Finally, when they were marooned in the middle of the bay, not moving, just drifting, a kayaker passed by and the couple yelled out for rescue.

"Can you give us a tow?" they asked, and they threw out a rope for the kayaker to tow in the party of four.

"And this is an America's Cup sailor!" the man who went on the boat exclaimed.

Clark Rockefeller was clearly adrift.

CHAPTER 18

"Find Out Who He Is"

In December 2006, four months after the Rockefeller family had moved to Boston, Sandra Boss decided to leave her husband. The last straw, she told the grand jury, was an incident involving their daughter.

"The school called Clark and me into a parent-teacher conference on, I think, December 2, 2006. They said they had been trying to get ahold of me and hadn't been successful. It turned out that Clark had given them a fake cell phone number for me, and had been preventing me from seeing them." She added, "He had been telling me that they didn't do parent-teacher conferences."

When Reigh's teachers finally got her mother and her father in the same room, they expressed some serious concerns.

As Boss recalled, "They said that she, while very intellectually impressive, was having a temper tantrum practically every day. She was really struggling socially. She was five at this time. She would go to the teachers and say, 'Please tell me what to play.' She really had been harmed at that point by his excessive control of her. I spoke to Clark the day after this event and said, 'We really need to follow the teachers' instructions to get some behavioral help for Reigh, and this is proof that we have to change how we're caring for her.' He screamed at me. He threatened me. He told me that I could never talk to the school again. He just went psycho."

"Just to be clear," the prosecutor asked, "what was his position about getting a therapist or a counselor for Reigh to address some of the issues that were raised at school?"

"Unequivocal refusal. He wouldn't allow it under any circumstance."

Leaving Clark Rockefeller was no simple matter, however. It would require careful planning if she wanted to exit the marriage with her daughter, and she was determined not to allow the child to remain in her husband's custody. She spent a week trying to find suitable legal representation.

"It took a lot of strategy to figure out how to get me out," Boss said. "I was quite worried about my safety, and, frankly, he was stalking me in the night and doing a lot of crazy stuff before I left. It was very, very dangerous. I was advised by a psychotherapist brought in by my lawyers that I couldn't take [Reigh] out right away—that it would result in severe danger for all of us."

She wasn't asked to elaborate on the "crazy stuff" that her husband was doing, and she didn't. Instead, she outlined her plan of attack to regain control of her daughter and of her own life. He was taking care of their daughter two-thirds of the time. Sandra immediately claimed two days a week. "Then we started the procedure to get her out. The only thing I focused on was taking care of Reigh. My obsession was her safety. I immediately expressed my concern that he would kidnap her."

On January 17, 2007, almost two months after she had determined to leave Clark, her attorney filed the divorce petition. Both parties' lawyers quickly filed a child custody claim (Sandra paid all of Clark's attorney's fees). Thus began what would turn out to be a full year of contentious negotiations. Sandra moved into an apartment in a building across from what is now the Taj Boston hotel. "I was able to see Reigh two days a week, and the defendant was seeing her five days a week at that time," she said.

Rockefeller was like a wounded lion. When he wasn't tending to his daughter, he roared about the various sins he said his wife had committed against him. He moved into a small apartment overlooking the school bus stop on Beacon Street (the town house on Pinckney Street was to be sold) and entered his financially struggling single-father phase. It wasn't pretty. "He was *furious*!" said one friend. A fellow Southfield parent remembered, "When they were going to get divorced, I asked him, 'How are you going to divide things up?' He said, 'Everything is going to have to be sold. I can't believe this is happening. I can't believe she's doing this.' Looking back on it now, his whole cover was about to be blown. Sandra was the money that allowed him to have the antique cars, the artwork, the clubs, and when she pulled the plug, he was incredibly distraught."

Rockefeller vowed to interview every divorce lawyer in Boston so that Sandra wouldn't be able to hire any of them due to conflict-of-interest restrictions. But she had secured a lawyer, and a good one. Strapped for cash, he asked people to buy back the antique cars they'd sold him or buy furniture that he'd received from Sandra after their split. Don MacLeay, the elderly Cornish excavator, was the recipient of one such request. "I had sold him a '91 Buick, and he called me up and said Sandy was getting a divorce. He said, 'Gee, Don, I want you to go down and pick up the Buick and send me the money.' It was $4,500. I'm thinking, 'Somebody who has been spending all this money, why the hell is he worried about $4,500?' By this time my wife was seriously ill. I said, 'Clark, I've got a lot of problems.' Two or three nights later, he called me: 'Did you pick up the car?' I said, 'No. I'm not going to. I've got troubles too!'"

Rockefeller snapped, "Well, you're no longer my friend!"

Rockefeller also spoke to the art dealer Sheldon Fish, another friend, about his divorce. "He told me, 'Sandy only wanted my money. She married me because I'm a Rockefeller,'" Fish recalled. "He said, 'She used my name, and now she wants everything. Maybe I can trade the paintings for custody of Reigh.'" Soon after that he made a second call to Fish, who was then living in Peru. "He said, 'I had to give Sandy all the paintings for custody of Reigh. I don't have anything. I'm down to my last two million, which is nothing today. I'm in bad shape.' I said, 'Come down to Peru. Two million here is worth a lot more than two million there.' He kept changing the stories. He told so many, and twisted them all around."

His writing partner, Amy Patt, also noticed the change during Rockefeller's divorce proceedings. First, he said he was looking for a job and his search wasn't limited to the weaponry or ballistics fields. "He mentioned that the Dexter Southfield School was talking with him about hiring him as a publicist for the school," she told the grand jury. He was so distraught about the divorce and the prospect of losing his daughter that he couldn't concentrate on writing the sitcom anymore. Finally, they decided to abandon the project, but not before Rockefeller confided to Amy what he planned to do if indeed Sandra was successful in moving Snooks to London: interview for a job with overseas companies, he said. In fact, the Chinese government had recently approached him to work for their missile department.

"That's what I do, Amy," he told her, alluding to his background in ballistics and adding that the Chinese had offered him a three-year contract worth $1 million a year. And if things got rough in the divorce, he assured her, his powerful friends in the Chinese government would step in "and help me take care of the situation."

When she asked what he meant by "the situation," he would only say, "It was something about his daughter, something like 'to get my daughter back.'"

Later, he asked Amy to lie to his daughter's guardian ad litem, the person designated by the court to protect and oversee visitation rights with a child in a divorce case. "To say that I was his girlfriend," Amy explained. "He felt that it would show him in a good light, that he was in a stable relationship." Amy refused.

Even the architect Patrick Hickox, Rockefeller's most ardent defender of all the people I met, noticed a disturbing change in him after Sandra cut him off. Hickox told me about a trip the two of them took to visit Rockefeller's home in Cornish around the time of his divorce. "We went driving up in my little sports car," Hickox said. "He put me up in this guesthouse that he had." The genteel architect blanched the moment he set foot into his lodgings. The house was vacant, mattresses sitting on the bedroom floor. "There were sheets that had never been used that he took right out of the plastic bags. I drove him up the hill and dropped him off at his house, and when I went down it was a little bit after midnight. I went around the house and systematically checked all the windows and all the doors and locked everything. I have a knife that I kept under my pillow."

"A knife?" I asked. "Why in the world would you feel the need to do that?"

"I didn't have a good reason. I just thought, 'I don't know about this person.'"

Back in Boston, Rockefeller complained to one of his Beacon Hill neighbors that he couldn't even spend $200 to trim the ivy on his Pinckney Street house, which was then on the market, without the approval of his wife and her lawyers. Sandra had "bled" him of his riches, he told anyone who would listen. His carefully cultivated façade of the rich, powerful, and entitled aristocrat slowly began to fall apart. As a final indignity, he had to resign from the Algonquin Club, where he had been a director; he was reduced to entering his beloved club on a reciprocal membership.

"He was talking, for the first six or seven months, [about] a house-husband position, and arguing that he should be supported forever and care for Reigh," Sandra Boss testified. "I obviously knew that that was dangerous for her."

The divorce proceedings were stalled for a number of months, with motions flying back and forth. Rockefeller threatened his wife with the specter of testimony from their Boston and Cornish neighbors, who had watched him on a daily basis and seen that the vast majority of the time he had been the one lovingly caring for Snooks.

Then, suddenly, a breakthrough for Sandra came from Seattle. Her father, the retired Boeing engineer William Boss, "stumbled upon some information that was very helpful," as she put it. Rockefeller, who had originally told his wife that his mother was the late Mary Roberts, from southern Virginia, had in recent years changed that story. Two years before the separation, Boss said, he talked about "his mother having been a child actor, Ann Carter."

She continued, "It's interesting, because when he started talking about her having been a child actor, I thought it was funny. I hadn't heard about it before." When she questioned him about it, he said, 'I just never brought it up.'

"I said, 'But that's not what you said your mother's name was.' He said, 'Don't be stupid.' He just insulted me and said I was wrong, and said he'd only mentioned her name once because she was dead. He just said I was an idiot. So what happened was, he had told us all about his mother, Ann Carter, looking so much like Reigh, and blah, blah, blah."

William Boss, apparently angry with his son-in-law for putting his daughter through hell for twelve years of marriage, and for dragging her through what was turning out to be a very bitter divorce, began surfing the Internet. He typed in the name Ann Carter and a Wikipedia entry popped up. Not only was Ann Carter alive, she was doing a documentary for TBS.

William Boss called his daughter with the news. "He said, 'It's a miracle. Clark's mother isn't dead. Something's wrong here.'" Ann Carter, it would turn out, not only didn't have a son named Clark Rockefeller, she had never even met the man.

A few months earlier there had been another incident that caused Sandra to question her husband's identity. It was early 2007, and the couple had to prepare to pay their taxes.

"He was still pretending to be nice to me in an attempt to get me to come back to him," Boss explained. "At that time, I said, 'I'm going to call Phil [their longtime accountant] so I can get the taxes done.' He started slamming Phil as being incompetent and the wrong guy, and we shouldn't use him."

"Why don't I get somebody else?" Rockefeller suggested.

By that time, Boss wasn't interested in her soon-to-be ex-husband's opinion. "I'll just call Phil," she told him.

"I did, and he and I exchanged some e-mails. I said, 'By the way, I need to make sure that my taxes are okay, because Clark has been working with you, and one thing I'm worried about is, I don't know if you know that I have a six-year-old daughter named Reigh.'

"He said, 'Oh, yes, I do know about that. Your brother told me.'

"I found that Clark had been telling the accountant that he was my brother so the accountant would acquiesce to what he wanted on the tax forms."

"Meaning he would file it as a single return instead of a married return?" Boss was asked.

"Exactly," she said.

At last, after more than a decade of glaring warning signs, Boss began to suspect that her husband was a fraud. "I hired a private investigator and gave the private investigator every single thing that Clark had told me about himself . . . and said, 'Go find out who he is.'"

Boss asked her attorneys to find her a good private eye, and they suggested Frank Rudewicz, a former police detective with more than two decades of experience.

He agreed to meet me for dinner in Boston, and while I waited for him to arrive I read a transcript of his testimony in the Clark Rockefeller case, in which he described his business: "We are a licensed private-investigative firm. So [we] do anything from surveillance to internal investigations and computer forensics and litigation support across the country." His online bio noted that he was also a "Certified Anti-Money-Laundering Specialist" and had extensive experience "investigating fraud, workplace incidents, and employee misconduct."

I was expecting a hard-boiled detective in the Columbo or Mannix mold, but instead I encountered a big, friendly, clean-cut guy in a business suit. He was more than happy to relate the story of the strangest case of his long career—even stranger, he noted, than a famous case that was featured on the TV series *Forensic Files*, in which Rudewicz unmasked a man who used false names and assumed identities to fake his own death in Mexico and collect $6 million. (The detective's work enabled the insurance company to avoid paying the bogus claim, and the scammer to be caught and punished.)

"I got a phone call from a lawyer representing Sandra Boss," Rudewicz said. "I didn't know who their client was. The lawyer told me, 'We want to engage you to do an asset search.'"

Other than the fact that it involved a Rockefeller, the job was a routine one. An asset search is commonly performed in divorce cases when one (or both) of the parties is suspected of squirreling away cash. It involves scouring public records, tracing bank accounts, and cross-referencing databases in an effort to follow the money trail to any hidden assets. "There were a lot of construction projects going on, and she thought he may have struck private deals with the contractors and gotten kickbacks." Rudewicz assumed the voice of his target overseeing the never-ending construction jobs on his Cornish estate: "'Look, this is a $400,000 project. You pay me a hundred, you keep three, and we're all set.'"

Rockefeller had dug deep pits—security bunkers, he called them—all around the Doveridge property in Cornish. His wife suspected that he might be literally hiding money in their backyard. The investigator wasn't only looking for hard cash but also boats, cars, anything hidden. And Sandra was convinced that he had hidden something, Rudewicz said, because there was so much money flying out of her checking account—and frankly she had been too busy working to check on where it had all gone. Now, at long last, she wanted answers. "She was saying, 'Before I give this person money—and I know I have to give him money to settle our divorce—I want to know if he has already stolen from me. I want to know if he's stashed some money, so instead of offering a million, if I know he has five hundred thousand already, I can offer less.'"

Based on Rudewicz's limited interactions with Boss, he found her to be a "very organized, driven individual who was, in my opinion, used to dictating and determining what she wanted and what she got. At least in this context." In other words, a very tough cookie, except, as she admitted on the witness stand, when it came to her husband. Initially, though, she was less interested in who her husband was than in whether or not he had stashed any of her cash. As she told Rudewicz, millions of her hard-earned dollars had flowed through Clark Rockefeller's hands. The private investigator went to work.

"We started with his name, date of birth [which Sandra had given as the leap day February 29, 1960], and address," Rudewicz said. Entering this information into a few databases typically produces a list of prior addresses, potential relatives, neighbors, and, in some cases, places of employment.

The search results showed his addresses with Sandra in New York, Cornish, and Boston, but absolutely nothing from before 1994, when he met Sandra. "That was strange," Rudewicz said. "This wasn't a seventeen-year-old kid who was just starting out in life. This was a grown man with a high-profile name, who, from his own account, had a very substantial life prior to meeting Sandra Boss."

Rudewicz didn't find any hidden assets; he didn't find *any* assets whatsoever in Clark Rockefeller's name. Nothing that Boss and her attorneys had told the private eye about Rockefeller could be verified: not where and when he was born, although his birth certificate certainly should have been easy to find if he had been born in a New York City hospital, as he had always claimed; not who his parents were and how they had died; not his father's $50 million legal dispute with the U.S. Navy; not his admission to Yale, at fourteen or at any age; not his (or any Rockefeller's) having lived at 19 Sutton Place; and not his relationship with his "godfather," the late Harry Copeland, who Rockefeller claimed in an affidavit had given him most of the information he possessed about his long-deceased parents. (Rudewicz tracked Copeland's supposed widow, then in her nineties, to a Virginia nursing home, but never got to interview her.)

Rockefeller had no employment history, no relatives, no addresses, no passport, and no credit cards that weren't paid by Sandra Boss. There was not even a marriage license issued to Clark Rockefeller and Sandra Boss. He had, in short, absolutely no trace of a pre-Sandra life.

Most of his lies, however, had some kernel of truth behind them.

"The brilliance of Clark Rockefeller, if you can call it that, was that almost everything he told people had some semblance of fact—not true, but some facts," said Rudewicz. "Was there an Ann Carter? Yes. Was there a Rockefeller born on February 29, 1960? Yes. There was a Scott Rockefeller, who lived on Long Island and was born in New York City. So now I'm thinking, 'He's done his research and has picked somebody who has that birth date with the same last name, so that anybody who checks is going to get to a certain point, and that will keep buying him time.'"

Rudewicz handed me a piece of paper from his briefcase. It was a copy of an entry from the 1978 Yale yearbook for James Frederick Clark, a young man distantly related to the Rockefeller family with three of the same names that Rockefeller went by, as well as some of the honors and affiliations he claimed—Yale dean's aide, marching band, drama club—the implication being that Rockefeller had gone through the Yale yearbook, found someone he admired, and simply used him as clay for the character he was building.

Rudewiciz checked the records on Rockefeller's cell phone bill. Nothing suspicious, and nothing that could give him any solid leads. They tried to get his computer, where surely he kept his secrets, but Rockefeller had taken it with him. "He never let me near the computer," Sandra told the investigator, who searched blogs, social networks, anything and everything that might show where—or with whom—he was communicating. Again, nothing, other than technical geek Web sites and one book review he had written for Amazon.com.

By the second day of his investigation, Rudewicz smelled a rat. "I told Sandra Boss's attorney, 'There is no record of this guy, there are no addresses.' We had to be careful about how we would communicate this back to the client. This was her husband. We couldn't just say, 'You married this stone-cold, boldfaced liar.'"

"So what did you tell her?" I asked.

"I said, 'Look, we don't know who he is. We know he's not Clark Rockefeller, but we don't know who he is.'"

Despite the mounting evidence that he was not a Rockefeller, Clark continued to cling to the name, as Rudewicz explained in his testimony. "As we kept running into dead ends and asking for more information, it became known to Clark that a private-investigative firm was engaged. We had asked for birth-certificate proof. We were told that it was [issued in] the city of New York, a hospital in New York, he could not remember which. Vital records required an application and an affidavit, which we were provided, signed by Mr. Rockefeller."

Rudewicz was asked to produce the addendum to the affidavit, then to read it aloud:

J. Clark Rockefeller under oath do depose and state, Sandra L. Boss (Sandra) and I met on February 5, 1993, and ever since then she has known me by my one and only name, James Frederick Mills Clark Rockefeller. If I indeed had a different name, one would find it difficult to imagine that in all the years she has known me such a name would not have come to light, particularly since Sandra, throughout our life together, met many persons who have known me by that same name for much longer than she has known me.

"Mr. Rudewicz, let me ask you, how many of these deep background checks have you done in your entire career?" the investigator was asked before the grand jury.

"This is a significant portion of our business. It would be thousands," he said.

"Among those thousands, how often have you come to this result, where you simply cannot find information about a person?"

"Never."

Sandra Boss summed up Rudewicz's findings in her grand jury testimony: "The private investigator proved (a) that nothing Clark had said was provable; (b) he couldn't figure out who he was."

"Do you remember any of the specific details that you told the private investigator that he then told you were not true?" she was asked.

"Sure," Sandra replied, and she began to list some of her husband's many lies:

"He hadn't grown up at 19 Sutton Place. That had actually been a multifamily building for a long time.

"He hadn't gone to Yale.

"He hadn't gone to any of the other schools that he had said he had gone to.

"He hadn't worked for First Boston.

"He didn't have a birth certificate that said he was born in 1960 in New York, New York."

In short, Boss stated, "Every single thing that he ever said."

If she was humiliated, as a Harvard Business School graduate and a young partner of McKinsey & Company, to have fallen prey to such a monstrous con, she didn't show it in the courtroom. And she didn't act humiliated when she got the news. Instead, at last, she took control. Her days as a cowering wife under the sway of her powerful husband were over.

In consultation with her lawyers, Boss settled on a plan. She knew that Clark despised courtrooms. "I noticed that when we went in front of a judge on a minor issue he got very nervous," she said. So she decided to make what she called "a big play." Her lawyers put "every single thing about all the bad treatment," as well as the endless and unfathomable lies, into an affidavit, which they filed in the probate court where the Boss/Rockefeller divorce was being handled. Then they waited to see how Rockefeller would respond.

Her husband "completely freaked out," Boss said. Two days later, his attorney called Boss's and said, according to Boss, "Clark wants to settle. You can have Reigh. You can take her to London. All he wants is a million dollars."

She had an escape hatch in her job. A while back she had been offered a position in the London office. Now she told her superiors, "If that offer is still open, I'd like to take it." "Because I thought he was an incredibly scary person who had no identity, and that I needed to get her out of the country so that he would not kidnap her."

Moving from the Boston office to the London office came with a pay cut of more than $1 million, but for Sandra, being able to put an ocean between her and her soon-to-be ex-husband was well worth it. She told Rockefeller's attorney, "I'm really glad that I can have full custody of her. Let's talk about the number.'"

She countered his million with $750,000. He shot back with $800,000. "We settled on eight hundred, and he also wanted two cars, a dress, and my engagement ring," said Sandra. What dress—and why he wanted it—was not discussed at the trial. But from that point forward, Rockefeller, unwilling or unable to produce documentation to prove his identity, never stood a chance. Boss got everything: the historic house and church in Cornish, the town house on Beacon Hill, and, most important, custody of Reigh.

The judge approved her request to take the child to London, where mother and daughter moved into a lovely home in the well-heeled Knightsbridge neighborhood, limiting the doting father to three court-supervised visits a year.

"Why did you want supervised visits?" Boss was asked.

"Because I thought he would kidnap her. I knew that he was good at privacy. I knew that he didn't have the identity that he said he had. I found it entirely possible to believe that he had a scary other identity."

Rockefeller had no choice but to agree to her terms, which she enumerated for the grand jury:

"I [would] have full effective legal custody of Reigh. He would get

$800,000 in three payments. Bizarrely, that neither of us would write a book, and that he could have three supervised visits a year, either in Boston or in the city that he could prove he was living."

The visits would be strictly structured. "No overnights. For the first of what was to be three annual supervised visits, he was allowed to see his daughter for eight hours a day over three days, sequentially. He had to meet with her therapist beforehand and after. All the terms of the visit had to be agreed upon in advance."

Sandra and Reigh Boss moved to London on December 23, 2007.

"She was taken from me four days before Christmas, which was evil," Rockefeller would later say. "I just want to be with her. I want to get her up in the morning, send her off to school, walk her to the bus, wait for her when she comes back. Give her something to eat at night, and put her back to bed, and the next day the same thing again."

"On the day of the [divorce settlement] hearing he sent me a text message: 'I've just signed the Treaty of Versailles,'" remembered Clark's Starbucks friend Bob Skorupa, referring to the treaty that ended World War I, which Germany signed under protest. John Greene, another member of the Starbucks group, added, "He gave up all rights to his kid in return for $800,000, plus there would be no due diligence—that is, no investigation of his true identity. We would be here at Starbucks, and his kid was gone, legally taken to London. I think he took the money from her and then had regrets. I think the moment he took the money he started planning on how to get his daughter back."

CHAPTER 19

Chip Smith:
Baltimore, Maryland

A seemingly broken Clark Rockefeller walked the streets of Beacon Hill during the 2007 holiday season. His third-floor bachelor's apartment at 73 Beacon Street, where he never even unpacked boxes or arranged furniture, would be paid for by Sandra for six months. But though he had a temporary place to stay, he claimed to be rootless without his daughter, his Pinckney Street town house, and the clout he had enjoyed for so long, thanks to his wife's seemingly bottomless bank account and her credit cards.

"He told me he'd spent $800,000 on the custody fight and also had to pay Sandy's attorney's fees of $1.2 million, and he was completely broke and was going to have to start looking for a job, which I found funny because he had never mentioned having to have a job before," said one friend who watched Clark's slow decline.

Rockefeller spent the Christmas of 2007 with the artist William Quigley and his family at Quigley's sister's house in Boston. There were children at the celebration, which seemed to compound Rockefeller's misery. "It just makes me so sad seeing all those children running around," he told the Quigleys. "I miss Snooks so much." In the course of the evening, someone asked about the status of his modern art masterpieces in the divorce. "I had to give my whole collection to the family trust, so I no longer own it," he said. If that weren't stressful enough, he added, his ex-wife now wanted him to pay her even more money, up to $15,000 a month. The artist's brother-in-law asked Rockefeller why he didn't just move to London to be near his daughter. "You're a Rockefeller!" he reminded him. "You can do anything you want." Rockefeller replied sadly, "Everything is depleted." Quigley remembered, "He kept saying, 'I just miss her so much!' He was completely devastated and ripped apart."

He seemed to find some solace in impressing women, however. "He was always with some pretty girl," said his friend Sheldon Fish, the art dealer. "He introduced me to one of the Dixie Chicks." Another friend added, "He loved blondes." He put the full-court press on my friend Roxane West, the young woman from a West Texas oil family, after she collided with him at a party at an art gallery in Manhattan. After one lunch together, he began "text flirting," as he called it, proposing meetings while brooding that he was unable to travel from Boston to the city because all of his private clubs' residential facilities were booked and he, as a Rockefeller, couldn't stay in a commercial hotel. "I hope you had a good Mother's Day," he texted on one occasion. On June 1, he texted, "Please please PLEASE do not feel ignored. Very busy week. Just coming to an end. Would LOVE to see you. Will call tonight. Just returned from Bermuda. Rented summer house there. Excellent time."

He went to great pains to present an elaborate charade. At one point while on the phone with Roxane, he even acted as if he were speaking to his daughter, who was, of course, already living in London. By the time she received her last text message from him, Roxane was certain that he was a charlatan whom she intended never to see again. "I just thought it was all bullshit, that he wasn't who he said he was," she said.

One of his last social appearances in Boston was at a dinner party in the home of Paul and Helen Wessling, on Commonwealth Avenue. During Rockefeller's trial, a fellow guest at that dinner, the veteran financial portfolio manager Nathan Peltz, took the stand. "We had cocktails, and I was told another guest was coming," Peltz testified, identifying the

guest as "the defendant." Asked if Rockefeller had disclosed his occupation, Peltz said he had thought he had something to do with investments. "I never got a clear answer as to the name of the company. My
understanding was it was probably a private fund. Our host was also
in the same business. I'm used to having people say, 'I work for X, Y, Z
company.'"

Peltz also testified, "He said he lived on Beacon Hill and had just
experienced the loss of his child. He had a little girl, whom he referred
to as Snooks, or Snookums. He said he had the child out of wedlock in
England, and that the woman who had mothered the child had come to
some sort of resolution. He was raising her as a single parent. He said
the mother had decided she wanted her child back. He said his child
had been taken back to England by a court order by a judge here in
Massachusetts. . . . He never said anything about having a wife. It was
clear he was distraught and he felt he had been unjustly treated by the
court, to the extent that the court had granted the mother custody."

The cocktail hour had segued into dinner, during which Rockefeller
couldn't get off the subject of Snooks. "He talked incessantly about losing her," Peltz told the court. "He was very angry about it. I suggested,
why couldn't he go back to the court and talk to the judge? He indicated that if the court couldn't resolve this he would probably go back
to England and bring the child back. I took it to mean the equivalent of
kidnapping."

While one carefully cultivated persona, Clark Rockefeller, was dying,
another was being born. The process of reinvention began in November
2007, even before he lost custody of his daughter, with an e-mail to Obsidian Realty in Baltimore. Julie Gochar, an owner of Obsidian Realty,
who received the e-mail, later testified during Clark Rockefeller's trial.

A blond young woman in a white cotton summer dress, Gochar was
at least six months pregnant at the time of the trial. After some preamble about her company, which she owned with two partners and ran
with twenty-seven independently contracted agents in the greater Bal-

timore area, she was asked by the prosecutor if she knew the individual sitting with his lawyers at the defense table.

"Yes, I do," she replied.

"What is the name by which you know him?"

"Chip Smith," she said, adding, "He sent an e-mail to the office through our general inquiry. He was interested in relocating to Baltimore. It was mid- to late November 2007."

"In the initial e-mail, did he provide any information about himself at all?"

"Just that he was in Chile and would be at some point in the spring of the following year coming up by boat and staying in Baltimore."

"Did you respond to his e-mail?" she was asked. Of course, she said. The Baltimore real estate market was red-hot and intensely competitive in the fall of 2007, and any Realtor with a heartbeat would recognize that an e-mail for a relocation from Chile seeking a house in the half-million-dollar range was a slam dunk for a sale. "He asked for help in learning about Baltimore and the neighborhoods, and that's my job," she said.

He hadn't given her his name at that point, just his e-mail address: svshenandoah@gmail.com. "There was a lot of information provided back and forth," said Gochar, the result of "the usual probing questions on my part to get to know him . . . to help him with where he would want to live. . . . He had a daughter. Needed certain housing to accommodate that. Wanted to be in the city and would be working under contract, I believe for some sort of construction, catamarans."

Gochar was asked what the sailor said about his daughter, whose name he said was Muffy. "I knew he had a seven-year-old daughter. On the boat with him."

"Did he tell you how he was able to raise a seven-year-old on a boat?"

"Only in the context of schooling. She was homeschooled on the Calvert School Program, actually headquartered in Baltimore. He wanted a city-row-home kind of feel with a roof deck, ideally close to Camden Yards, so he could engage in his passion for baseball." Because he was sailing around Chile, he said, e-mail service would be difficult and intermittent."

"What did he tell you about the girl's mother?"

"The mother was a surrogate, and he had destroyed the papers on her identity," she said, adding that he had burned the birth records to ensure that his daughter wouldn't ever discover her mother's identity. "She doesn't need to know," he told the Realtor.

The night after receiving the e-mail, Julie Gochar told her husband about her prospective new client, the ship's captain named Chip Smith. "He's a sailor," she said. "How does he have the money to buy a house?"

"Those contract captains make a lot of money," her husband answered. And that was good enough for Julie Gochar, who immediately began searching for suitable properties to show the captain when he arrived in Baltimore.

After e-mailing and instant-messaging for a few months, the captain finally gave Gochar some specific directions. "In early February we were talking logistically how he would be locating from another country and where he would stay. Would he stay in a hotel with enough time to find housing, or would he need some sort of temporary short-term housing? So we set him up in short-term housing . . . two-month lease on a row home around the corner from our office."

"Why a rental instead of a hotel?"

"He didn't like hotels," she said, because, he explained, he didn't trust them. She set Chip Smith up for a two-month rental at $2,000 per month just behind her real estate office on South Wolfe Street, beginning in April, when he would arrive. She drew up the lease in the name of S. V. Shenandoah, assuming the e-mail address was the captain's name. "That's funny," he e-mailed back. "That's the e-mail address of my boat. My name is actually Charles Smith." She testified, "He told me he loathed the name Charles." He instructed her to call him Chip. Before his arrival, Chip had several boxes of his belongings sent to Julie Gochar's real estate office, big boxes with a Boston return address, which he explained were filled with clothing, "because I won't have any northern wear when I arrive." When she asked him why the boxes were shipped from Boston when he had told her he was originally from Wisconsin, he replied, "Oh, when I was at Harvard, I left some of my personal belongings there, which Harvard alums are allowed to do."

They set up a meeting in the realty office. When Smith strolled in, Gochar did a double take. "It wasn't at all what I was expecting. . . . I thought he would be a tall, tanned, sailor-looking guy. . . . He wasn't at all." His accent reminded her of Thurston Howell III from *Gilligan's Island*, although, she would later admit, she had never heard a Boston Brahmin accent before. The other thing that struck her was that he seemed much too slight to be a sailor, much less the captain of a massive ship. Her husband had attended St. Mary's College in southern Maryland with a group of real sailors, strong and robust men who were nothing like the fey gentleman who stood before her wearing a baseball cap and thick black-rimmed glasses, with extremely red hair that looked as if it had been dyed. "I certainly wasn't picturing five foot nothing, pale . . ."

He had warned her in advance that he wouldn't be tanned, because his trip was spent mostly in the rain. "I can't believe I've been sailing for as long as I have and don't even have a tan to show for it," he said.

He was alone. He said his daughter was spending some time with his two sisters in Wisconsin and would be arriving later in the summer. He said he wanted a list of suitable properties to visit. It was April and he needed a home fast so he could relocate immediately to start his new job: he was under contract with a Baltimore boat company, designing, building, and selling a new brand of state-of-the-art catamarans.

Since he lived practically next door, and because Julie Gochar makes it her business to be available "24/7" for her clients, Chip Smith quickly came to be a welcomed regular presence in the offices of Obsidian Realty. Sure, he was a bit odd, in his salmon-colored khaki pants, some embroidered with little fish, and his boat shoes, always worn without socks. But he was a client, and for Julie Gochar the client was king. "He was there even when it wasn't pertaining to us having a meeting," she said. "Doing research. Looking at his own properties, property values. Other things. He just kind of came in and hung out in the office."

They let him use an office computer. They even gave him his own e-mail address: chip@obsidianrealty.com.

"At some point did he have greater access to your computer system?" she was asked in court.

"Yes, he did."

"How did he get greater access?"

"I gave him a key," meaning a key to the Obsidian Realty offices. "So he could come and go as he pleased. Because there was a lot that he needed to get at. He didn't have a computer where he was staying. . . . And to be frank, I didn't want to meet him down there every time he had the need to go and do some research."

Smith would often spend hours in the office. "It was almost like he was working in the office with us," said Gochar, adding that he would sit at the computer "looking at designs of boats and values of gold and stock and stuff like that."

Of course, it didn't hurt that he had money for a substantial real estate purchase. Gochar realized that early on, when she asked him to complete the standard prequalification loan papers for the half-million-dollar value of the properties he would be seeing. "And he indicated that he would not be financing the transaction, he'd be paying cash."

"Look, I can trust you now," he told his Realtor as they prepared to look at properties. "I come from a lot of money. I just don't want people to know that I have money. Because everybody's always coming at me with their hands out."

"Well, you're in the right place," Julie Gochar said. "Because nobody here cares if you have money or not."

She was referring to the low-key South Point neighborhood of Baltimore, where money didn't impress people. "You have to understand that you're going to be sitting next to a tugboat captain on one side of you and an orthopedic surgeon on the other side. They almost prefer if you have money that you don't rub it in their faces." He hardly toned it down, though. When Gochar invited him to an office mixer—"It's a great way to meet people!" she said—he demurred, saying, "I don't have any party clothes," only to show up in a big white floppy sailor's hat and pinkish pants, which the office staff came to call "Chip Smith's Party Pants."

There were other idiosyncrasies. Chip Smith ate only "white" food: things like chicken salad on white bread, white potatoes, white sliced turkey, the whites of hard-boiled eggs. "And don't put anything on it," he would tell the waitress when ordering a chicken sandwich at lunch, turning to Julie Gochar to add, "I can't have tomatoes because I'm allergic." While they looked at houses, he was always on his cell phone, texting or having loud and animated conversations about things like money and diamond rings and about how his daughter didn't like her name, "Muffy," and he might start calling her "TLO—The Little One." As for his choice of homes, he explained, the name of the street was extremely important. He couldn't live on Boston Street, he told Julie Gochar, but he could see himself living on Montgomery Street, and they quickly found a house he loved at 10 West Montgomery in the Federal Hill section of the city, which was owned by an attorney, whose library Chip Smith admired.

"He loved the neighborhood and he loved the street name," said Gochar. But he felt the house needed $100,000 worth of renovations. "I'm going to lowball it," Chip Smith told his Realtor. "I'm paying cash and I should be able to get it for $100,000 less."

His low-bid offer was rejected and another buyer immediately swooped in to offer almost the asking price. He offered $150,000 more than his original offer. Still the buyer went with the other offer, even though it was $50,000 less, which sent Chip Smith into a rage. "I just don't lose," he said. Gochar saw another side of Smith that day. "Kind of a temper tantrum almost. 'I want that house! I don't understand why I can't have that house! I'm paying *cash* for this house!' My personal impression was that he was used to getting what he wanted."

When he didn't immediately get it, Chip Smith went around his Realtor and contacted the seller directly, which didn't hold much sway with the seller, but succeeded in infuriating Gochar. By then, she said, she was beginning to wonder if Chip Smith was worth all the endless time and trouble she was enduring in trying to help him find a house.

By early May, he wanted a sailboat, a catamaran. Not for his job, which he said was designing catamarans, but for other reasons. He began looking at the boats docked at the Anchorage Marina, which billed itself as "Baltimore's Premier Yachting Center." As reported by Annie Linskey in the *Baltimore Sun:* One day in the marina, he met Bruce Boswell, the owner of a twenty-six-foot catamaran. He introduced himself as Chip MacLaughlin and asked Boswell whether he was interested in selling the boat, which, being somewhat dilapidated, was worth half the $10,000 cash the stranger offered. "Chainsaw food" was how the boat would later be described. "I was happy to sell it," Boswell told the *Sun.*

They retired to a neighborhood bar, where MacLaughlin spun "a big story," Boswell was quoted as recalling. He said he had come to Baltimore to be closer to his sister, who lived in the city. He bragged about his membership in the private Century Club in New York and said he planned to buy Baltimore's historic Mayflower Theater and restore it to grandeur.

As for the purchase of the boat, Chip suggested that they close the deal in his office, Obsidian Realty. It was night when they arrived there. Chip MacLaughlin punched in the after-hours security code and opened the door with his own key. While counting out the cash— $10,000 in twenty- and fifty-dollar bills—he mentioned that he *owned* Obsidian Realty. If Boswell had bothered to check, he would have discovered that one of Julie Gochar's partners in the company actually had the name MacLaughlin, but his first name was Henry.

Chip insisted that the boat be registered in the name of Chip Smith, Boswell later said, because "he didn't like the name MacLaughlin." The deal was consummated, and the catamaran remained docked in the slip owned by Bruce Boswell's brother Harry, to whom the new owner would pay $2,200 annual rent.

On June 6, Rockefeller called the owner of Boston Bullion, a precious-metals brokerage in the Boston suburb of Arlington. "He was looking to purchase some gold," said the proprietor, Kenneth Murphy. The caller identified himself as Clark Rock, gave his address as 217 Commonwealth Avenue, Boston, and said he wanted to convert the approximately $2 million he'd just won in a patent lawsuit into gold. He said he needed $465,000 in gold immediately, $300,000 more on June 30, and $1.235 million on July 31.

Clark Rock asked Murphy to meet him on June 9 at the Harvard Square Starbucks in Cambridge. "He looked like a college professor to me, kind of preppy, Ivy League," Murphy remembered. He had wired $465,000 to Boston Bullion that day from his bank account, listed under the name of Clark Rock. Once the funds arrived in Murphy's bank account, Rock could collect his gold, which he wanted in South African Krugerrands. Ten days later, on June 20, Rock arrived at Boston Bullion to pick up 527 Krugerrands, which weighed almost forty pounds. He put them in his briefcase and asked Murphy for a ride back to Boston.

The next day, June 21, Rock called Murphy again, saying he wanted to sell twenty-four of the Krugerrands. But three days later, Rock called to say he'd changed his mind. "He told me he was unhappy with the Krugerrands altogether and wanted to exchange them for American Eagle gold coins," the official gold bullion coin of the U.S. Mint, on the face of which is Augustus Saint-Gaudens's "Lady Liberty." American Eagles have no IRS or other reporting requirements and are thereby untraceable. On July 7, Clark Rock returned to Boston Bullion with his briefcase full of Krugerrands and left with a briefcase full of American Eagles, which have a face value of $50 each but sell for the going price of gold, making each one-ounce coin worth more than $1,000. A week later, on July 14, Rock wired another $300,000 to Boston Bullion, to order approximately three hundred more American Eagle coins, which he would pick up a week later, on July 21.

Chip Smith finally found a suitable place to live in Baltimore, a carriage house behind a large home that had been converted into an apartment building. The address was 618 Ploy Street, in the Mount Vernon neighborhood. Julie Gochar almost didn't show him the house, because she was certain he would dislike the street name: Ploy. To her surprise, he loved it. The price was $450,000, inclusive of upgrades being completed at the time of the sale, among them a kitchen renovation and new carpeting. Smith insisted that the house be put in the name of his limited liability corporation, P1OY St. Parking, LLC, a corporation he said was registered in the state of Nevada.

"After the offer was accepted, did the defendant continue to spend a lot of time in your office?" the prosecutor asked Gochar.

"No," she answered. "He went home to Wisconsin to visit his sisters and his daughter.... Both his sisters had been divorced once or twice.... My overall impression was that he didn't believe in their tactics for marriage and getting divorced. They kind of made him a workhorse whenever he got home. So he didn't want to go home all the time."

The original date for the closing on the house was June 27. "But it continued to get postponed for multiple reasons, some from the seller's side . . . some from our side," Gochar said. "[Chip] had been traveling through Europe and fell ill and was not going to make it in time for settlement. He was able to get in touch with me via e-mail at one point, when he was well enough to do it and had access."

She was asked if she had received word of Smith's becoming ill while abroad from him or from other sources. "No, it was him telling me. It was either Switzerland or Sweden. . . . It turns out that they couldn't really identify what the problem was for four days. It was a flu, which turned out to be a reaction to sun-dried tomatoes."

At that, a roar of laughter rose in the courtroom. Gochar remained straight-faced. She still had much more to tell.

He told her he had flown in from Chestertown, the private airport just outside of Baltimore, on a private plane he had chartered—and piloted himself. He couldn't wire the money for the purchase. "Because I can't wire money out of this trust account," he explained. So the $450,000 sales price had to be paid via cashier's check. The sale of the carriage house closed on July 18, 2007. Gochar was asked if he moved in immediately. "I don't know," she replied. "I know that he was going home to pack up and make the drive down. He had left some belongings in Boston while he was abroad, so he was going to pick those up and do his formal move throughout that week."

"Do you know who helped him move?"

"Yes, Beth Grinspoon. She's another agent in our office."

The Boston police detectives who would later work on the case, Ray Mosher and Joseph Leeman, told me about Grinspoon, who was twenty-five, with the greatest admiration. She moonlighted from her real estate job as a waitress and bartender at the Annabel Lee Tavern. She was a triathlete. Her picture on the Obsidian Realty Web site showed a fit, attractive, dark-haired woman in a brown polo shirt and turquoise earrings.

The agents at Obsidian Realty soon came to know that Chip Smith was cheap, and they recognized that some of his stories—such as the one he told about appearing in a Backstreet Boys video—were a little far-fetched. But he was offering several thousand dollars, plus transportation to the Boston area, where his belongings were stored, so Beth Grinspoon said she would enlist a friend and help him move. He flew them from Baltimore to Boston on AirTran, the cut-rate airline, and put them up in the Royal Sonesta Hotel, in Cambridge. He kept the whereabouts of his storage facility a secret until the next morning, when a cab took the movers to a Boston suburb, to a house with a two-car garage, which was packed with Smith's belongings.

It was July 22, one day after the man calling himself Clark Rock had picked up his $300,000 in American Eagles from Boston Bullion.

He rented a twenty-six-foot U-haul truck, but when it became obvious that it was much too small for the load, he returned to rent a five-foot-nine-inch trailer as well. Almost everything was packed in large boxes, which were very heavy.

"What do you have in these boxes, gold?" Grinspoon asked him, according to the detectives.

"Books," Smith replied.

Soon the owner of the house, whom Smith identified as his aunt, returned home and urged him to finish as quickly as possible. "I've expired my welcome on using the garage," Smith told his moving team, imploring them to hurry. When they had finished loading the truck and trailer, Smith, who remained in Boston, sent Grinspoon on to Baltimore. He still owed her $1,400. On July 23, Beth Grinspoon unloaded the truck at 618 Ploy Street. As per Smith's instructions, she had a locksmith change all the locks and give her the new keys. All the while, she received regular e-mails and text messages from Smith asking, "Are you done?"

That day, July 23, Chip Smith was back in Boston as Clark Rockefeller. Embarking on the most audacious act of his life, he began setting up people like pieces on a chessboard.

That evening, he called the driver Darryl Hopkins and booked him for a trip the coming Friday to New York City, where Rockefeller said he had to attend a board meeting. "He wanted to leave at seven a.m., shoot down to the board meeting, vote on something, leave, and try and be back in Boston by three or three-thirty," Hopkins would later testify. Though Hopkins had another corporate client on his schedule that day, he chose to drive Clark, because he was a Rockefeller, and a Rockefeller would "make the phone ring more often." The charge was $700.

While his driver sped toward New York, Rockefeller made calls on his cell phone in the backseat. "One of them was about spending the weekend in Newport, in particular with Senator Chafee's son," Hopkins remembered.

"Do you know who Senator Chafee is?" Rockefeller asked Hopkins after hanging up.

Certainly, he did: he was the former Rhode Island senator Lincoln Chafee, known as a Rockefeller Republican.

"I'm friends with his son," Rockefeller said, adding that he and his daughter, Snooks, had been invited to go sailing that weekend with the senator's son in Newport. Would Darryl be able to drive them?

"Yes, of course."

Rockefeller instructed Hopkins to drop him off on the corner of Central Park South and Sixth Avenue and said he would walk the block or so from there to his board meeting. Fifty minutes later, he called to say he was finished and told Hopkins to pick him up in front of the Plaza Hotel. Next he wanted to zip over to the J.G. Melon restaurant for a take-out lunch—"steak tahr-tahr," the driver later imitated him saying—and then back to Boston.

Wolfing down the raw meat with his hands—the restaurant had neglected to include utensils—Rockefeller made phone calls along the way, all the while griping about how he was "sick and tired" of board meetings. He said he didn't need the headache or the meager fee the company's directors were awarded for their attendance. Besides, he said, "I don't work anymore." When he had worked, he always told Hopkins, it was carrying out high-level duties "for the Defense Department."

Another cell phone conversation that Hopkins overheard on the way to Boston concerned a "clingy" friend named Harold, who was certain to be a thorn in Rockefeller's side during the upcoming weekend of sailing with Snooks and Senator Chafee's son. "Oh, I'm stuck with him again?" Rockefeller groused loudly on his cell. "Do I *have* to do this?"

Once he hung up, Rockefeller talked about how he might ditch Harold. "He said that Harold was a friend of the family, gay, and very— he always described him as being very clingy, very sort of possessive," Hopkins recalled. "He said that he was a pain in the ass and that he was getting stuck with him again because of some family relationship."

Rockefeller didn't go into details, and the driver didn't dare to pry. "Why don't you get a restraining order?" he asked. Rockefeller said, "This guy's too dangerous. He might hurt me and, God forbid, he might hurt Snooks."

Then Rockefeller said, "Darryl, look, I know you're down on your luck. And you know I can help you out. I'd pay you $2,000—I'd pay you *$2,500*—if we can get rid of this guy for the day."

What could Hopkins say but yes? He later gave his reasoning to the grand jury: "Knowing that I was going to be returning to Florida, that my business was falling apart because of the economy—I mean, I was working in negative territory, not enough to even make car payments and the insurance for livery plates, which is over $5,000 a year. It was summertime, it was really slow, and my wife and I had made the decision: this isn't working anymore. So if the ship's going to go down, we'll go down together as a family."

And right there, in the backseat of his car, was the answer to his problems. "I don't think there's anybody in America that doesn't know the name Rockefeller," said Hopkins. "This guy doesn't work for a living. He lives on Beacon Hill. His daughter goes to the Southfield School. Everything—the steak tartare, board meetings in New York, there was nothing about this individual that did not say that he was a real honest-to-God Rockefeller. Even the way he talked."

Hopkins didn't hesitate to accept the offer. He would have ditched a battalion of clingy Harolds for Clark Rockefeller. "If you want to get rid of somebody, we'll get rid of somebody," Hopkins told him. The next day they met to rehearse their plan. Rockefeller even practiced leaping into the limo with Snooks in front of the valet parkers at the Algonquin Club. After dropping him off, Hopkins called his wife. "I couldn't wait to call her and tell her that Clark Rockefeller was willing to help us out," he said.

After Hopkins dropped him off at the Algonquin Club, Rockefeller called Aileen Ang, his friend from the Boston Sailing Center. Like Darryl Hopkins, she believed everything Clark Rockefeller told her.

"He was a venture capitalist, an entrepreneur, and he was losing $10 million in some deal," the seemingly innocent, moonfaced Ang testified. He told her he was a single father whose extremely problematic ex-wife worked at *Vogue* magazine. They had been married in a ceremony on Nantucket, he said, but his witch of a wife "never filed the papers." She deserted him and his daughter when Snooks was three, and "only comes around when she needs money." That Clark Rockefeller had money was immediately apparent to Ang. He had so much money, in fact, that he could indulge in things that ordinary people couldn't even dream about, such as arranging to have a second child at a birthing center in California, which Ang said he had described as an "egg farm," where his sperm could impregnate an egg from a respectable mother fed a special diet. Such a child, he told Ang, would truly be "all mine." Women were lining up to date him, he added. "One even tried to trap me in her house and wouldn't let me go."

Ang had come to know him quite well in the time they had spent together at the Sailing Center and elsewhere around Boston, always as friends, never intimates. She learned he was developing a television show while "going for his Ph.D. at Harvard . . . astronomy or looking at the stars or something," she said. Rockefeller told her he wanted to know his stars when he sailed around the world in his new seventy-two-foot sailboat with his daughter. He invited Ang to join them on their trip around the world. She could give Snooks piano lessons on the boat, he said.

On July 25, coming out of a movie theater in Ipswich, Ang discovered that Clark had left her a voicemail. When she returned the call, he asked, "Are you ready to go sailing? I'm not going to be mad at you if you don't come, but I need to know now."

She couldn't possibly, she told him, adding, "I enjoy my life on land." He told her he and Snooks needed to go to their new sailboat, which was docked in New York, the next day. Could Aileen drive them to New York City for $500? Of course, she said, but not on Saturday. She'd be helping out with a fund-raiser for a friend's charity, she explained. "Well," Rockefeller said, "I really want to go on Saturday, but let me try to rearrange my schedule."

He called the next morning to say that Sunday would work. "How about we leave at noon from the Boston Sailing Center?"

"I'll meet you there," Ang told him.

When Rockefeller called Ang Saturday morning, he was minutes away from moving the third pawn in the chess game he was playing into position: the court-appointed veteran social worker he had described to Darryl Hopkins as the "clingy friend," whose name he told Hopkins was Harold (instead of Howard) Yaffe. Rockefeller had advised the social worker that he "was traveling up from Florida," and Yaffe had no reason to disbelieve him. He knew that Rockefeller was an extremely busy man. He had canceled the first potential visit with his daughter after his divorce, scheduled for April. Finally, the day of his first supervised visit with Snooks—Saturday, July 26—had come.

At 11 a.m., Howard Yaffe picked up Snooks from Sandra Boss on the corner of Commonwealth Avenue and Exeter Street and walked the little girl across the street to meet her father at the Algonquin Club. Later, it would become clear that Aileen Ang and her charity work had thrown a monkey wrench into Rockefeller's plans. Therefore Rockefeller, Snooks, and the social worker ambled leisurely around the Algonquin for a couple of hours.

After leaving the club, Rockefeller bought stamps at the post office, and then the trio went to a bookstore. At 3:30, they were at Fenway Park, presumably to see a Red Sox game, but when Rockefeller went to pick up the tickets he had ordered, he said they wouldn't give them to him without a picture ID. Later it would be revealed that there were no tickets waiting for him. It was all a ruse. The real plan for the day, foiled by Aileen Ang, would have to wait until the following day's visitation, Sunday, July 27.

Sunday morning began just as Saturday had: Snooks and Howard Yaffe left Sandra Boss to meet Rockefeller at the Algonquin. They walked around the club for a bit, then strolled over to Clarendon Park so that Snooks could play for a while. "We pushed her on the swings," said Yaffe. As usual, Rockefeller had calls on his cell phone. "About a deal that was going through in Florida," Yaffe recalled. Around 12:30, the social worker suggested that it was time to get Snooks some lunch.

At 12:45, they were walking down Marlborough Street, Snooks on her father's shoulders, Yaffe close behind. When Rockefeller put Snooks down, complaining that his back was hurting, and pointed out something on a historic building to Yaffe, who turned to look, Rockefeller's plan was set into motion. "I remember being shoved and pushed by Clark," Yaffe would recall. "It was sort of a body block. As I got up and turned around, I saw a black SUV with the door open."

As Rockefeller had practiced the night before, father and daughter leaped into the limo. Snooks's doll and backpack flew out of her hands, and Rockefeller screamed to the driver, "Go, go, *go!*"

"I had my hand on the open back door," said Yaffe. "I'm trying to climb in, and then the SUV started to take off."

Everything was going precisely the way Rockefeller had planned it. Clingy "Harold's" hands slipped off the door handle and he crashed to the pavement, where he lay dazed and bloody in the street. Darryl Hopkins expertly followed Rockefeller's directions—"Right, left, right, left!"—until he was ordered to drop them in front of a White Hen Pantry grocery, where a cab was waiting, ready to ferry Rockefeller and Snooks to the Boston Sailing Center, where Aileen Ang was in position in her SUV to drive them to New York. At last they made it through the crowded freeways and into the city, only to be stuck in traffic in front of Grand Central Terminal, where Rockefeller threw an envelope with $500 in cash in it on Ang's front seat and, without saying good-bye, grabbed his daughter and disappeared into the traffic.

Within hours, Darryl Hopkins and Aileen Ang would realize that they had been duped into being accomplices in a parental kidnapping. Back in Boston, Howard Yaffe, possibly with a concussion, was still muttering, "He got the girl." And Sandra Boss, whose divorce settlement of $800,000 had financed the events of that frenetic day, was crying hysterically, telling police, "You'll never find them now!"

En route to Baltimore that evening, Rockefeller, having reverted to being Chip Smith, called Beth Grinspoon.

"Where are my keys!?" he asked. "I need them. I'm *desperate!*"

"Where's my money?" snapped Grinspoon.

"I have it, but I won't get in until midnight," he said.

She knew how tense and anxious he could be when he was not getting his way, so she agreed to deliver the keys to Ploy Street before he arrived. He texted her at 9:17: "Beth, terribly sorry. But I had to get in tonight. Gladly pay for the cab [to Ploy Street]. Mission accomplished?"

"Yes, jackass, on my way," Grinspoon texted back.

Within two minutes, Smith responded, "Did I ever tell you I think of you as really great?" Later: "Left Pittsburgh 7 p.m., will probably arrive at midnight. Do keys to the door work?"

"Jackass," Grinspoon texted him.

"Thanks for all your help," he texted back.

"Stop it," Grinspoon replied. "You're making me mad. On my bike. Keys in the box. Piss off."

The next day Grinspoon texted him again about the outstanding $1,400: "Am I going to see you today?"

"Yes, this evening," he replied.

"I'm at work at the Annabel Lee Tavern," she texted him at 5 p.m.

He didn't respond until 9:52: "Just returned. Are you still at the Annabel Tavern? If not, where do I find you?"

"Still here."

"See you soon."

He arrived at 10:10. The tavern was jammed. He strode up to Grinspoon, who was still on duty, gave her a hug and $1,400 in cash. "Are you going to stay for a drink?" she asked.

"I'm in a big hurry," he said and left. "You look gorgeous," he texted her once he was in a taxi, headed back to Ploy Street, where, unbeknownst to Grinspoon, his daughter, Reigh "Snooks" Boss, was waiting for him. Also unbeknownst to Grinspoon and a long list of others whom he had snared in the events of that day, he was the subject of an Amber Alert.

Chip Smith, a.k.a. Clark Rockefeller, was suddenly the most wanted man in America.

CHAPTER 20

The Manhunt

To those he had left behind in Boston, Cornish, and New York, Rockefeller was merely off on another of his adventures, this time on the high seas. He told one friend he was sailing to Peru; he informed another that he was traveling by boat to Alaska. To others he said he was headed to the Turks and Caicos, Bermuda, or the Bahamas. His unwitting friends became part of his elaborate escape plan, creating a vast network of possible trails to throw off anyone who might come looking for him.

July 29, 2008, MSNBC News Services:

Boston—Police on Tuesday were investigating the disappearance of a father and daughter amid concerns the dad, involved in a custody dispute, may try to flee the country on a 72-foot yacht, possibly to Bermuda.

July 30, 2008, CBS News:

Police in Delaware are looking into a claim that a state worker saw Clark Rockefeller and his daughter, Reigh Boss, at a car dealership in Smyrna on Tuesday. A state worker reported the sighting to police. She claims she saw a well-dressed man—believed to be Rockefeller—and a little blond girl wearing a flowered dress in the corner of a car lot. The woman said they had red suitcases with them. When the woman turned her car around to snap a picture of the pair, they were gone.

August 1, 2008, the *Sunday Times* of London:

The mysterious Clark Rockefeller and his abducted daughter have been spotted in a Caribbean island, having arrived by yacht on Thursday, the FBI has been told. Mr. Rockefeller, 48, had been on the run since snatching Reigh Boss, 7, during a contact visit in Boston, Massachusetts, last Sunday. The manhunt turned to the Turks and Caicos Islands yesterday. [The Turks and Caicos police would later confirm two sightings of Clark Rockefeller and his daughter, Reigh, after two store clerks at a NAPA Auto Parts and a 7-Eleven convenience store reported seeing the pair. Police showed workers pictures and the clerks identified them. They said the child was a girl, but had her hair cut short to look like a boy. At one store, the man used a Visa credit card bearing the name David M. Gibson.]

August 2, 2008, the *Daily Telegraph*, London:

Apparent sightings of the pair were reported across America and abroad. For the past six days, people who thought they knew him—including his former wife, who had custody of their daughter—have been trying to work out not just where he is, but who he is. Not many Americans reach the age of 48 without a driving license, a social security number, a job or a single penny paid in tax.

Throughout his life in America, the immigrant had depended on the kindness—and often the gullibility—of women, from his first wife, Amy Jersild, to his landlady Didi Sohus, to the widows of San Marino, to Sandra Boss. Now, however, a string of women were hot on his trail, led by Noreen Gleason, of the FBI, which took command of the case once it became clear that Reigh Boss had most likely been taken across state lines.

Twenty-four hours after the kidnapping, Gleason was on the phone with a representative of the Rockefeller family, assuming that the fugitive she and her fellow agents were seeking was indeed a member of the famous family. "There was no reason for me not to assume that he was a Rockefeller," she said. "But this really didn't fit the profile of how a Rockefeller would conduct himself."

"We've never heard of him," the Rockefeller representative told Gleason.

Months later, when I spoke to her in her Boston office, Gleason was still marveling over how Rockefeller's many bogus destinations tripped up a squadron of FBI agents. "We would start going down one avenue, one lead, and we would get to the end of it and there would be nothing there," she said. She mentioned his supposed destination of Peru as an example: "He had contacted the Peruvian government, so when we looked into all the things that we normally trace and track, there were bread crumbs that indicated that he did go down this lane. And then we would get to the end of it and we would know: he didn't do this! So we would go all the way back out and get another lead, go down that same avenue of intense vetting and investigation, and find another dry hole. And it's not like we started off down that avenue and stopped after only going five feet. We'd go the five feet and there would be something else that made us keep going, a little piece of cheese. He had talked to somebody, somebody would actually confirm it: 'Oh, yeah, Clark told me he was going to do this. He showed me a map!'"

Even where he spent the night before the kidnapping seemed to be, upon reflection, a ploy. Most assumed that Rockefeller had spent the night in a room at the Algonquin Club, where he met his daughter and the social worker on the morning of July 27. But he had actually stayed in the home of a woman with whom he was having a love affair. "I had just returned from Dubai, and was jetlagged and hung over, but I did manage to wrest up enough energy to have dinner with him that night," the woman said, adding that Rockefeller had seduced her over the course of a year with his good manners, compliments, proficient Latin, and the attentiveness he showed her children. He was too cheap to stay at the Algonquin, she added, so he frequently stayed with her, most recently leaving empty boxes of gold on her dining room table and saying urgently of his daughter, "I *have* to get her back!" They had dinner at The Palm steakhouse on the night before the kidnapping, then returned to her house. "The next morning he was gone," the woman remembered. Some time over the course of that evening, he stopped by the house of yet another friend, where he drank a glass of water. When the police arrived a few days later, the friend hadn't washed the glass Rockefeller had used, and the police were able to lift a fingerprint from it.

While the prints were being analyzed, the authorities released pictures of the kidnapper and his daughter to the media in hopes that someone might recognize him. On July 31, Sandra Boss recorded an impassioned video plea to her former husband, which was aired on television stations across America. She wore a simple green top, and her hair was a mess.

"Clark," she said in a weak and cracking monotone, "although things have changed, you will always be Reigh's father and I will always be Reigh's mother. We both love her dearly and have only her best interests and well-being in our hearts. I ask you now, please, please, bring Snooks back. There has to be a better way for us to solve our differences than this way."

Then she addressed her daughter: "Reigh, honey, I love and miss you so much. Remember, you're always a princess."

The video, coupled with a Wanted poster showing Clark Rockefeller's picture, brought calls from all over the country. In Berlin, Connecticut, Steve Savio (Ed's brother) told the Associated Press that he was "100 percent certain" that the man police were seeking was Christian Gerhartsreiter, a foreign exchange student his family had hosted thirty years earlier. In Milwaukee, Amy Jersild's husband confirmed to a *Pasadena Star-News* reporter that his wife had been married to the alleged kidnapper, "but said it only lasted a day." The *Boston Herald* contacted Amy's sister, Beth, who told the newspaper, "It wasn't like they dated. To me, it seems like it was kind of on the quick side."

In San Marino, California, the Swedish hairdresser Jann Eldnor told reporters that the fugitive was Christopher Chichester, a British aristocrat who lived in San Marino in the 1980s, claimed to have been related to Lord Mountbatten, and disappeared without a trace. "When I see the picture, right away I knew it was the guy," said Jann. "The hair, the head—I worked on that head for years." In Greenwich, Connecticut, veterans of the financial industry recognized the mystery man as Christopher C. Crowe, a TV producer who had worked for at least three investment firms in the late 1980s before suddenly vanishing. And scores of people in New York, Cornish, and Boston knew him as Clark Rockefeller, a distinguished if somewhat eccentric member of America's most famous family.

The accounts of all the people who had known the fugitive in the past, however, were of limited usefulness to the authorities. What they really needed was a verifiable sighting of Clark Rockefeller—or whoever he was—since his dramatic flight from Boston.

"We had no idea that he was [still] in Baltimore," the real estate agent Julie Gochar said. She had more or less tried to forget her peculiar client Chip Smith, who had bought the carriage house at 618 Ploy Street. She figured he had taken off on the yacht he was always talking about or had gone to visit his sisters in Wisconsin. Then she got a call from one of her associates at Obsidian Realty, Cindy Neuberger, who had been watching a report about the Rockefeller kidnapping on the *Today* show.

"I think that's Chip on TV!" Neuberger said on a voicemail message she left for Gochar. By the time Gochar checked her messages, there were several more from Neuberger. "She said, 'Urgent! Urgent! Call me! I'm freaking out!'" Gochar remembered.

Gochar kept her cool and checked out the *Today* segment online. There was definitely a resemblance between the wanted man on the screen and the persnickety ship's captain who had driven her batty, but she wasn't entirely sure they were the same person. "I don't know if that's him," she told Neuberger. Gochar was uncertain, she explained to me, because Chip Smith "was in a hat and glasses the whole time."

But Neuberger was insistent: it *was* Chip Smith. "We've got to do something," she said.

Beth Grinspoon, the Obsidian Realty employee who had helped Smith move his belongings from Boston to Baltimore, agreed with Neuberger. She had also seen *Today*, and she told Gochar that Smith had met her at the Annabel Lee Tavern just a couple of days earlier to pay her money he owed her for the move. "So he actually came out of hiding to give Beth money, which doesn't make sense to me," said Gochar. "I mean, why? I guess because he really planned on not getting caught and wanted to pay off his debts to people here—he didn't want to make a bad name for himself and didn't think anyone was going to find him."

She was right about his belief that he had succeeded in creating yet another new life. He would later tell an interviewer that the time spent with his daughter in Baltimore represented "six days of intense fun," adding, "I wanted to change my life altogether. I could really no longer afford to live in Boston. I always loved Baltimore. I wanted to have a boat that I could sail. In Boston, that's almost an impossibility. In Baltimore, that's very possible."

"Were you going into hiding?" he was asked.

"That's perhaps an extreme way of saying it," he replied. "I just wanted to live an obscure life."

Yet, he lamented, those peaceful days "ended rather abruptly."

Although her fellow Realtors were insisting that Clark Rockefeller was their own Chip Smith, and they had to advise the FBI, Julie Gochar still wasn't sure. She later admitted that she was "stressing" about calling the authorities.

"Beth said, 'We've got to call!' And I said, 'Beth, I've got a baby! You know, if the guy's out there, I don't want it to be on the news that we tipped them off that he's in Baltimore! And they don't catch him! I don't feel right about putting my family in jeopardy.'"

But that night, while watching yet another television report about the case, Gochar became convinced that the man who had kidnapped his daughter was her client, Chip Smith, when one reporter mentioned that the suspect had a patch of white hair on the back of his head, a trait she had noticed on Chip. That did it for her: she knew she'd been had. She knew the supposed highfalutin ship's captain was a fraud who had chosen what he considered a nowhere place where "us podunk, laypeople live," and chosen "a small, local agency like ours" on which to pull his final scam. All the bullshit—the posing, the never-ending neediness, the temper tantrums, the lies—put Julie Gochar on high boil.

"He was hiding out in Baltimore the whole time?!" she later exclaimed. "Excuse my French, but I almost shit the bed when I heard that. I mean, he's actually *here*? We thought he was in Turks and Caicos."

She and her husband placed an anonymous call to the FBI's national tip line, but with the flood of calls they had been receiving, he got no response. Then Grinspoon called the bureau's Baltimore branch. "I know where Clark Rockefeller is," she began. At six o'clock the next morning, Gochar was in the FBI office. "I told them everything," she said, from minute details about the house on Ploy Street to the location of her client's broken-down catamaran. Gochar put the agents in touch with her brother, who allowed them to stake out the marina from his house. "I gave the agents the local cell phone number that [Chip Smith] had been using, and I think they pinged that," she said, meaning they used the number to pinpoint the wanted man's whereabouts. Grinspoon and Neuberger cooperated with the FBI as well.

A string of different women had been instrumental in the fugitive's rise in America. Now three women in Baltimore were going to be the key to his downfall.

Surveillance of the house at 618 Ploy Street began at 1 a.m. on Saturday, August 3. It was a brown-brick two-story home, sparsely furnished, strewn with boxes yet to be unpacked. Through the large oval windows the agents could see an open case of sherry and a small painting leaning against a wall. Chip Smith and his daughter were thought to be inside, but in nearly twelve hours of watching the place, the surveillance team hadn't detected any motion. Noreen Gleason, directing the manhunt from Boston, took this to be a bad sign. She knew that Rockefeller was an insomniac who often worked on his computer throughout the night. "We'd gone down so many avenues, we were afraid maybe he had been there and left," she said.

Their first priority was getting the child out safely. "We wanted her to remain inside the house, but we wanted him to come out," said Gleason. "That's where the ruse came in."

Julie Gochar had shown investigators her client's beat-up catamaran the previous morning. Through a window of the boat, they could see a file labeled "Chip Smith," presumably the plans for the new identity he was setting up. So they knew they had their man. To lure him out of Ploy Street alone, the FBI had the manager of the marina call Smith on his cell phone and say that his boat was taking on water.

"I'll be there," came the reply.

As more than a dozen police officers and federal agents with assault rifles stealthily surrounded Smith's house, his neighbors watched with curiosity but little surprise. According to the *Baltimre Sun*, one of them, Lauren Gritzer, a twenty-six-year-old researcher at Johns Hopkins medical school, had already heard from the new arrival through his Realtor—he demanded that she remove a barbecue grill that was blocking his view of her building. "He said he was going to call the fire department and that I was going to get fined," Gritzer told the *Sun*. "I was like, 'Whatever.'" There were shades of the imperiousness he displayed in Cornish. She added that Smith's house was always dark. "There were no lights, not even at night."

After Smith received the phone call from the marina manager, Noreen Gleason said, "It took him fifteen to twenty minutes to get ready, and at that time we could actually see the little girl, Reigh, walking around. The agents were telling me, 'We can see her, Noreen.' I said, 'Does she look okay?' and they said, 'Yeah, she looks fine.'"

The fugitive emerged from the house and headed toward the marina.

"Hey, Clark!" an FBI agent yelled.

He turned around.

"Where are you going, Clark?" the agent asked.

"I'm going to get a turkey sandwich," he said. It would be the last lie he told before a group of agents wrestled him to the ground, while others stormed the house and got the girl.

Later that day, Clark Rockefeller sat in an interview room in the FBI's Baltimore office. He was dressed in the same clothes he had worn for his two consecutive supervised visits with Snooks in Boston the previous weekend: a sky blue Lacoste polo shirt with khaki trousers, no socks. Now the clothing was dirty, and his upper arms were pale beneath his short sleeves, in contrast to his sunburned forearms. He wore heavy, black-framed glasses. He was unshaven, and his left hand was handcuffed to the wall. But as always, he assumed the position of being absolutely in control.

FBI agent Tammy Harty and Detective Ray Mosher had been selected to interview the suspect. They had been involved in the investigation from the beginning, Harty as a member of Child Abduction Rapid Deployment Team and Mosher as the lead detective for the Boston police. They had been in Washington, D.C., where they were preparing to go on the television show *America's Most Wanted* to talk about the case, when they got the call saying that the kidnapper had been captured.

"Are you willing to speak with us, Mr. Rockefeller?" Harty asked after having read him his Miranda rights.

"Yeah, within a limited extent," he said, adding, "Call me Clark."

"You've kind of given us a run for our money this week," Harty told him. "You've put some of the best of us to the test."

"I could say thank you, but . . ." he said.

Harty said that she and Mosher wanted to get to know him a bit, so he told them something about himself. He said that he had made extra money writing term papers for college students; that he had amnesia about his childhood, but he believed it had been spent in New York City; that one of his few early memories was of going "to Mount Rushmore as a child in a Ford Woody Wagon, a Country Squire"; that he had audited classes at various Ivy League colleges without actually enrolling or having to pay tuition; that he had been given the name Rockefeller by his "godfather," the late Harry Copeland.

He was still in full spin mode, and it appeared that he fully felt that he would extricate himself from this situation as easily as he had from so many others. He not only steadfastly clung to his identity as far as the name Rockefeller went, he confided in the investigators the power that the Rockefeller name gave him, saying the name worked "like a charm" on everyone who heard it. "It was easy to get into the clubs by just saying you are a Rockefeller," he said at one point. "It would enhance a club if a Rockefeller was on the board."

Was it a slip on Rockefeller's part? Perhaps. But he went no further. The investigators weren't going to get him to confess anything, especially about how he came to assume the famous name. Harty and Mosher quickly got the sense that he used the big name in part to compensate for his small stature; he kept talking about how short he was. "Nobody notices a short man," he said at one point.

"How tall are you?" Harty asked.

He wouldn't say, but at one point when he mentioned his height, he stood up from his chair and quickly sat down again, so that they could see for themselves, Harty said.

Besides his name, the prisoner said, the key to making himself larger than life was his extraordinary art collection. He said an "opportunistic" friend had given it to him, and the art fooled everyone, including

his wife. (Later, his attorney would say that the art was fake, "derivatives, basically worthless.")

He also admitted that his daughter had been his undoing. "Reigh
was like a little me," he said. "They have a way of getting to your heart.
My goal was to be reunited with Reigh."

They offered him something to eat. He insisted on turkey on white
bread, because, he explained, he ate only white foods. As the interview
stretched on, he turned increasingly evasive, then demanding, dictating what he wanted his daughter to have for dinner. His interviewers
began to lose their patience as he tried to defocus from the interview.

"You just wanted to jump across the table and wrap your hands
around his neck, because he just irritated the hell out of you," said
Harty. "He had those beady little eyes."

The vast majority of parental kidnappings, Harty was aware, aren't
about the child, but about the spouse—one parent using the child to
get revenge on the other. That scenario made perfect sense in the case
of Clark Rockefeller and Sandra Boss. "Because he went eight or nine
months without visiting [Snooks]," Harty observed, adding that Rockefeller hadn't even called or e-mailed his daughter. "Nothing. Zero."

So when he kept repeating, "I just want to be a good father," Harty
cut him off.

"Knock off the bullshit," she snapped. "This isn't about you."

They had told him earlier that they needed to know his true identity
because someday his little girl would want to know about her heritage.
Tell us who you are for the sake of your daughter, they had pleaded. Now
they tried a tougher approach. "Everything you have told us is bullshit,"
Harty said flatly. She stood up and wrote on a piece of paper in big
block letters, THIS IS ALL ABOUT REIGH. He still wouldn't divulge his
identity.

Harty kept hammering away. "You need to start telling us the truth
and stop playing games," she said. "You have been lying over and over
again throughout the course of this interview, and if you think you can
pull one over on us when we have fifty FBI agents out there determin-

ing who you are . . . We are going to figure it out. We are damned good at what we do."

She recalled, "He just sat there and blinked at me again and said, 'I'm sorry, I'm sorry.' I said, 'Don't be sorry, tell me who you are!'"

Still nothing. Harty looked over at Mosher. "Ray, what is the first thing you think when somebody does what Clark has done?" she asked. "Hiding your identity. Not telling your child who you are. Not telling your wife who you are. Using multiple aliases."

"I would think he's got something to hide," said Mosher.

"What are you trying to hide, Clark?" asked Harty.

He said nothing.

"Did you steal something from somebody?"

No response.

"Did you rape somebody? Are you a serial jaywalker? Are you a serial murderer?"

Harty later said she had hoped that he would "bite" on the murder line "and tell me about the California thing at that point. But there was just no way. I think he was still hoping that he could continue with the charade he had been playing, because it had worked so well for him for so long."

He may have believed he could escape this unfortunate situation just as he had escaped so many others, by sticking to his mantra: the bigger the lie, the more people will believe it—even if you are lying to the FBI and the police.

Finally, near the end of the four-hour interview, he admitted, "Clark Rockefeller does not exist."

"Really?" asked Harty. "Then who am I talking to?"

"And I went down the whole list of aliases," she remembered. "I said, 'Who is Christopher Crowe?'"

"He doesn't exist," said Rockefeller.

"Who is Christopher Chichester?"

"Doesn't exist."

"Who is Christopher Mountbatten?"

"Doesn't exist."

"So who am I talking to?"

"I don't know," he insisted. "I don't know my name."

A few days later, however, investigators would; the results of the FBI's fingerprint analysis confirmed that he was, as they had suspected, Christian Karl Gerhartsreiter. It was under that name that he would stand trial in Boston almost ten months later.

CHAPTER 21

One Last Con?

He never ceased being Clark Rockefeller.

When he emerged from the Baltimore holding cell to be escorted back to Boston to face charges that included kidnapping of a minor and assault and battery with a deadly weapon (the SUV he used in his escape), he was outgoing, erudite, eager to meet and greet. Boston police sergeant Ray Mosher drew the duty of escorting him home, and when a handcuffed Rockefeller walked outside with his guards, reporters surrounded them, screaming, "Mr. Rockefeller! Mr. Rockefeller!" The prisoner seemed eager to speak to them, but Mosher stopped him and guided him toward the car that would take him to the airport for an AirTran flight to Boston.

Shackled on the plane, he spoke nonstop with Sergeant Mosher, most notably about a startling murder conspiracy he said he had uncovered while going through the books in an office where he had worked in New York City. It was called Operation Hat Trick, he whispered, and it involved the deaths of three major politicians—U.S. senators John Tower and H. John Heinz III and Republican political strategist Lee Atwater—all of whom had died over an eight-day period in 1991. "Can you give me your word that you'll look into it?" he asked Mosher.

Perhaps he believed that by giving the sergeant a bigger case to investigate he could divert his attention from the one at hand. It didn't work. Mosher asked a flight attendant if she had a newspaper, and when she brought him that day's *Boston Globe*, he handed it to his prisoner.

FINGERPRINTS DEEPEN A MYSTERY: AUTHORITIES LOOK AT POSSIBLE LINK BETWEEN KIDNAP SUSPECT, CALIF. SLAYING, read the August 5, 2008, front-page headline, alongside a scruffy mug shot of Rockefeller. The story referred to the possible murder of missing persons John and Linda Sohus, although their names had not been released at that point. Rockefeller read the paper carefully, solemnly, then handed it back to Mosher.

"Well, what did it say?" asked the sergeant.

"I don't want to talk about that," said Rockefeller, uncharacteristically quiet for the first time on the trip. "You'll have to read it yourself."

From the moment he landed in Boston, however, he couldn't seem to *stop* talking. The lawyer he chose to represent him, whose fees would be paid from what he had left of his divorce settlement, was the veteran Boston criminal attorney Stephen Hrones. As the media storm grew, both in the United States and abroad, Hrones actually encouraged him to keep talking. "Fight fire with fire," Hrones later said. "We had to get out and tell his side of the story, emphasize the loving-father aspect. That was his strength. I pressed that at every point: how can you kidnap your own child?"

There was a larger question, however, which Sandra Boss had asked after she learned that her daughter was safe and her ex-husband was in custody: Who is he? "He is a mystery man, a cipher," said Suffolk County assistant district attorney David Deakin during Rockefeller's bail hearing, adding that he was a spinner of stories "literally so numerous and varied that they are proving to be difficult to keep track of, even with a database."

Rockefeller declined to meet with California authorities, who had revived their investigation of the Sohus murder case following his arrest. But he was the old charmer again when he and his attorney went on NBC's top-rated morning show *Today* in his first attempt to present his side of the story. The show's crew, led by correspondent Natalie Morales, set up a studio in the Nashua Street Jail. When Rockefeller walked in wearing his jailhouse scrubs, he acted as if he were entering one of his private clubs, shaking every crew member's hand, working the room. Sitting down for the interview with Morales, he crossed his legs, cocked back his head aristocratically, and confided to her, "Normally, I would enjoy this moment."

His memory was sketchy when it came to his past, but he did recall some scenes from his childhood. "I remember clearly going to Mount Rushmore in the back of a Woody Wagon," he said grandly. "Being an aficionado of station wagons, I believe it was a '68 Ford with the flip-up headlights. I have a clear memory of picking strawberries in Oregon."

"Did you kill John and Linda Sohus?" Morales asked at one point.

"My entire life I've been a pacifist," Rockefeller replied. "I am a Quaker, and I believe in nonviolence. I can fairly certainly say that I have never hurt anyone physically." Asked what he would say to his daughter if she happened to be watching, he said, "She should wish that we be reunited." Eyes welling up and voice trembling, he added, "That there's hope for the two of us." Then Morales asked him if he believed he would see Snooks again. He straightened and replied, "Natalie, I cannot predict the future. . . . I only hope so, and I wish for it." At the end of the first segment of the two-part interview, he recited a portion of "Address to a Haggis" by Robert Burns in a Scottish brogue.

In a subsequent installment of the *Today* show, investigative criminal profiler Pat Brown, interviewed by Morales, marveled at Rockefeller's television performance. "Most people have not heard a man talking this much, to expose himself this way, who is what I would call a psychopath," she said. "He's a pathological liar. He's spinning his tale. He wants to be the center of attention." She described him as an individual without "empathy for other people," whose only concern was himself, who could be dangerous to anyone who stood in his way, even his own child, whom he had used "as a pawn to get back at his wife." Rockefeller's show of conviviality, introducing himself to everyone in the studio, was evidence of a con man "selling himself," casing the room to see "who [his] marks are."

Rockefeller's next and last interview, with three reporters from the *Boston Globe*, gave credence to the profiler's analysis. The *Globe*'s resulting front-page story, with the headline I'M NOT QUITE SURE WHAT I'M SUPPOSED TO REMEMBER. I DON'T LOSE MUCH THOUGHT OVER IT, began:

> He burst into the room smiling, with the cheerful demeanor of a host welcoming guests to a party. "Clark Rockefeller," he said, fixing his gaze on a visitor and extending a hand. His nails were manicured. He wore tasseled loafers with his jail-issued scrubs. He turned to another visitor and another, bowing slightly to each. "Clark Rockefeller, Clark Rockefeller," he said in a Brahmin accent. "Nice to see you. How are you, everyone?" . . .
>
> Peppering his speech with verbal filigrees such as "quite so" and "rather," he rambled on about the "five or six or seven" languages that he speaks, the historical novel about the roots of Israeli statehood he is writing, and his work as a researcher of "anything from physics to social sciences." He painted himself as a devoted father.

Two months later, when Stephen Hrones visited his client in the Nashua Street Jail after a court appearance on his behalf, Rockefeller told him that he had decided to switch attorneys. He said his friends didn't agree with Hrones's fight-fire-with-fire, get-your-story-out approach. He had already hired a new legal team, led by Boston criminal attorney Jeffrey Denner, who had come up with a defense radically different from the "loving father" one Stephen Hrones was preparing.

Rockefeller would plead insanity.

"This case isn't about what happened, but *why* it happened," Jeffrey Denner said in his opening statement, on May 28, 2009, in a courtroom packed with media and spectators. A lanky, well-regarded attorney with wiry hair and a deep baritone voice, Denner, along with his young associate, Timothy Bradl, would make whatever blistering attacks the prosecutor levied against his client seem even worse, by *admitting* that Rockefeller had indeed kidnapped his daughter and *enumerating* the various personas Rockefeller had invented during his thirty-year reign of deceit in America.

However, Denner submitted, his client wasn't a calculating con artist but a mentally ill individual who couldn't tell right from wrong. He exemplified a certain "narcissistic personality disorder and delusional disorder, grandiose type," which had intensified over the years, guise by guise, lie by lie, until the pitiable defendant was living in a "magical, insane world."

"Along with every identity change there is also an incredible biographical change," the attorney informed the court, with these changes steadily increasing in "grandeur" and culminating in his pitch-perfect performance as a Rockefeller, with "billions of dollars' worth of art, keys to Rockefeller Center, and so many other things that are so blatantly, blatantly ridiculous to anyone other than [a person] in the throes of this kind of mental illness."

The kidnapping of his daughter wasn't a calculated, elaborately planned operation, Denner insisted. It was the result of a "psychotic break," triggered by the loss of that daughter four days before Christmas in 2007, "that pushed him over the edge.

"He believed that he was telepathically communicating with his child. He believed that she was secretly signaling him, basically saying that she needed to be saved . . . that she wasn't being cared for, that [she was] in danger." Walled off from his memories and separated from the one person he cared about above all else, Denner said, Rockefeller, in his deluded state, felt he had no choice but to "rescue his daughter."

The defense would introduce expert witnesses, a psychiatrist and a psychologist, who had carefully examined the defendant and could confirm that he was insane. "You don't have to be a rocket scientist or, respectfully, a psychiatrist to know that something is very wrong with him," Denner told the court. "This is not a man playing with a full deck."

Denner concluded, "If in fact after hearing all the evidence in this case you do believe that the defendant at the time of the offense was suffering from a mental illness or defect that substantially affected his ability to appreciate the criminality or the wrongfulness of what he was doing, then the judge will instruct you that he should be found not guilty by reason of insanity."

I looked over at the defendant, sitting in his blazer and khaki pants, and he did indeed look crazy, mumbling to himself at times, his complexion so pale it was ghostly. It was as if, after a lifetime of lies, he had finally run out of stories to tell. For someone who usually talked nonstop, in court he would not say a word on his own behalf. Through his attorney, however, he was now telling perhaps his greatest story yet. I kept thinking of what the criminal profiler Pat Brown had said on the *Today* show: he enters a room and introduces himself to everyone, seemingly out of friendliness but actually in order to case the room and see who his marks are. In this case, the potential dupes were the members of the jury and the alternates—seven men and nine women.

The expert witnesses paid for by Rockefeller and his defense team tried to paint the picture of a psycho. "His father called him 'human refuse,'" testified Dr. Keith Ablow. The celebrity psychologist said he had spent twelve to sixteen days examining Rockefeller, who told him that his father insisted that he switch his studies in Germany from music, which he loved, to "the vocational track." Ablow continued, "He openly questioned whether Mr. Rockefeller might be a homosexual in front of him." Ablow also said the father questioned whether or not he was truly his biological son, verbally attacking him so viciously that the boy had no choice but to escape and reinvent himself in America.

The second expert witness for the defense, forensic psychologist

Catherine Howe, said, "What's fascinating about Mr. Rockefeller is that not only does he meet five or more [of the criteria for delusional-disorder, grandiose-type insanity], he meets *all* of the criteria."

At that point, prosecutor David Deakin held up *The Diagnostic and Statistical Manual of Mental Disorders*, which had been referred to over and over by the defense. "And there's no diagnosis for liar?" he asked.

"There's nothing in there under that word, no," said Howe.

The psychiatrist for the prosecution, Dr. James Chu, testified that in his interviews with Rockefeller, it had become apparent that the defendant was faking mental illness. Rockefeller had told him that 70 percent of the time he found himself in places where he would have no idea how he had gotten there, which would have rendered it impossible for him to function. He gave "untruthful," "exaggerated" answers to questions but "clearly understood the wrongfulness of his conduct."

For two weeks, a dizzying parade of witnesses and psychological experts passed through the courtroom, analyzing the mental state of the defendant, making him once again the center of attention, the star of his own world. David Deakin invariably asked witness after witness, "Any sign the defendant might be hallucinating?"

"No" was the usual answer.

"Any signs that he was delusional?"

"No."

In his closing arguments, Deakin told the court, "This is not a case about madness. It's a case about manipulation. . . . Don't let him get away with that. Don't let this insanity defense be the culminating manipulation of a lifetime of lies designed to try to get what he wanted. Don't shy away from the facts. See the truth before you."

Most of the jurors were quite young—maybe only four over thirty—and seemed extremely impressionable. As I watched them, I thought, "They can be conned." They took their duties very seriously, though, following the judge's instruction not to discuss the case among them-

selves until they had heard all the evidence. At the end of the twelve-
day trial, however, when they retired to an upstairs room to deliberate,
they exploded.

"I felt like I was in a John Grisham novel! You couldn't believe that
the guy had done what he'd done. That the wife [Sandra Boss] had fallen
for it. The [limo] driver, poor guy. He was just trying to make a living
and thought he'd found a cash cow. The detectives . . . Are these people
real? It was like they were cast for their parts! . . . Our mouths were
open as we heard all of the stories," one juror said later.

Everybody on the jury was perfectly sure that Clark Rockefeller was
a fraud, and there was no doubt that he had kidnapped his daughter.
But once again he had brilliantly positioned himself, in perhaps the
only way out of his present situation, by putting the jury in a quandary.

"He's crazy!" more than one of them said more than once. "There's
no way anybody in their right mind would do something like this!"

The group included a lawyer, a fireman, a social worker, several college students (including two nineteen-year-old freshmen), and a young
woman on her way to medical school, and over five days of deliberation
they debated the notion of insanity. Yes, Clark Rockefeller was definitely crazy, but was he crazy to the point of insanity, of not knowing
right from wrong? They went around and around.

One of them tried to put herself in the shoes of the con man. "Okay,
suppose I'm Clark Rockefeller, and I have this little girl, and I felt what
had happened to me in the divorce was unfair," she told herself. "And I
love this little girl, and I've been having her in my life for so long, and
I get to have her. I get to do whatever it takes to get her. I can do this.
I can take this divorce money. I can find a house. I can manage to get
ahold of her, and we can go live happily ever after in Baltimore. Cool.
Because I want it, it's okay."

She knew that he showed all the signs of the classic narcissist, who
lives by the creed that what's important to him or her is the most important thing. "The world revolves around what I need and what I want.
And so I make a plan and carry it out," she said, putting herself in the

mind of the defendant. "Yeah, it's illegal. But illegal schmillegal—I get to do what I want.

"This isn't something that someone in a psychotic state can really do," she continued. "They can fantasize about it, but they can't really do it. He was a planner. I think he was really smart! Certainly this was an elaborate plan."

The next day, the jury reached an agreement: what Clark Rockefeller had done wasn't the work of a delusional nutcase; it was the carefully orchestrated plan of a self-centered narcissist who had gotten what he wanted for so long that he thought he was entitled to get his $800,000 divorce settlement from Sandra Boss and take his daughter too. He wasn't insane; he was guilty.

On June 12, the jury foreman presented the verdict to the court: guilty on the most serious charges—kidnapping of a minor and assault and battery by means of a dangerous weapon—which Rockefeller received standing, wild-eyed and blinking, but saying nothing. His attorneys succeeded in having one of the charges dropped: providing a false name to the police, arguing that he had used the name Rockefeller for so long that there was no better identification to give. The defense argued for a light sentence: less than two years, which Rockefeller's lawyer deemed fair for a "mentally disturbed individual" who "loved his daughter too much and made huge mistakes in trying to express that love." The prosecution argued for the maximum sentence, up to fifteen years, and read a statement from Sandra Boss to the court, which included the following: "While Reigh was gone, I faced a mother's worst nightmare—the possibility of losing a child without a trace. The emerging horrors about her abductor's nefarious past only heightened my concerns that she might come to harm."

Later that day, Judge Frank Gaziano brought the proceedings to an end: "The defendant displayed no regard for the rule of law. He thought he would be able to outmaneuver Sandra Boss by taking her money and then at the right time taking his daughter. The defendant committed this crime with complete disregard for the anguish this would cause

Ms. Boss." The judge sentenced Rockefeller accordingly: four to five years for kidnapping and two to three years for assault with the SUV, to be served concurrently.

Massachusetts Department of Corrections offender No. W94579 began serving his sentence at the minimum-security state prison housed in a turn-of-the-century mental hospital in Gardner, Massachusetts, on June 14, 2009. He was given a cell on the third floor—basically a bed, toilet, and sink—which he grandly inflated to friends: "I have my own two-room suite!"

He spent his time reading, writing, and preparing his appeal. He asked a friend to send copies of his favorite periodicals—*Sailing World*, *Cruising World*, *Sail*, *Latitudes & Attitudes*—and said, "I don't know who to trust (except you). Right now, I worry that someone might cheat me."

Although he confided contritely to one friend about his youth in Germany, stressing that his father's bullying had driven him to flee to America, he clung to his Clark Rockefeller persona in public, showing up one year after his trial in a tweed jacket for a court hearing, where his petition to reduce his sentence was denied. Regarding the disappearance of John and Linda Sohus, Rockefeller's defense attorney Jeffrey Denner said, "Mr. Rockefeller has absolutely no involvement in that case whatsoever."

For me, the Clark Rockefeller story ended in a suburban basement, where I had been invited to see where many of the earthly possessions of Christian Karl Gerhartsreiter had somehow come to rest. How and why these things found their way to the basement I wouldn't know for certain. But it was all there: his birth certificate; his German passport; the tortoiseshell eyeglasses he wore as Christopher Chichester and the black Ray-Ban Wayfarers he wore as Clark Rockefeller. There was a well-worn brown Ghurka leather wallet with more than a dozen membership cards to private clubs—the Algonquin Club and Harvard Club in Boston, the India House and Metropolitan Club and Lotos Club in New York City. An enormous pack of credit cards—some in his name, some in the name of Sandra Boss—was held together by a rubber band.

A large and impressive collection of Rockefeller memorabilia was gathered in a box: booklets listing the members of the famous family, one dating back to 1932; personal photographs and newspaper clippings of the clan leaders, John D. Sr. and Jr., Nelson, and David; stock certificates from the family's Chase Manhattan Corporation (signed by David Rockefeller); missives from John D. Rockefeller Jr. ("Dearest, thanks for your beautiful and understanding letter . . ."); and other family artifacts that seemingly only a Rockefeller would have.

Some pieces of artwork, but not the major pieces he loved to show off, were scattered about: some crated, some framed, and some just lying on the floor, including *Abrupt Break*, the small painting by his friend William Quigley that Rockefeller had supposedly found in a secondhand store. His clothing, all from J. Press, was stacked in a large pile—a tuxedo, several bold-plaid sports coats, all in plastic travel bags. For some reason, I reached into the inside breast pocket of one of the jackets and found, to my astonishment, a small glass dildo. There were new J. Press shirts, still in their original packaging, and several pairs of lace-up shoes from Church's, the British shoemaker, size 9. Thrown casually into a paper bag was the preppy outfit he wore day after day during his trial—the blazer, the white shirt, the khaki pants. The whole lot comprised a sort of do-it-yourself kit for an impostor. Without him, though, it was all just a lifeless collection of stuff.

Were these artifacts of the fraud Christian Karl Gerhartsreiter perpetrated upon America destined for the scrap heap? Or would the prisoner, upon his scheduled release in 2013, pick them up and begin anew, in a new city, with a new identity?

The answers are pending in California, where agents for the Los Angeles County Sheriff's Department and the FBI continue their investigation, interviewing an infinite cast of characters who have become entwined with Christian Karl Gerhartsreiter, in the hope of completing the "thousand-piece jigsaw puzzle" of his multiple lives and, more important, answering the ultimate question: what happened to John and Linda Sohus?

Their spirits live on in a modest house in Southern California, where Linda's loyal best friend, Sue Coffman, keeps a constant vigil. "They weren't allowed to die in a respectful way," she says. "They didn't get a service. They didn't get a farewell. They got nothing." She hopes to give them a long-overdue memorial someday, once answers to their deaths have been found and justice for their killer has finally been done.

On March 15, 2011, Christian Karl Gerhartsreiter was charged with the murder of John Sohus. The indictment came after Los Angeles County sheriff's investigators claimed to have amassed enough evidence in the case, including positive identification of the remains found in the San Marino backyard as being those of John. Whatever happened to Linda Sohus was not addressed in the indictment. After visiting his client in prison, one of Gerhartstreiter's attorneys told the media that Gerhartsreiter was "absolutely innocent" and would vigorously fight the charges.

Before receiving the news, Gerhartsreiter had been working on appealing his conviction on kidnapping charges. He told friends that he was confident he would win early release from prison and was looking forward to resuming his life, possibly in the television industry.

Upon hearing of the murder charge, the cast members of Gerhartsreiter's lifetime reunited, calling each other from around the world, all waiting to see which face the enigmatic impostor would put on next—or whether standing trial for murder might, somehow at last, reach whatever was left of the real man inside.

Afterword

After this book's publication, I received more than 150 e-mails from readers. Many of those who contacted me had known Clark Rockefeller in his various guises, and many of their stories were new to me, even after my years of investigating Rockefeller and tracking every possible lead I discovered.

Some wrote about his talents as a con man: "I was Clark Rockefeller's first contact in Boston and one of the last to see him on that Saturday before he snatched Snooks," wrote one Back Bay Brahmin. "It took me almost a year to realize he was not who he said he was."

Others marveled over their own gullibility: "Mark, I just read *The Man in the Rockefeller Suit* and liked it. I wish I had met you before you wrote it. I was 'Clark's' locksmith in Boston, and I also went to Cornish to help him transport a 'telescope' after I rented a van for him. I think now it was the paintings. [His daughter] Snooks was on the trip. He also contacted me about some other job he wanted me to do, which I told him, over supper on Charles Street, was illegal and I would not do for him. I think he was looking for people to help with the kidnapping. Hindsight is 20/20. If you ever do a revised version, I'd love to give you a page or two. Peace, Bob Whitelock, Owner of Beacon Hill Lock & Key."

I called the locksmith. "He hooked me from the get-go," he said, explaining that Clark paid his first locksmith's bill with a platinum American Express card while dressed in lime green pants, a white belt, and pink Izod shirt with the collar up. "I thought, 'Nobody but a Rockefeller would dress like *that*!'" said Whitelock. He loved Clark's stories about his years of late-night visits to Rockefeller Center to watch his beloved *Saturday Night Live*, which was filmed at NBC Studios in the building, although as a locksmith Whitelock questioned his claim of having the only master key to the mammoth complex. "He told me, 'When the Japanese took over Rockefeller Center, they took my key away.'" He recalled driving Clark and Snooks to Cornish in the rented van to retrieve a collection of giant metal tubes, which Clark claimed were parts of a telescope, but which Whitelock now believes were his modern art paintings. And he was entranced when Clark and his daughter sang complicated and intricate interpretations of popular songs on the drive back to Boston. "They would sing the words to Led Zeppelin's 'Stairway to Heaven' to the tune of the theme song from *Gilligan's Island*," he remembered. "Like a lot of people in your book, I fell for it. I wanted to believe that he was a Rockefeller and I could be the locksmith to the stars."

Many readers wanted to know more about Rockefeller's fabulous collection of fake modern art. "I am the director of the Robert Motherwell Catalogue Raisonné Project, as well as president of the Dedalus Foundation, which was founded by Motherwell," wrote Jack Flam, the director of the esteemed foundation. "A few years ago, a painting supposedly by Motherwell that belonged to Clark Rockefeller came to the notice of the Project; at the time, one of our researchers wrote to (his wife) Sandra Boss, who informed us simply that she did not own a painting by Motherwell. While reading your book, I became very curious about the origins, and fate, of the paintings Rockefeller owned that were purported to be by Motherwell, Rothko, and other abstract expressionist artists. In particular, I wondered whether it is known where he acquired those paintings. And after he was exposed as a fraud, I wonder what happened to the paintings. I am, of course, most interested in the 'Motherwell' painting; but the whole matter intrigues me, and I would very much like to know more about the collection as a whole." (I replied, saying that Rockefeller had freely admitted to the police that his collection was composed of fakes. Rockefeller's friend, the artist William Quigley, had told me that there was a Motherwell hanging above Clark's fireplace mantel in New York. However, how he acquired the paintings and the current whereabouts of the "art" were unknown at the time of our e-mail exchange.)

More people shared stories with me as I crossed the country on a book tour. At the Greenwich Library in Connecticut, the wife and daughter of Stanford Phelps, who had given Rockefeller (as Christopher Crowe) his first investment-company job, attended the reading, and afterward Phelps took my call. He told me how the man calling himself Christopher Crowe came to work at his investment firm, S. N. Phelps and Company, as a computer programmer—submitting a résumé that stated he had been born and raised in San Marino, California, had attended the Polytechnic School, a prep school in Pasadena, and USC, and had worked in the film industry. Once Crowe started working at his firm, Phelps said Crowe tried to make himself "indispensable," and refused to give him details about files on his own computer. "At that point, I said, 'You're out of here,'" Phelps told me.

One of the most revealing e-mails came from Mason Sherwood, an architect living near the University of Wisconsin-Milwaukee, where the impostor supposedly attended college and where he married his first wife for a green card that would grant him U.S. citizenship. Sherwood said he was "amazed" when he read about the book in the *Wall Street Journal*. "This character was a boarder (albeit briefly) in my home when he was in Milwaukee studying film. (I'm thinking midsummer of 1979 to October of that year.) He used a ruse of acquaintanceship of a friend of a friend and showed up at my door in Delafield.

He called himself Chris Gerhart, but in later times said that his name was Christopher Kenneth Patrick Roth (or Ross, my memory is not perfect) Gerharts-Reiter De Longchamp. He explained his accent by saying that while he was from Connecticut, he went to school in Germany and then Switzerland. He paid a little bit of board money up front and then was always waiting for his father to send his (stupendous) allowance."

Sherwood recalled the young man arriving at his doorstep in the affluent Milwaukee suburb of Delafield one rainy night. "He presented himself and indicated that he was a student of the University of Wisconsin-Milwaukee and was looking for a place to live," Sherwood wrote. Since he said he'd been referred by a "dear friend" of Sherwood's mother, Sherwood rented a room to the then-eighteen-year-old for $75 a month, plus a $300 security deposit. Neither his allowance nor another rent payment came. Letters did, though—dozens of them—all from his father, in German, one of which Sherwood later had translated. "It was, 'We miss you. Why don't you write? Your mother and I are concerned,'" Sherwood told me.

"He seemed to go to school, but I came home from work to find him glued to the TV, watching inane sitcom reruns and sitting with my dog," Sherwood continued. When months passed with no allowance from the De Longchamps, Sherwood gave him a deadline for payment, which came and went. "So I packed his stuff. While packing, I found his German passport for Christian Karl Gerhartsreiter. . . ."

Sherwood got angry. Not only had he been stiffed for what had by then amounted to more than $600 in back rent, but his boarder had lied to him. He packed up Rockefeller's possessions—passport, letters, an electronic solo chess game, and books about Boston and Connecticut—and locked them in the trunk of his car. "In a doorstep confrontation, I told him he could have it all back as soon as he paid up. He never came back."

Embarking on what Sherwood called a "campaign" to get back his money, he contacted the bursar and admissions office of the University of Wisconsin-Milwaukee, hoping to find a forwarding address. "They could find no record of him being a student," said Sherwood.

Of the many mysteries I encountered while writing this book, a most intriguing one was trying to trace Gerhartsreiter's whereabouts from 1989 to 1992, when the impostor, posing as Christopher Crowe, disappeared. He had taken off after being sought for questioning by the Greenwich Police Department about trying to sell the truck that had belonged to John and Linda Sohus, the couple that was missing in Los Angeles.

From another reader and from his preliminary hearing in early 2012, though, I learned where Gerhartsreiter was for most of this time. He emerged in his new persona as early as October 1989—less than a year after his disappearance as Christopher Crowe—at a hostess desk at a restaurant in Camden, Maine, where he suffered the indignity of waiting interminably for a table. Suddenly, an idea bubbled up.

"Rockefeller," he lied smoothly, impressing the hostess with the famous American family name.

"Clark Rockefeller."

Magically, a table became available, and then Christopher Crowe, aka Christopher Chichester, aka a series of other aliases, became Clark Rockefeller from that moment on.

He must have marveled at how easily the great name could be seized, and how quickly people fell for it, with no questions asked. Even an old colleague at Nikko Securities, where Clark ran the bond department as Christopher Crowe, bought the new name. When I called this man and questioned him about it, he said he thought that the "migration of the name," from Crowe to Rockefeller was odd, but nothing suspicious, not during their days as two bachelors on the make. At that time, Rockefeller's former pal added, anything that gave a guy an edge was okay if it got you laid or got you ahead in the dog-eat-dog business world of Wall Street.

The name worked beautifully, e-mailed a woman named Candice

Leit, who was one of the first to be introduced to Rockefeller as Clark
Rockefeller. They met at Saint Thomas Church, the most privileged
Episcopal church in midtown Manhattan, a sanctuary that would serve
as a key to the young man's ascent in Manhattan society and investment circles.

"I was working as a children's book designer at Grosset & Dunlap,
which is now an imprint at Penguin," she wrote to me. "One evening I
was killing time before a dance class uptown and I went to a weekday
Evening Prayer service at Saint Thomas. This preppy young man struck
up a conversation with me afterward. Within minutes, he extracted
some vital information from me. He asked whether I was a member
of Saint Thomas. I replied no, but offered that I was on the vestry of a
church downtown, the Church of the Holy Apostles. With that, I now
realize I became a target but was ultimately fortunate that I did not
have the amount of money or earning potential that he was seeking."

It was October 1989, less than a year after he disappeared as Christopher Crowe, but he was hardly hiding out. "What really struck me is
how he played up the Rockefeller connection," she said, adding that he
crowed about being a Rockefeller even in front of her aunts and uncles,
who knew David Rockefeller. "Clark showed no concerns about dropping his 'Uncle David's' name and talking about the Rockefeller Estate,"
she said. "Clark made a point of going to the Metropolitan Museum of
Art with me and touring what he called his 'cousin's' [the late Michael C.
Rockefeller's] collection. He claimed to have raced Matchbox cars down
the center of the hollowed-out canoes (in which Michael Rockefeller disappeared in New Guinea) before the family donated them to the Met."

Life was not easy being a Rockefeller, Clark told his new friend
Candice. "Clark complained about a magazine listing him among
New York's most eligible bachelors," she said. "After the article ran, he
claimed that he had to separate his trash into public and private trash
as people were ransacking his garbage. He would allegedly burn the
private trash in his fireplace."

She sent me pages from her diary, filled with notations about Clark: "He finished his physics degree at Harvard, sold his place in Maine, and will be fixing up his early 18th-century home in Massachusetts. He replaced the main summer home with one in Nantucket. After that conversation, I dreamed of receiving a red Christmas card from Clark."

Other e-mails arrived in my inbox. One from Rockefeller's daughter Reigh's teacher in Boston. Others from members of Trinity Church in Cornish, New Hampshire. Still others commented on how parts of Clark's biography, which he related to Natalie Morales on the *Today* show after his arrest for kidnapping—especially his story about going to Mount Rushmore in "a woody wagon" as a child—were appropriated straight from a scene in the film noir *North by Northwest*, by Rockefeller's favorite director, Alfred Hitchcock. But all roads eventually led back to San Marino, the Los Angeles suburb where the most disturbing chapter of the impostor's life was now unfolding.

In wealthy, urbane, ultrafriendly San Marino, the locals who knew Rockefeller as Christopher Chichester threw a garden party to celebrate the publication of my book. I had a wonderful time at the party, which was held in the backyard of one of the town's leading citizens and his wife. Everything was impostor-themed. There was a life-size cutout of Chichester (behind prison bars) and a buffet festooned with beer steins, sauerkraut, handcuffs, and signs lampooning the con artist who had so utterly bamboozled the town back in the 1980s:

"Dip the Chip! Free food for Christopher Chichester, Clark Rockefeller (Or Whatever His Name Was While He Was Painting the High School)" read a sign beside the chips and dips.

"Christopher Chichester is a Cheeseball" read a sign beside a cheese ball.

One neighbor had constructed a mammoth replica of the Chichester Cathedral—which the impostor had bragged that his family owned and he was going to import to San Marino—out of bologna.

I read from the book at Vroman's Bookstore in nearby Pasadena one night. Afterward, a woman whispered in my ear. "You missed a big part of the story," she said. "Chichester lived in South Pasadena before getting to San Marino."

She was referring to the scruffy by San Marino standards section of Pasadena just a few miles away from the bookstore. I was, of course, immediately compelled to find out more. She said she would check with those who knew him during this period and get back to me. Which is how I came to the home of Reverend Harold Frank Knowles, a tall, thin, white-haired veteran of the cloth in his seventies, who on the day of our meeting was dressed casually in a white shirt and white slacks with a silver medallion around his neck.

We met in his house, a pleasant, book-and-memento-filled home, where he showed me his collection of first-edition murder mysteries, including many of the works of Agatha Christie. Knowles leaned into the tape recorder and began speaking, as if reciting a long-rehearsed speech, which, he said, he told to the police investigating the missing couple, John and Linda Sohus, back in the 1980s.

"I'm the Reverend Harold Knowles, one-time rector of St. James's Episcopal Church, South Pasadena, where I served from 1969 to 1989," he began. "The man giving his name as Chris Chichester attended St. James's church from August 1981 until February or March 1982. The first time I met Chris, as he called himself, was my first Sunday back from summer vacation, which was always the Sunday following Labor Day, in this case 1981."

He paused dramatically and began to paint the picture of the day he met the charlatan. That year, he had spent two weeks in England, a highlight of which was seeing the *Gipsy Moth IV*, the historic sailing ship on which Sir Francis Chichester sailed around the world in 1967. When he returned to his church in South Pasadena, Father Knowles found young Chichester waiting for him at the front doors. He led him into his office for the usual interview he always gave to prospective new members, and the reverend began the interview by telling the young man about his vacation.

"Two weeks ago, I had my hands on the side of the *Gipsy Moth*," Father Knowles said. "Are you familiar with the *Gipsy Moth*?"

"No," said Chichester.

"It's a sailing ship that Sir Francis Chichester sailed around the world back in the 1960s," said the reverend.

Still, the young man's face drew a blank. "He had never heard of the *Gipsy Moth*," Knowles said. "Nor had he ever heard of Sir Francis Chichester."

Chichester gave the reverend the standard details of what had by then become his adopted identity: "He told me his father was an architect, and his parents lived in Greenwich, Connecticut, and had a great deal of money, and he was estranged from his parents because they didn't approve of his being in film school at USC," said Knowles. "He got monthly stipends from his parents. But sometimes they would be angry with him and the checks wouldn't arrive. That was the excuse he used, apparently, in borrowing sums of money from people in the parish."

His membership was approved. As always, Chichester gravitated toward a true believer. In this case, it was the highly respected bachelor C. Buford Lewis, who had retired from a lifetime of service to the Santa Fe railroad to generously donate his time to St. James's. "He was a lovely older gentleman from Mississippi, known to many people as 'Mr. St. James,'" said Knowles. "He was not only our head usher, but he was always on the lookout for people who were new, and he would introduce himself and say, 'Won't you come to our parish coffee hour and get acquainted?'"

C. Buford Lewis not only did all of this for Chris Chichester; he also leased him an apartment at a favorable rent in the complex he managed. Very quickly, Chichester was a fixture at the front doors of the stately old church. Prayer books in hand, he would stand beside C. Buford Lewis, his fellow usher known as Mr. St. James, and was immediately accepted and soon loved and trusted by all—especially by those Father Knowles called "the lonely and the widows," and especially by the wealthy ones.

He seemed to be everywhere at once: ushering beside C. Buford Lewis on Sundays, setting up tables at church events, making and serving coffee at the parish breakfasts, closing the church after potluck suppers, doing everything, in short, to "make himself indispensable," said Knowles.

The priest had an inkling about the true nature of Christopher Chichester when C. Buford Lewis arrived in Father Knowles's office in an uncharacteristic snit.

"I have to be circumspect in what I say because you understand that these were things that were confided to me by parishioners and it's under the seal of the confessional even if it isn't a confession, if people confide," Knowles said. "But a number of people came to me with complaints that they felt Chris had befriended them and taken advantage of their friendship. The first person to do so was Mr. Buford Lewis, the elderly gentleman who was the manager of the apartment complex where Chris lived.

"He said, 'Well, Father Knowles, I just have to tell you I'm very much disillusioned by our young friend Christopher Chichester, who we thought was such a wonderful young man.'

"He told me that he had not seen Chris around the apartment complex for a week or more. And then he saw some young girls, perhaps in their twenties, going in and out of Chris's apartment. Buford finally questioned them and was told that Chris had *sublet* the apartment to them—*at a profit* . . . which is illegal. I began to get complaints from individuals," Knowles continued. "Petty complaints," he added. "You know, 'He hit me up for fifty dollars last month and said that I would have it back when he got a check from his parents and now he is avoiding me when I see him in the parish hall!'"

The pastor said he had heard this complaint from at least a dozen people, and if a dozen people had complained, he knew, from his "years in the ministry," that there were at least a dozen others who had kept quiet. After head usher C. Buford Lewis gave Chichester the boot, he found free lodging with a young church lady with whom he had become "chummy," said Knowles. She and her psychiatrist husband gave the young man free room and board in their "Pasadena high-rent district" home in exchange for his being a nanny to their three children. "A lovely home," said Knowles. "Then she came to me very angry and claimed that Chichester had taken some things from her home and was into her for a good deal of money."

Next he went to live with another doctor and his wife, who rented out rooms in their spacious home to students in need. Once again, Chichester was thrown out amid accusations of theft. "The lady of the house felt there were some items missing," said Knowles.

He sighed. "Chris was always crying poor mouth . . . hitting people up for money because his parents hadn't sent his check," added Father Knowles. "He was always finding excuses. People were always inviting him into their homes for free meals. . . . He was a con man. He was a thief."

Knowles gave me a list of several parishioners who were supposedly ripped off, in hopes that they would see me. However, none of them wanted to discuss Christopher Chichester, save for one: an elderly woman and her young adult son.

"Father Knowles *loves* England," said the son. "Occasionally in his sermons somehow England would get into it." He remembered Father Knowles proudly introducing Christopher Chichester, who had deep familial roots in Great Britain, from the pulpit. "I just remember looking over to Chris and he was smiling."

The mother had prepared a list of her impressions, pretty much covering everything I had heard before: he was "charming," her late husband loved him, and he left behind a chattering chorus of burned landlords and landladies, who awakened to find things missing in their homes. But her son, now an accountant, had a new chapter to tell. He was twelve when Chichester took South Pasadena by storm, telling everyone that he was a student of film at the famed USC School of Cinematic Arts. "He took an interest in all of the kids at that time," the son said. "He wanted us to help him write a screenplay. He had this children's book that he wanted to make into a movie, and he and all of us stayed after church and helped him develop the screenplay."

The son set the scene: a handful of children in the church's guild room, sitting before the great Christopher Chichester, in his tan suit and Hollywood sunglasses, taking the kids on a wondrous cinematic journey. Chichester passed out copies of a children's book he planned to adapt for the screen, and began lecturing.

"I want your input," the son remembers Chichester telling the children, while scribbling notes, stage directions, and ideas on index cards. "I remember him saying he had met Steven Spielberg and George Lucas, and he liked Lucas more," said the son. "He said, 'Lucas is more down to earth and Spielberg is kind of cocky.' That was the time of *Star Wars* and *Raiders of the Lost Ark*. So those were huge movies."

"Wow!" is all the kids could say.

"I was a big fan," said the son.

"He kind of strutted," added the mother.

We were sitting at the kitchen table for our conversation, the very place where Chichester sat during his visits with the family. Some nights, they would turn on the television; their late husband and father loved to watch the popular nighttime soap operas, especially *Dallas* and *Dynasty*, but Christopher Chichester was repulsed by these.

"Those shows aren't worth watching," the son recalls Chichester snapping. He insisted that they instead switch the channel to what he deemed the "greatest show on American television": *The Greatest American Hero*, which the son described to me as "the story of some guy who overnight found he had supernatural powers and he would go around saving people."

Perhaps that's how Christopher Chichester saw himself: as some sort of superhero, to whom ordinary people owed everything.

After being thrown out of his third residence in South Pasadena, Chichester seemed to disappear. "From there I don't know where he went to live," Father Knowles continued. "I do know that after 1982 his attendance at church became sparser and sparser."

By then he had taken the good members of St. James's for their lodgings, money, and friendship. He had also adopted a choice nugget of biographical information from Father Knowles's account of his vacation to England, where he put his hands on the legendary *Gipsy Moth IV* in which Sir Francis Chichester sailed around the world.

"By March 1982, he was claiming to be Sir Francis Chichester's nephew," said Father Knowles. "The former rector of St. James's, Gil Prince, an eminent yachtsman, came up to me and said, 'I have so much enjoyed meeting your new member, young Mr. Chichester. I am just amazed to think that he is the nephew of Sir Francis Chichester, who sailed on the *Gipsy Moth.*'"

The reverend shook his head. "I just simply said, 'Gil, I don't think you should believe everything the young man tells you.'"

Soon after that, he was gone. "Sometime in the spring or early summer of 1982, I received a request from the Church of Our Saviour of San Gabriel (the church attended by the superwealthy of San Marino), saying that Chris Chichester was now attending service there and would like to have his membership transferred," said Knowles. "I can remember very distinctly signing his letter of transfer and telling my secretary, 'Mary, get this letter in the mail before he changes his mind.' . . . I was glad to see the end of him."

As always, the impostor moved onward and upward to even more affluent San Marino, and into the home of the alcoholic Didi Sohus and her son, John, and his wife, Linda, who would, like the possessions in the homes of South Pasadena, go missing.

Hoping to learn more about John and Linda Sohus, I spent time with their friends on the phone, in their homes, and at the Pasadena Public Library, where they mourned John and Linda twenty-six years after their disappearance. They recalled their friends as two tormented puzzle pieces that fit so perfectly together: John, the short, nerdy computer geek, and Linda, the big-boned, headstrong, strawberry blonde. They told me of Linda's fierce determination and John's paranoia. "He felt the government was out to watch and find out what everyone was doing, and he didn't want to have anyone knowing about him," said a childhood friend. "He didn't like going to the dentist because of dental records." What he did like was collecting sci-fi arcana: phasers and lightsabers from *Star Wars*, science-fiction and fantasy books, and, most of all, his computer and the places that wondrous machine led him. He had been obsessed with computers since his scouting days— he was a member of the Jet Propulsion Laboratory's explorer troop instead of the Boy Scouts—and he landed a coveted job at the Byte Shop of Pasadena, the area's first computer store where John Sohus found himself at the forefront of the computer revolution, even if he was only a drone running the shipping and receiving department. From there, it was computers all the way, leading to what would be his final job as a computer programmer at Dual Graphics. All were giant strides for the physically frail young man suffering from such advanced type 1 diabetes that he was warned to not drive because of the danger that he might pass out.

As for Linda, her friends added nuance to my earlier reporting. She could have sprung from the mind of a science-fiction author, they said: a quirky, sci-fi obsessed artist who clerked at Dangerous Visions bookstore and seemed sent from sci-fi heaven to be John's wife, lover, and protector—a protector even from his mother, the drunken Didi Sohus, in whose home John was embarrassed to still be living. They were that short on money, which is why, friends believed, they might have been the perfect dupes for the guesthouse snake charmer, Christopher Chichester.

None of their friends seem to have seen, much less known, Chichester, universally referred to by the couple's friends as "the guy in the guesthouse." They didn't recognize him as the master manipulator who had, according to the Los Angeles County Sheriff's Department's lead homicide investigator quoted earlier in this book, manipulated Didi Sohus into moving into a trailer park, eventually selling her home and disinheriting her son, John, which Didi did after John and Linda took off on their "secret mission."

The friends recalled events in the days before John and Linda departed. One friend ran a small, independent magazine called *Fantasy Book*, for which Linda was going to contribute one of her fanciful art paintings, as soon as she and John returned from the "secret mission" they were taking overseas for a few weeks. Something odd happened before the trip. I had known and written about Linda leaving behind her beloved cats in a kennel and never returning. But, the magazine publisher said, "There was a bigger red flag: her horse. She had scrimped and saved to lease a horse at a San Gabriel farm and the horse, which she studied for her drawings and rode as her obsession, was her life. It was her responsibility to feed, groom, and care for the horse. There was just no way she would have left without making arrangements" for the horse, said the friend. "It was totally out of character and a major red flag."

"They were both very excited about things, in love with life and in love with each other," said another friend. "You could see it in the way they looked at each other, the little bits of affection. She was his protector. She was taller and stronger and I believe she had some self-defense training. My expectation is she probably got killed trying to prevent John from being killed."

John and Linda left earlier than expected, without even packing their belongings, a suddenly mad dash to who-knows-where. As for Chichester, at least when he left San Marino, he apparently had plenty of time to pack and get his effects in order. A criminalist would later testify that four large bloodstains were found inside the guesthouse that Chichester left behind in 1985—along with human hair and small remnants of a human scalp.

This being good-hearted, all-trusting San Marino, nobody seemed to suspect Christopher Chichester of anything more than stealing free lunches, until the bones, presumably of John Sohus, were unearthed from the San Marino backyard in 1994. By then, Didi was dead, and Christopher Chichester had morphed into Clark Rockefeller, still more than ten years away from the Boston kidnapping that would finally expose his lifetime of lies.

During the five-day preliminary hearing in the superior court of Alhambra, California, in January 2012, to determine whether there was enough evidence for the impostor to stand trial for murder, prosecutor Habib Balian called twenty-nine witnesses and introduced seventy-five pieces of evidence—including, most extraordinarily, old and shocking photographs of the plastic book bags in which the dismembered bones and fractured skull of John Sohus were buried. One of the bags bore the logo of the University of Wisconsin-Milwaukee ("UWM Bookstore"), which, the prosecutor pointed out, was a logo used by the university from only 1979 to 1982, during the time when the man now calling himself Clark Rockefeller lived in Wisconsin, was supposedly a student at the university, and married his first wife in Milwaukee to obtain a green card. "There is only one reasonable conclusion, and that is the defendant killed him," said Balian of Sohus's murder. Another bag bore the logo of the USC Trojan bookstore, which was used when Chichester frequented the university, claiming to be a film student.

Adding to the Alfred Hitchcock overtones, Lynne Herold, senior criminalist for the Los Angeles County Sheriff's Department, testified that the flannel shirt encasing the bones found in one of the bags was cut several times by a weapon or tool capable of "sharp force." Forensic medical examiner Frank P. Sheridan testified that the victim died from three strong blows to the head. "The individual was alive when these fractures occurred and died very shortly afterwards," he said. "[The blows were] very strong, suggestive of an object," which, he added, could have been "a baseball bat with a rounded top."

One witness testified about Chichester borrowing a chain saw; another about complaining to him after she noticed black, rancid-smelling smoke billowing from the Sohus guesthouse's fireplace. (Chichester told the neighbor that he was burning carpet.) The San Marino couple Bettie and Robert Brown said the man then known as Christopher Chichester attempted to sell them a small oriental rug soon before he left town in 1985. When they pointed out that it had what appeared to be a small bloodstain on it, he rolled up the rug and drove away. Robert Brown also recalled that Chichester, while claiming to be a USC film student, asked him for advice about a good location to bury a drum filled with what he claimed were film-processing chemicals. (Brown recommended the San Gabriel Mountains.)

Then came Susan Mayfield, the mother of Linda Sohus. Now elderly and infirm, she arrived in court in a wheelchair with an oxygen tank. Mayfield testified that Linda dropped out of high school and moved in with her grandmother, and that the last time she saw her daughter was February 1985, when Linda asked if she could leave her truck at her mother's home when she and John went on their strange trip to the East Coast. (Mayfield said no.) When Linda and John hadn't returned after two weeks, Mayfield called the police, who "blew me off," she said.

The most explosive testimony came from Mihoko Manabe, the woman I called by the pseudonym Rose Mina in earlier chapters of this book. She is a petite, dark-haired, Asian New York City business-woman who appeared in court in a neat gray suit and frameless glasses. She met the man calling himself Christopher Crowe when they both worked at Nikko Securities in the World Financial Center in downtown Manhattan in the late 1980s. She worked at Nikko as a translator, Crowe as the head of the corporate bonds desk. I had tried numerous times to reach Manabe by e-mail, phone, and letter with no response. Under subpoena, she was clearly uncomfortable about being on the witness stand, quietly telling the story of how Christopher Crowe transformed himself into Clark Rockefeller.

"He said he was from Pasadena, went to Caltech, and studied film at USC," said Manabe of her introduction to the impostor. He told her that his real name was Chichester Mountbatten, but was using "Crowe" professionally, and that he had been involved in the new *Alfred Hitchcock Presents* television series. He also claimed that his father was an anesthesiologist, and that his mother had been a child actor. "He said he had a grandmother in England," Manabe said.

After a year of friendship, they became romantically involved in a relationship that lasted a total of seven years, living together on both West 69th Street and in the east-side Manhattan neighborhood of Tudor City. But like his later relationship with Sandra Boss, the impostor soon became verbally abusive to Manabe, even after he abruptly left his job at Kidder Peabody and she began paying all of their bills. He initially said he was writing a book, Manabe said, but actually spent his time overseeing the household, paying their bills (with her checkbook), caring for the dog, and shopping for groceries. Virtually all financial records and accounts were under Manabe's name. Crowe didn't even have an ID or a checking account.

"How did he treat you?" she was asked on the witness stand.

"Not well," she said.

"He had a temper, but not in a physically violent way. He was just very caustic, and derogatory. He could be very mean. . . . He was also very disdainful of people doing menial work. For example, if we ordered food to be delivered and it was late or cold, he would send it back with some words."

On one occasion, the emotional and verbal abuse rose to the physical, when he grabbed her by the arm after she mistakenly left his Gordon setter, Yates, locked in a hot car.

She was asked at one point in the questioning if she loved him. "I guess," she replied.

"I just wanted to protect him," she would also say, and told a story of taking that protection to extraordinary lengths.

One day in 1988, the telephone rang in the apartment Manabe shared with Crowe. Manabe answered. The caller identified himself as Detective Dan Allen from the Greenwich Police Department, and he was hoping to question Crowe about the truck that belonged to the missing couple, John and Linda Sohus. When Manabe told her boyfriend about the call, he panicked—and, as always, had an explanation. It wasn't a policeman who had called. It was "somebody bad and that he was going to get him and not to tell him he was there," she told the court. "He said that his parents had gotten into trouble. They were in danger and because of that, he was also in danger.

"He said he had to go into hiding," she said.

Manabe believed the story and followed his request to help him dye his hair and eyebrows blond (he also grew a beard and "scrapped" his trademark eyeglasses for contact lenses and "abandoned" his car). She followed other directions, too, including transferring their mail to a post-office box in Pennsylvania, shredding their papers, dumping their garbage in public places like shopping centers, and walking on opposite sides of the street in New York City.

"He insisted that I disassociate myself from my friends and my family," Manabe said. Why would she go along with it? "The gist of it was because he was going to put me through all this, he might as well marry me."

Soon after the phone call from Detective Allen, Crowe proposed marriage. Manabe accepted, and soon after that he suggested they move to Germany. After a visit to the German embassy, she noticed his green German passport printed with the name "Gerhartsreiter," which she did not recognize. "He said he had a fake passport made and we were going to escape from whatever it was pursuing him and putting him in danger," Manabe testified.

The wedding was to be held in Camden, Maine, where Crowe and Manabe traveled in 1989 to visit an inn as a potential location for the ceremony. It was here that her fiancé made the restaurant reservation

under the name Clark Rockefeller, and was struck by the magical attention that famous name brought.

That dinner marked the beginning of Christian Karl Gerhartsreiter's greatest con.

"Eventually, he became Clark Rockefeller," said Manabe.

They were never married. "Several months after he proposed, he
changed his mind," she said. However, they continued living together
for several more years, until Manabe met the man who would become
her husband in 1994. Shortly after she left Rockefeller, he showed up in
her new apartment with a gift. "He came to bring me a painting he had
painted," she said.

At the end of the five-day hearing, Alhambra Superior Court judge
Jared Moses ruled. "I have reviewed all seventy-five of the people's ex-
hibits," he said. "There is sufficient evidence; it is ordered that the defendant be held to answer."

Bail was set at $10 million. The trial is expected to begin in the fall
of 2012.

So who is the prisoner in the blue jumpsuit, now facing a murder charge in the Alhambra, California, courthouse? Perhaps he is a
twisted aberration of the boom years on which he thrived, the years in
which people felt entitled to do whatever it took to win. Life was a game
and the man calling himself Clark Rockefeller saw himself as a victor,
above the rules, the ultimate narcissist in the golden age of narcissism.
For him, everything and everyone became objects to be manipulated,
especially his wife of twelve years, Sandra Lynne Boss. He told investigators that although his fabulous collection of modern art was filled
with fakes, he *had* to maintain the facade that it was real, to keep his
friends, his wife, his life. Without the art, and the millions of dollars
people believed it could bring on the open market, who would he be? In
his world, he needed to be the center of everything, and he needed to
pull the strings and levers to make the world dance around him.

Now he sits in his cell, discussing the price of gold and the euro and his bitter dislike of Washington politics. Still, in his pose as Clark Rockefeller, he denies any wrongdoing and awaits justice and yet another jury, whose members will decide at long last whether Christian Karl Gerhartsreiter is merely a devious impostor or also a cold-blooded killer.

Acknowledgments

First and foremost, to Alessandra Lusardi, my brilliant editor at Viking Penguin: Thank you for your wisdom, enthusiasm, editing expertise, and patience in our journey to assemble what has been called "the thousand-piece jigsaw puzzle" of a life. And to Viking Penguin president Clare Ferraro, thank you for becoming an early and ardent champion of this book.

The story of Clark Rockefeller was first published in the January 2009 issue of *Vanity Fair* magazine. For that, I want to thank the incredible Wayne Lawson for his editorial genius and guidance, first in editing the magazine piece and later this book; *Vanity Fair's* great editor Graydon Carter for originally sending me on a quest to find the truth about Clark Rockefeller and showing such enthusiasm for the resulting *Vanity Fair* piece; and Matthew Pressman for his invaluable and intelligent work on both the magazine story and this book.

Thank you to my incomparable literary agent, Jan Miller Rich, of Dupree Miller & Associates, and to my close friend, great story scout, and esteemed adviser Jeff Rich. I treasure your friendship.

Almost every story begins with a source, and in the case of Clark Rockefeller my original source was Roxane West. Having met Rockefeller in New York, Roxane called me one afternoon shortly after he had kidnapped his daughter, literally screaming her insistence that I *had* to write about him. Thank you, Roxane, for that pivotal call and for all of your help, insights, and recollections along the way.

Thank you to Elizabeth Suman, for your indefatigable and invaluable research talents every step along the way; to John Ruddy, for your continued assistance; and to Tom Colligan, for fact-checking the maze that led through so many people and places.

To the staff of the wonderful Taj Boston hotel: Your gracious hospitality and stately accommodations provided me with a second home in Boston. And thank you to Sheila Donnelly & Associates for all of your assistance in Boston.

This book is the product of almost two hundred interviews with people whose paths crossed with the man eventually known as Clark Rockefeller. Many of those who gave me their time and insights have asked to remain anonymous. What follows, then, is a partial list.

In Germany, I was accompanied by Marten Rolff, a newspaper reporter who wrote about Rockefeller there. Thank you, Marten, for your help with translation, introductions, and background information. And thank you to all those in the town of Bergen who spoke to me, a stranger from America, with special thanks to the men who meet to drink beer throughout the day and night at the *Stammtisch*, the regulars in the beer garden in the center of town.

In Connecticut, thank you to Edward Savio, Chris Bishop, Wayne Campbell, Greenwich police lieutenant Daniel Allen, and Jeff Wayne.

In San Marino and elsewhere in California, thank you to Jann Eldnor, Peggy Ebright, Elmer and Jean Kelln, Sue Coffman, Los Angeles County Sheriff's Department sergeant Timothy Miley, Frank Girardot (Metro editor for the San Gabriel Valley Newspapers), Wayne Kelln, Kenneth Veronda, Dana Farrar, Carol Campbell, Bill and Cori Woods, Meredith Brucker, Carol and Warner J. Iliff, Steven J. Biodrowski, Professor Geoffrey Greene, Bernice Sadamune, Tricia Gough, Lilli Hadsell, Marianne Kent, Lydia Marano, Ralph Wikke, the producers of the *Unsolved Mysteries* television series and the members of the Los Angeles Science Fantasy Society, who so fondly recalled John and Linda Sohus.

In New York, thank you to Anthony Meyer, Martha Henry, William Quigley, Venanzio Ciampa, Lawrence Steigrad and Peggy Stone, Sharlene Spingler, Dave Copeland, Richard Barnett, Stanley Forkner, Bob Brusca, Eric Hunter Slater, Ralph Boynton, Sheldon Fish, Jeffrey Richards, and Brittney Ross.

In Cornish, New Hampshire, thank you to Peter Burling, Alma Gilbert-Smith, Merilynn Bourne, Don MacLeay, Nancy Nash Cummings, Laura White, Charlie White, and Gregory Schwarz.

In Boston, thank you to Jake Wark, Stephen Hrones, Patrick Hickox, Boston police sergeant Raymond Mosher, Boston police detective Joe Leeman, Bob Skorupa, John Greene, John Sears, FBI special agent Noreen Gleason, Gail Marcinkiewicz, FBI special agent Tamara Hardy, Frank Rudewicz, Gretchen Berg and her colleagues at NBC, *Dateline,* and the *Today* show, Boston Police Department deputy superintendant Thomas Lee, Suffolk County assistant district attorney David Deakin, defense attorneys Jeffrey Denner and Timothy Bradl, Jessica Van Sack, Jonathan Saltzman, Denise Lavoie, Victoria Block, Maria Cramer, and the staff at the Algonquin Club.

In Baltimore, thank you to Julie Gochar.

Thank you to Nancy Doherty, Annie Laurie Hines, Carolyn Hines, Keenan Delaney, and Tom Rizer.

Last but far from least, I would like to thank my family: Evelyn Abroms Kraus and Melvin Kraus, the late Berney Seal, Eddie and Melissa Seal and family, B.J. and Alana Seal and family, Brandon and Jennifer Blocker and family, and all of the many members of the extended Seal, Abroms, Kraus, Blocker, and Gambini clans.